SAGE was founded in 1965 by Sara Miller McCune to support the dissemination of usable knowledge by publishing innovative and high-quality research and teaching content. Today, we publish over 900 journals, including those of more than 400 learned societies, more than 800 new books per year, and a growing range of library products including archives, data, case studies, reports, and video. SAGE remains majority-owned by our founder, and after Sara's lifetime will become owned by a charitable trust that secures our continued independence.

Los Angeles | London | New Delhi | Singapore | Washington DC | Melbourne

Diversity beyond Tokenism is the best book on diversity that you'll find. It's the first time that I see an open, honest and objective approach about such a complex and difficult topic. It gives a unique perspective to most of the common doubts and questions we have about diversity and makes us think and reflect about them with a different mindset. Its holistic and deep analysis on how organizations should think and act about diversity is bold and outstanding. It's a must-read for every leader.

Miriam Manrique
General Manager, Uber, Central America

A courageous and incisive attempt at breaking down the dogmas and myths surrounding diversity and inclusion (D&I) and constructing a positive argument using the inherently contradictory strains in this field. I would recommend this as a reading in business schools, to understand what constitutes D&I and how one can truly build inclusive organizations. As HR professionals, this book forces us to look at practices within our organizations that provide mere lip-service to the concept of diversity. It goads us towards deeper questions, which, when answered truthfully, would lead us to build cultures and organizations which are truly inclusive. An extremely thought-provoking, oftentimes discomforting, but supremely pertinent piece of corporate writing.

Aditya Vellore
Chief of Staff, Intel, Greater Asia

'D&I' is an important mantra of the contemporary workplace. In this provocative book, Swati and Hari go beyond the standard clichés to explore the why and how of D&I. You may or may not agree with them, but this is an important read for anyone involved with diversity, which is just about all of us.

Rishikesha T. Krishnan
Director, IIM Bangalore

There is a lot spoken about diversity these days, but here is a book that makes you sit up and reflect. It questions our assumptions and points out our biases and beliefs that we are living with, which can truly impede diversity. The book explores a variety of issues on diversity in the Indian context, and I am sure that you, like me, will come out with renewed commitment to diversity and not mere tokenism.

Krish Shankar
Group HR Head, Infosys and President, NHRD, India

Scholarly, forthright and written with a journalistic rigour—finally we have a book that is not another 'me-too' on this important subject of building diverse and inclusive societies and workplaces. I highly recommend it.

Dushyant Goyal
Director HR, Novartis, US

Swati Jena and T. N. Hari make *Diversity beyond Tokenism* an easy-to-read book. They have made the understanding of diversity simple but not simplistic. The book is well-researched with ample references making the overall point that diversity is not just about gender but dealing with multiplicity of viewpoints. I especially liked the quick summary at the end of each chapter by way of 'big ideas'. Overall, a thoroughly enjoyable read and something for keeps in the long term.

Raj Raghavan
Senior Vice President and Head of Human Resources,
Indigo Airlines

The lethal duo of Swati and Hari, courtesy this book, has debunked innumerable politically correct myths and left a trail of realization in their wake. Reading and reflecting on their brilliantly presented and forthright perspectives, one is overcome with a strong sense of subliminal resonance to relate seamlessly with the 'big ideas'. I believe this book will provide the much-needed pivot in re-calibrating mindsets across organizations.

Rohit Manucha
CHRO, SIH-AGH, UAE

As a French woman engineer, daughter of an Algerian immigrant and CEO of one of the first women-led open innovation agencies in India, I am utterly aware of the devastating effect of the drivel that leaves the topic of diversity misconstrued. The book *Diversity beyond Tokenism* cuts through the clutter and boldly addresses the various sub-themes underlying this topic. The book is a combination of rigour and storytelling. The key takeaways (the big ideas) at the end of every chapter serve as ready reckoner for a practitioner. I found the book insightful and thoroughly enjoyable. I would recommend this strongly to anyone interested in deconstructing this complex topic.

Souad Tenfiche
CEO, Link Innovations

Swati and Hari have unlocked a much-needed dialogue around the true meaning of diversity. They capture issues realistically and raise pertinent questions. The two most powerful ideas put forward are 'equal but not same' and the 'mindset of no'. A must-read for those who desire to bring about a change in and around themselves.

Smitu Malhotra
*Associate Dean, Student Affairs (Women students)
and Ex-Chairperson of Committee
Against Sexual Harassment (CASH)
at XLRI, Jamshedpur*

Fascinating, provocative and insightful book; it speaks to the reader's head, heart and soul! Highly engaging and fresh perspective from non-experts, taking a rational look at some of the well-renowned D&I research studies and the root causes of inequality in the corporate and civilized world. References from history, mythology, evolution, education, government, legal system, arts, business, society and the universe are thought-provoking. A must-read for leaders, D&I beginners, enthusiasts and practitioners who want to build a resilient and future-proof organization.

Monika Navandar
Global D&I Expert, NeoSeven Solutions

I have two terms for this book—'politically respectful' and 'refreshingly honest'. *Diversity beyond Tokenism* portrays the most original aspects of diversity and its practices at workplaces. It is as insightful as it is addictive. It pushes our capability to see, feel and comprehend issues around D&I like never before.

Saurabh Nigam
CHRO, Omidyar Network India

SAGE Response, our business books imprint, celebrates its silver jubilee this year. As we reflect on this transformational journey that began with a single title, we thank everyone who has helped us to produce content that is topical and relevant across a varied audience of aspiring managers, working professionals, practitioners and students. We feel privileged that eminent management and leadership experts, professionals and stalwarts from academia supported and trusted us with their work. Over the years, SAGE Response has built an enviable list of practice-based, reader-friendly books that provide creative strategies to keep pace with the rapidly changing global scenario. As we grow and evolve with the times, it is our endeavour to continue to publish books that offer innovative solutions, approaches and perspectives to the disciplines that we serve.

DIVERSITY
BEYOND
TOKENISM

Why Being Politically Correct
Doesn't Help Anyone

SWATI JENA · T. N. HARI

Los Angeles | London | New Delhi
Singapore | Washington DC | Melbourne

First published in 2021 by

SAGE Publications India Pvt Ltd
B1/I-1 Mohan Cooperative Industrial Area
Mathura Road, New Delhi 110 044, India
www.sagepub.in

SAGE Publications Inc
2455 Teller Road
Thousand Oaks, California 91320, USA

SAGE Publications Ltd
1 Oliver's Yard, 55 City Road
London EC1Y 1SP, United Kingdom

SAGE Publications Asia-Pacific Pte Ltd
18 Cross Street #10-10/11/12
China Square Central
Singapore 048423

Published by Vivek Mehra for SAGE Publications India Pvt Ltd. Typeset in 11/14.5 pt Sabon by Fidus Design Pvt Ltd, Chandigarh.

Library of Congress Control Number: 2021941447

ISBN: 978-93-91370-63-3 (PB)

SAGE Team: Neha Pal, Shruti Gupta, Shivani A. Damle and Ginkhan Siam

To my mom, who told me stories as a child,
but only half—so I would figure out
the rest of it on my own.
That was my first lesson in seeking.

To my alma mater, XLRI, Jamshedpur,
for believing in old-world values of ethics and Magis,
which I can hopefully live by.

To my sister, my constant cheerleader,
who generally owns half of anything I have.

To my dad, who bought me the best books
he could find, even those he couldn't afford.

—Swati Jena

To my mom and dad—who did their best
for me despite all the challenges life threw at them.

To Niroop Mahanty, Sanjeev Aggarwal, Raghunandan
G. and Shradha Sharma—for being with me at the
turning points in my career.

To Neelam Ahluwalia and Tanuja Tewari—
for letting me fly and pursue my dreams.

—T. N. Hari

Thank you for choosing a SAGE product!
If you have any comment, observation or feedback,
I would like to personally hear from you.

Please write to me at **contactceo@sagepub.in**

Vivek Mehra, Managing Director and CEO, SAGE India.

Bulk Sales

SAGE India offers special discounts
for purchase of books in bulk.
We also make available special imprints
and excerpts from our books on demand.

For orders and enquiries, write to us at

Marketing Department
SAGE Publications India Pvt Ltd
B1/I-1, Mohan Cooperative Industrial Area
Mathura Road, Post Bag 7
New Delhi 110044, India

E-mail us at **marketing@sagepub.in**

Subscribe to our mailing list
Write to **marketing@sagepub.in**

This book is also available as an e-book.

CONTENTS

Foreword by Sairee Chahal ix

Foreword by Ravi Venkatesan xiii

Preface xvii

1. An Ideological Echo Chamber 1

2. Does Diversity Really Help Business? 17

3. Dissent and Diversity 45

4. Discrimination and Diversity 63

5. Equal, Not Same 99

6. Women in Senior Management 129

7. #MeToo 151

8. Bias Is Pervasive 205

9. Beyond Tolerance 225

10. Rewiring for Diversity 251

About the Authors 275

As a young girl growing up in a small town, my experiences led me to observe, first-hand, the inequities that come with a lack of access. Large pockets of women and other marginalized communities continue to be deeply underserved in our country, even today. While new schemes and frameworks are continuously being announced to reduce this inequity, the impact of these initiatives does not reflect in the gender gap indices.

In the World Economic Forum's *Global Gender Gap Index* 2019–2020, Iceland ranked number 1 while India ranked 112. India dropped four places since 2018. On the health and survival parameter, India ranked 150th of 153 countries!

This is definitely alarming. Optimism inspires one to expect things to get progressively better and not worse. But this is not the case.

Simultaneously, diversity is a term that's continuously being thrown around in boardrooms, policy conversations and international forums. The term first made an appearance in public discourses in 1978. It was part of a landmark decision by the American Supreme Court in the University of California v. Bakke. Quotas were struck down by the court, which instead upheld the need for affirmative action towards ensuring more racial diversity on campuses.

In India, diversity is a major conversation in the context of boardrooms, senior management, technology and other spaces of traditional male dominance. A kind of unspoken quota system has emerged at workplaces, while in other ecosystems, actual quota systems exist. The impact of such systems is uneven and, sometimes, sketchy. There are several cases where those in positions of authority are puppets with no voice or power to shift the narrative for the marginalized group they represent.

From a larger perspective, it is the lack of access that is a setback, not a lack of talent, capability or potential. Equal opportunities need to be curated by design, on a massive scale, at various entry points of the hierarchy across all ecosystems. We need interventions as much at the grassroots level as we do at the higher echelons of corporate, political and other hierarchies, so that our cabinets and boardrooms resemble the world we live in.

There's also a great need to view diversity in a more inclusive way. In a melting pot like India, we need to factor in gender, religion, race, disability, as well as socially constructed and economic hierarchies.

Technology is a key driver of access that can be a great friend to a country like India. Affordable data and the reduced cost of smart devices are already a game changer in several pockets, and as penetration increases, they can be leveraged to create more equal opportunities.

Another great investment is access to entrepreneurship training. Imagine that networks like Self-Employed Women's Association and Grameen Bank are replicated and scaled online. Some of the traditional ecosystems where technology is creating access in a massive way include healthcare, education, skills training, mental health, entrepreneurship and finance.

We also need more advocates to drive diversity conversations— people with empathy, skills and an in-depth understanding of issues, who are committed to triggering change.

Swati Jena, through her analytical, unapologetic, yet, mindful writing, has shone the spotlight on several issues connected to diversity and inclusion—from maternity laws and their effectiveness to casual sexism at work. Work culture plays such a key role in shaping inclusion at work, and Swati has played the devil's advocate in questioning common practices and leadership that is detrimental to work culture. Her writings call out deep-rooted mindsets that contribute to exclusionary work environments.

T. N. Hari has been a powerful voice for equal opportunity through his phenomenal career journey. An engineer by qualification, blessed with a sharp, analytical mind, he brought fresh perspectives to the HR function. His keen interest in the interplay between human psychology and business performance has helped shape his understanding and commitment to prioritizing work culture as a leader. He has also been a strong advocate for safer workplaces and is one of a handful of male corporate leaders who have been outspoken about the need for better execution of POSH laws.

Diversity beyond Tokenism: Why Being Politically Correct Doesn't Help Anyone is an exploration of what's redundant in our systems, mindsets, behaviours and what needs to get done to progress the diversity narrative. I invite all stakeholders to read and engage with fresh actionable ideas, experiences and experiments that can help us design more equitable systems for future generations.

Sairee Chahal
Founder and CEO, SHEROES—
The Women-Only Social Network

I am grateful to Swati and Hari for inviting me to read and write a foreword to their book on diversity. Diversity and inclusion are vitally important and urgent issues not just for businesses but also for societies which are getting increasingly polarized in many parts of the world.

I grew up in situations that were at once very diverse and homogenous. I studied at an all-boys school in Chandigarh. The only South Indian in my class, I was precocious in science and a failure at sports. I was an oddity and teased a lot. IIT Bombay, where I studied engineering, was a microcosm of middle-class, aspiring India but there were exactly four women in a cohort of about 350 students. Like much of my class, I immigrated to the US in search of opportunity and a better life. It gave me the profound experience of being a minority. There were just four Indian students in my graduate program in 1985 (this has changed dramatically since). Friday evenings were particularly lonely as everyone partied and we stayed late in the labs writing code. I then worked as a manufacturing leader in gritty factories of Cummins Engine Co. in Indiana, South Carolina and Georgia. I was starkly different from almost everyone else in ethnicity, language, education and aspirations. For the first time in my life, I experienced prejudice, overt racism and tokenism. It was no fun at all, but it made me a better person—more sensitive and empathetic and able to work across differences. I believe that such crucial experiences that get us out of our comfort zone, force us to work with and understand people who are unlike us and get us to experience what it feels like to be in an 'out-group' are an essential part of our development as humans and especially as leaders.

At Cummins, I had the good fortune of working for and with a CEO who has a passionate moral conviction about diversity and inclusion. Tim Solso did, of course, believe that diversity was good for business. How can an enterprise flourish if it walks away from half the talent in the world and if its workforce fails to mirror its customers and the communities in which it operates? But to him, this was all just rationalization; being inclusive, providing equal opportunities to all was morally just. Diversity at Cummins under Tim was not about politically correct statements, grudging compliance and ticking the boxes. It was about leaders being role models and setting the right tone from the top. I remember a very difficult conversation with Tim in 1998; India was making no progress on gender diversity and he let me know in no uncertain terms that I was failing as an officer of the company despite turning in great business results. All my arguments that women weren't attracted to heavy manufacturing, that the few women who did pursue engineering preferred disciplines like software and electronics were dismissed as just excuses. He was right and this conversation focused my energies. One of the better outcomes was our investment into the Cummins College of Engineering for Women in Pune to make it one of the top engineering institutions in the country; we made a blanket job offer to all the graduating classes. Very quickly, more and more talented women made their presence felt in every function and at every level. Today, Cummins factories and offices are incredibly diverse in every dimension and the credit goes to Tim. He showed that diversity is a moral issue and that leadership really does matter. Having great role models like Tim are really important for inspiring lots of others.

One of the really important points made by Swati and Hari is that the mere presence of diversity doesn't mean diversity in thinking. It doesn't guarantee that diverse perspectives will influence decisions. This is an absolutely crucial point. I cannot count the number of times I have been in board meetings of iconic companies all over the world which ticked all the boxes in terms of diversity but where the leader (chairman) failed to create an inclusive and open environment where diverse and even dissenting perspectives were welcomed. There is a very useful exploration in the book of how you need to work to create such an environment.

The book explores other important and practical ideas. Why are affirmative actions and quotas essential? Why does the induction of more women (or any other minority) not automatically end harassment and result in a women-friendly culture? Why is it necessary to have a 'critical mass' of any minority group to reach a tipping point. While the authors don't always provide readymade solutions, they do a great service by asking questions that many of us may not have thought of or been hesitant to voice.

The world is waking up to the importance of biodiversity or diversity in natural ecosystems. No species—not the smallest mite or bacteria—is unimportant. Every species is the manifestation of nature, the divine and fills an important space and makes the world more beautiful and complete. The loss of a species diminishes everyone. The same logic applies to diversity in society and the workplace. It's not about the 'business case' for or the ROI of diversity; our commitment to a diverse society and workplace must come from a deep belief that it is the moral right of every human being to express their unique gifts and to pursue happiness. It must come from a conviction that diversity makes us collectively whole, richer and more beautiful. Compliance with laws and regulations can protect out-groups, but ultimately, real change requires such a shift in mindset. For this, we need more leaders to speak about and act out their convictions. We must celebrate diverse talent who breach glass ceilings and become role models for many others. But most of all, real change will happen only when more of us live and lead the change. This is where *Diversity beyond Tokenism* makes an important contribution by framing problems clearly, helping us think more critically about the fundamental issues underlying diversity and, most of all, by making the undiscussable, discussable.

Ravi Venkatesan
Member of the Board of Trustees,
Rockefeller Foundation and Founder,
Global Alliance for Mass Entrepreneurship

Love, itch, precision, courage.

1. These four words don't fit into a pattern.
2. These four words describe the *why, what and how* of the book.

Let's talk about the second point first.

Love: The idea of this book was love-at-first sight—an emotion writers are far too familiar with, when we are so consumed by the intellectual challenge of a subject, that we can't take our mind off it. It wasn't the idea of diversity, per se, that excited us. It was the idea of *relooking at diversity* that made both co-authors feel instantly that this book was meant to be. Herein lies the core essence of what this book is (and isn't) about. It is not a discourse on why diversity is important. The book rather seeks to explore: Does it matter? Why do we care? Is it worth the effort? As we wrote in the chapter 'Does Diversity Really Help Business?' Assuming diversity always helps or always hurts is incorrect. It is important to understand the business context and structure before weaving in diversity.

Itch: The origin of this book was an incomplete draft of a LinkedIn article titled 'Men and Women Are Equal Not Same' by one of the co-authors. When the idea of a book got discussed, both experienced what is, again, familiar to writers—an itch. It's the nagging feeling of thoughts growing in your head, waiting to be expressed. As we explored how this book could evolve, we realized how both of us had been witnessing the diversity saga with concerned scepticism, practical idealism and unassumed inquiry. And herein lies why we wrote this book. If organizations are a microcosm of the society, then diversity should be a natural part of it. However, the manner in which businesses are implementing diversity is rife with tokenism. We relooked at diversity using first principles. In that spirit, we have used questions as the tool of choice to explore how diversity could be approached within organizations. As we asked in the chapter 'Discrimination and Diversity', 'Is the narrative on discrimination driven by a reasoned voice, or are we drowning ourselves in reactive noise?' The question was driven by *concerned scepticism* on how much businesses feel pressured to act in a certain way by social media outrage, and how much that really serves to remove discrimination in the long term. We wondered, in 'Women in Senior Management', if the idea of mandating women board members was akin to a quota system, which is one of the common arguments against affirmative action. We dug deep into it with *practical idealism* by mapping a utopian situation against on-ground realities of hardwired stereotypes about women. In 'Beyond Tolerance', we plunged into the unedited realities of how organizations implement or bypass education and age-related diversity. We looked into it with *unassumed inquiry,* hoping to find wisdom on the larger question, 'Is focus on visible indicators of diversity misplaced?'

Precision: The process of writing this book was a lot like performing a precision surgery, having to take apart several intricately linked, seemingly paradoxical aspects of diversity. We had to make our arguments with care, constantly checking if one aspect contradicted the other. We observed how perspectives, seemingly at odds with one another, were essential parts of the whole we call diversity. Hence, while we argued in favour of affirmative action for women in 'Does Diversity Really Help Business?', we explored the principle of *absolute equality* in 'Equal, Not Same' and the need to address unspoken apprehensions of managers, in holding women professionals accountable for non-performance. On the one hand, in 'Women in Senior Management' we highlighted how women are bound by traditional gender roles to keep their career on the back burner and the need for that to change. On the other, in 'Discrimination and Diversity', we pressed upon organizational solutions for managers hesitating to hire women, instead of shaming and penalizing the apparently discriminatory behaviour. Addressing each of these aspects individually may have been easier (*relatively* easy to be precise), but arguing all the questions together in one book required us to understand carefully how each vein, artery and nerve of diversity interacted with the other. If diversity has to be discussed beyond tokenism, we cannot avoid understanding these complex interrelations. Our attempt has been to make that complexity simpler, discernible and amenable to an informed discussion among all stakeholders—as it should be, and not just remain the bastion of diversity experts.

Courage: It has taken a lot to write this book—time, painstaking effort and intense reflection. Most importantly, it has taken courage. We did not write this book as 'experts'. In fact, we would go a step further to say—this book could *not* have been written by experts. Because, as experts, we would have already committed ourselves to a point a view. Our focus would have been to tell, not ask. Our compulsion would have been to be politically correct. In the chapter 'Dissent and Diversity', we shared the story of Ray Dalio, whose business fall taught him to transition from 'I am right', to 'How do I know I am right?' That is the question we asked ourselves several times while writing this book. In the chapter '#MeToo', we played devil's advocate to the idea that inducting women necessarily means reducing sexual harassment. We asked the never asked question on this subject—can women perpetuate, aid and abet sexual harassment? We have called to question the role of HR and business leadership in prevention of sexual harassment. In 'The Ideological Echo Chamber', we pointed at the shaky grounds of popular diversity reports by the likes of McKinsey. Through the book, we have looked at what appears to be double-standard approach of admired companies such as Unilever, Google and Zappos. None of these are with the objective of criticism, which would be unhelpful to the overall objective of the book. We have taken the courage to do so in order to highlight that approaching diversity with tokenism leads even the best of organizations to act in a way that contradicts logic and their stated beliefs. We could not have explored these aspects from the lens of experts. We needed the courage to discard assumptions about diversity in popular narratives and see things for what they are. So, we have called out the emperor without clothes. We have pointed at the elephant in the room. We have belled the proverbial cat. We have done so to simply clear the way for all stakeholders to now ideate how real diversity can be implemented within organizations. It was not just writing a book. We wanted to have the courage to create *a turning point in the discourse on diversity*.

Finally, about the point we started this introduction with.

Love, itch, precision and courage are odd words. They don't lend themselves to the start of a serious business book. They don't even fit into a pattern. They don't rhyme. They don't start with the same letter. These words are just like diversity— people who can't be hammered into the same box coming together to fulfil a common goal. We said in the closing section of this book, 'Rewiring for Diversity', that the human mind in specific and the world in general is wired against diversity. That's because finding patterns makes it easier for the brain. If we know A, B, C, D fit into a pattern, once we have figured out A and B, we simply assume things about C and D. That is where stereotypes are born. As we cautioned in 'Equal, Not Same', 'men and women are not same, neither are women and women.' That's why pursuing diversity and truly benefitting from it will need rewiring both at an individual and organizational level. Perceiving diversity demands a higher level of intelligence and attention from all of us. In 'Dissent and Diversity', we quoted the king in *Alice in Wonderland*, 'Begin at the beginning. Go on till you come to the end; then stop.' If you are reading this book, remember what the king said. Begin at the beginning, and go on till the end, and *then* stop. Because this book and diversity cannot be understood in parts, unless we seek to understand all the parts held together with their complex interlinkages. Because the parts of this book, just like love, itch, precision and courage, don't make a predictable pattern. But together, they make sense. That, as we completed writing this book, we realized, is also the essence of *Diversity beyond Tokenism*.[1]

---

[1] Sections of the book where we have used 'I' reflect our personal experiences.

An Ideological Echo Chamber

The history of men's opposition to women's emancipation is more interesting perhaps than the story of that emancipation itself.

—Virginia Woolf, *A Room of One's Own*

In July 2017, James Damore, an employee at Google, published an internal memo claiming that biological differences prevent gender equality. The memo titled 'Google's Ideological Echo Chamber—How Bias Clouds Our Thinking about Diversity and Inclusion'[1] resulted in a highly polarizing debate which went beyond the confines of Google. The contents led to outrage across Silicon Valley and reverberated across the world. It also triggered debate on a contentious topic that had become overly sensitive and taken on overtones of a religious doctrine. Anything you say on diversity has to be weighed carefully, because you could be judged quickly. Hence people are extra cautious in what they say and went out of their way to be politically correct. In complete contrast, almost as if it was deliberate, Damore wrapped his explosive content in an inflammatory and polarizing style.

---

[1] https://felleisen.org/matthias/Articles/the-google-memo.pdf

Google, known for its relatively open culture, after a swift investigation, in a letter addressed to Google employees by CEO Sundar Pichai, said that Damore had violated the company's code of conduct and encouraged 'harmful gender stereotypes in our workplace'.[2] In his memo, Damore had also commented on Google's political bias and the absence of a more honest debate on contentious issues. From all accounts, Damore's memo was in response to the diversity team at Google seeking inputs and feedback on their diversity-related policies. What isn't clear is whether Damore circulated the document to a larger group or merely used the document as a basis for a private discussion with the diversity team or management at Google. What stood out, however, was the speed with which Google acted on it. In less than a week of publishing the internal memo, James Damore was fired from Google. One can't help suspecting that the haste with which Google acted was a reflection of an intolerance for a point of view that did not fit a certain perspective or doctrine. The contents of the memo may have been the product of an inadequate understanding of a nuanced subject, but it certainly merited a hearing, especially when feedback was explicitly sought. Diversity is not just about gender but also about dealing with multiplicity of viewpoints. Damore's memo was a perfect opportunity for dealing with questions that may have troubled many others who chose not to voice their concerns. Google's suppression of Damore's memo smacked of a shade of intolerance that is common in cults where there is no space for an alternate point of view. We'll circle back to this at the end of the chapter, but let's first look at the validity of Damore's assertions.

---

[2] https://fortune.com/2017/08/08/google-anti-diversity-memo-sundar-pichai-letter/

The content of James Damore's memo and the debates that ensued hold some deep insights on the topic of diversity, particularly gender diversity.

In a snarky summary at the start of the memo, Damore makes two rather sweeping conclusions: (a) differences in distributions of traits between men and women may, in part, explain why we don't have 50 per cent representation of women in tech and leadership and (b) discrimination to reach equal representation is unfair, divisive and bad for business. In our opinion, Damore's conclusions indicate an insufficiently researched point of view and a reflection of his own personal bias. The key question at this stage is: Has there been credible research that pointed to a fundamental difference between the genders? We were surprised to discover the extent of meticulous research on this topic, especially research that explores differences between the genders that are not socially constructed or have anything to do with discrimination of any kind. Unsurprisingly, almost all of the research was inconclusive. Even the most competent and perseverant researchers seem to have reached the conclusion that there was no evidence that pointed to any inherent and fundamental difference between the genders.

There are obviously some differences between the two genders which is clearly the reason why life evolved to create the two genders in the first place, but even amateurs in biology know that the mechanics of evolution work very opportunistically and defy logic or an attempt to fit observations into a 'cause–effect' framework. Some of these are discussed at length by Richard Dawkins in his highly acclaimed book *The Selfish Gene* in the chapter titled 'Battle of the Sexes'. Like Stephen Hawking's *A Brief History of Time*, Dawkins' *The Selfish Gene* brings an extremely complex topic down to the level of the layman, making for an exceptionally interesting read. Even someone of Dawkins' prowess and reputation in the field of biological evolution has not been able to establish any fundamental difference between the genders, though he lays out interesting possibilities on why evolution created the two sexes. It was Kurt Vonnegut, an American novelist and short story writer, who had said, 'History is merely a list of surprises. It can only prepare us to be surprised yet again.' After devouring Dawkins' and Darwin's writings, we can say with reasonable certainty that 'evolution is merely a series of progressive changes to life. It can seem tantalizingly within grasp, but the complexity and random nature will always elude our understanding.' Most of the apparent differences between genders, that have origins in evolution, are not beyond reasonable doubt and do not pass the test of more serious scrutiny.

Almost all research on the differences in aptitudes and capabilities between genders concludes that differences, if they do exist, are almost completely a result of the interplay between several factors including upbringing, culture, stereotyping since childhood and the unconscious nudges in particular directions rather than inherent differences attributable to gender (we have explored some of these differences in the chapter 'Equal, Not Same'). No researcher has been able to establish any significant correlation between gender and innate capability in any arena, with possibly the sole exception being in activities involving physical strength. Every research paper on this topic is inconclusive. Although from time-to-time, some research efforts have thrown up some findings which are admittedly tantalizing but, at best, ambiguous. But each of them, nevertheless, concludes that the differences are too insignificant to be called out. The American

Psychological Association, in a publication of 20 October 2005, concluded that,

> *Studies show that one's sex has little or no bearing on personality, cognition and leadership. A 2005 analysis of 46 meta-analyses that were conducted during the last two decades of the 20th century underscores that men and women are basically alike in terms of personality, cognitive ability, and leadership.*[3]

Which brings us to an important point, and that is about our ability to predict social outcomes far out into the future, including how a child may grow up to be. Those familiar with 'chaos theory', more commonly referred to as the 'butterfly effect', would understand this well. Some systems are not very amenable to predictions for the simple reason that even the minutest variation in the initial conditions can result in a huge variation in the end results. In other words, a very small variation in the initial conditions does not result in a very small variation in the outcome. Weather forecasting is such a system, and hence one can't forecast accurately for more than a few days irrespective of how much data you may gather and feed into a supercomputer farm. This phenomenon is more commonly referred to as the 'butterfly effect' where a metaphorical flutter of a butterfly in the Amazon rain forests could cause a cyclone in the Arabian Sea. Anyone who claims they can connect the flutter of the butterfly to the cyclone, and can actually predict it, is indulging in hogwash. If small differences in initial conditions, such as those due to rounding errors in numerical computation, can yield widely diverging outcomes even for deterministic systems where an approximate

---

[3] https://www.apa.org/research/action/difference

present cannot determine an approximate future, imagine how much more indeterminate and irrelevant would be the predictions for inherently non-deterministic and recursive systems like social behaviours and outcomes. Men and women were once boys and girls. The conditions that each individual, boy or girl, was subjected to at every stage, the biases they were exposed to, the stereotypes they were fitted into, all have a role to play in the way each individual evolves into an adult. This is a perfect example of the butterfly effect at play in real life. Viewing the impact of these conditions on the ultimate outcome and attributing the differences to gender or sex to the exclusion of everything else is like trying to conclusively establish if the flight of a butterfly in the Amazon rain forests would result in a cyclone in the Arabian Sea or a snowstorm in Vladivostok.

Damore wasn't the first, and certainly won't be the last, individual who tried to apply linear thinking—that may have held true in a single-independent and a single-dependent-variable scenario—to establish causation in a situation where the relationships between the variables were non-linear, recursive and an outcome of the interplay between hundreds of them. William Shockley, who shared the Nobel Prize in physics in 1956 for the invention of the 'transistor' with two other scientists, in his later years, applied this same faulty thinking to propound some outrageous theories like the American Negro's intellectual and social deficits are hereditary and racially genetic in origin. He even proposed that individuals with IQs below 100 be paid to undergo voluntary sterilization, because reproduction among the less intelligent would eventually result in a decline of civilization.[4] V. S. Ramachandran, one of the

---

[4] https://www.thoughtco.com/biography-of-william-shockley-4843200

world's leading neuroscientists, points out that no one with such warped and simplistic thinking would get very far in medical school or be allowed to practice as a physician, and yet, whole careers and political movements have been built on such absurd beliefs. Therefore, the entire debate of nature versus nurture can never be easily settled because almost every cognitive ability is an outcome of the complex interaction between different elements of nature and nurture, and the final outcomes are almost unrelatable to each of these variables just as a cyclone or a snowstorm in Asia or Europe is unrelatable to the flutter of a butterfly in the Amazon rain forest.

Coming back to Damore's memo, it is quite apparent that Damore reached a bunch of hasty conclusions. Using research findings conveniently in a one-sided way by citing findings, however inconclusive they may be, that justify your point of view is what psychologists refer to euphemistically as the 'confirmation bias'. This is also akin to the 'Texas sharpshooter fallacy', where differences in data are ignored and similarities overemphasized. This does not mean that anyone who is not an expert is not entitled to explore complex issues that call for deep expertise. An employee is entitled to bring up topics like company culture or company policy (on say gender diversity) with those responsible for crafting policies around these themes. It is possible that even after a lot of discussion, there could be differences that cannot be bridged. And the gap could remain unbridged for several reasons, including insufficient understanding of these issues on the part of those entrusted with explaining these to employees or intransigence and argumentativeness on the part of the employee or the custodians of these policies.

Many proponents of gender diversity, who disagreed with Damore, have argued that since there is not a shred of evidence from any credible research study to conclude that there is an innate difference in the capabilities of the two genders, Damore's conclusions are wrong. However, ironically many of the same proponents of gender diversity also argue that having gender diversity in leadership teams and at junior levels, too, increases the diversity of thought process and helps bring in different perspectives because men and women are different. You can't argue both ways based on convenience. If a 'hasty conclusion' (or stereotyping) of one kind is faulty, misinformed and harmful, then the reverse 'hasty conclusion' (or stereotyping) is equally faulty. Not just faulty, the reverse stereotyping gives credence to the original stereotyping and creates a fatal vulnerability in those who seek to fight it. A faulty logic cannot be fought with faulty logic just as one mystery cannot be explained with another mystery. Those who seek to criticize a construct cannot lean on the same construct to fight it. If there is no evidence to show that women aren't as decisive and tough as the men, and any attempt to paint men as being more decisive is a dangerous stereotyping, then arguing that having women in the mix would result in a better emotional balance is equally flawed. The truth is that there are men who are indecisive and women who are decisive, just as there are men who are emotional and women who aren't as emotional. If indeed there are any perceptible differences between men and women, it is because of all the other factors listed earlier, namely, upbringing, culture, stereotyping since childhood and the unconscious nudges in particular directions rather than inherent differences attributable to gender. Differences as a result of these factors are what every civilized individual agrees are not necessarily desirable. On the contrary, there is a need to eliminate most of the stereotyping and nudging. And therefore, how could one use differences that arise out of these factors to make a case for gender diversity? Simply put, gender diversity need not (and cannot) be justified on the grounds that it creates a diversity of thought process.

We'll now return to a point we left incomplete, namely, was Google as guilty as Damore, in making some sweeping assumptions about gender diversity? And therefore, was it a case of 'my sweeping assumption is superior and more politically correct than yours?' Damore's arguments may have been simplistic, but then who is not guilty of being simplistic? Every day, leaders take simplistic and politically correct positions on a whole range of issues. Far from being pulled up, they are rewarded. Duplicity is far more harmful than dissent. Many companies have been guilty of trying to take politically correct positions on this topic and, hence, tend to invite silent criticism or scepticism. Taking politically correct positions is no different from posturing. This precludes debate, discussion and questioning. When companies sidestep discussion and debate, even if there is visible acceptance of a policy by the employees, it may not always be wholehearted. And that could result in undermining the policy or the underlying beliefs. Once in a while, as a reaction to intransigence and an unwillingness to debate this contentious issue on the part of the companies, the criticism becomes strident and takes on rebellious overtones. For Google, it was apparent that defending gender diversity was more important than being transparent and encouraging freedom of opinion and expression, which too was quasi-religious. But in the face of a direct conflict between these two, gender diversity was seen as the bigger religion and ultimately prevailed. We believe Google could have handled it more maturely and used this opportunity to encourage debate. Treating something as holy, and beyond debate and discussion, borders on religious fervour, and this is not a good thing even in religion, leave alone in the corporate world. Ability to deal with dissent or multiplicity of opinions in an honest and transparent matter is the very foundation of diversity. Dealing with dissent calls for uncluttered thinking on one's part besides being open and humble. Absence of these is the main reason for avoiding discussion and debate. Every other form of diversity is built on this foundation. We believe Google failed the true test of diversity by taking a politically correct position and avoiding an honest discourse on the subject. We have discussed this at length in the chapter 'Dissent and Diversity'. Over the years, Google continued to do badly on handling dissent, and it's by now famous open culture was increasingly under threat. The company introduced draconian guidelines on what constituted acceptable speech in internal forums, and these guidelines severely restricted the ability of employees to question management actions. In November 2019, hundreds of Google employees protested against management attempts to silence employees who were involved with employee activism.

This is not an unbridled criticism of Google and its track record on diversity. We believe Google has demonstrated genuine commitment to diversity and inclusion, more than most other companies. It is not uncommon for companies to resort to subtle propaganda and create an impression that they are paragons of diversity. It is important to see through this propaganda by looking at a few indicators. The gold standard to assess a company's commitment to diversity, in our opinion, is the diversity in the apex leadership team of the company. The composition of the management team is a true indicator and no company can cheat on that. At Google, 7 of the 17 members of the management team are women. Google has also been very transparent in the way they have made diversity data and specifics of their programs available on their website. However, Google's response to Damore's memo, and its unwillingness to engage in a deeper discussion, was a big blow to their push for diversity, because diversity at the root is respect for diversity of opinions.

Stop Justifying the Need for Gender Diversity

We concluded earlier that gender diversity does not automatically drive diversity of thought process or multiplicity of perspectives. Therefore, one doesn't need to justify gender on the grounds that it would justify diversity of perspectives. Can you, for a moment, imagine having to justify women's right to vote, or say right to education, with an argument that it would promote diversity of political or academic discourse? Women have a right to vote and a right to education as much as men do, period. No justification is required.

Trying to justify gender diversity by resorting to imagined benefits, however well-intentioned, results in perpetuating another set of false notions and weakens the foundation on which a diversity program is built.

In a report titled *Why Diversity Matters*, published in January 2015, McKinsey concluded that:

> *Our latest research finds that companies in the top quartile for gender or racial and ethnic diversity are more likely to have financial returns above their national industry medians. Companies in the bottom quartile in these dimensions are statistically less likely to achieve above-average returns. And diversity is probably a competitive differentiator that shifts market share toward more diverse companies over time.*[5]

---

[5] https://www.mckinsey.com/business-functions/organization/our-insights/why-diversity-matters#

The hint of causation in this conclusion is certainly hasty.

Seeming to imply a diametrically opposite viewpoint, Aileen Lee in a *TechCrunch* article in 2013, (the rather famous article in which she first used the term 'unicorn', which caught the imagination of the start-up world), observed that one of the findings of the comprehensive study of 39 unicorns was that there was very little diversity among founders in the Unicorn Club. We don't believe she was implying that start-ups that are low on diversity have a higher probability of growing into unicorns. It was just an interesting observation that had caught her attention. However, unlike McKinsey, she was smart and, more importantly, intellectually honest, not to draw any hasty conclusions from this observation.

Exactly three years after the report *Why Diversity Matters*, in a similar report titled *Delivering Through Diversity*, McKinsey concluded that:

> *Top-quartile companies on executive-level gender diversity worldwide had a 21 percent likelihood of outperforming their fourth-quartile industry peers on EBIT margin, and they also had a 27 percent likelihood of outperforming fourth-quartile peers on longer-term value creation, as measured using an economic-profit (EP) margin.*[6]

While these reports contain the standard disclaimer that correlation does not imply causation, they end up misleading unwitting readers, many of whom seldom understand or differentiate *correlation* and *causation*. And some companies could end up concluding very simplistically that merely forcing diversity in boards and executive teams, without creating the

---

[6] https://www.mckinsey.com/business-functions/organization/our-insights/delivering-through-diversity

other ingredients, would drive financial performance and profitability. If a company is not deeply committed to diversity in thinking, then aiming for gender diversity could easily result in hiring women who are no different from the men in the company. And this is why most companies that pay lip service to diversity end up doing exactly this—creating superficial diversity. On the contrary, if a company is deeply committed to creating a diversity of perspectives and thinking, then the men themselves would not be a homogeneous lot. This eventually has a very high probability of resulting in gender diversity too.

In conclusion: Advocates of gender diversity in companies have, for far too long, tried to 'justify' gender diversity. Gender diversity needs no justification and is merely an outcome of pursuing the broader goal of creating an inclusive society and an inclusive culture in a company. Pursuing gender diversity blindly will *not* create diversity of thought. Gender diversity is also an outcome of eliminating long-standing biases against women. Biases that run so deep that it took centuries for them to be accorded the right to vote in most democracies. Biases that kept them locked in homes tied to household chores. We need to overcome these biases and do not need any justification to do it.

Gender equality and, hence, equal opportunities and equal pay for women should be a fundamental axiom that needs neither discussion nor justification—justifying essentially to male-dominated leadership on why they need to make some 'concessions' and 'accommodate' women a little more. If you really want to justify gender diversity, you don't need to go beyond the obvious fact that it immediately expands the range of the talent pool that is available to you and, hence, increases your chances of finding the best candidates; and half the consumers in the world are women. Over the decades, gender diversity has become the biggest driver of competitive advantage for acquiring talent. There cannot be a better signal to talented women that they have a fair chance of career advancement in a company than seeing women at all levels of leadership in the company.

Consultants like McKinsey have, through their well-intentioned studies, continued to naively justify how gender diversity is helpful for business. What a hopeless waste of time trying to establish a false sense of causation on something so complex when causation need not even be established. It is a sad state of affairs that even in the 21st century one needs dubious studies like these to induce change. For anyone who was born in an era where the right to education and the right to suffrage for women were universal (majority of the readers would fall into this category), reading the part of history where women had to struggle for these seems so incredulous and beyond comprehension. Let's apply the same incredulity when it comes to gender diversity at the workplace and ask ourselves as to why the same struggle needs a re-enactment and revalidation in a different arena. Why can't we, unconditionally and without any justification, accept, as easily as we now accept women's right to education, that gender diversity at the workplace is fundamental?

And finally, should we replace gender in this chapter with race, ethnicity or skin colour, the arguments essentially remain the same.

BIG IN THE CHAPTER
IDEAS

1. *Research on biological differences between men and women, w.r.t. capability, potential, etc., has been largely inconclusive:* Gender differences are more attributable to factors such as environment, societal norms, etc.

2. *If genetics-driven differences in gender are unproven, then it can't be argued that gender diversity necessarily adds to diversity:* Diversity business case cannot be built on the premise that a mere improvement in gender ratio leads to diversity in thought process.

3. *Duplicity is more harmful than dissent:* Companies are guilty of taking politically correct positions, that preclude debate and discussion, implying any visible acceptance of diversity policy may not be wholehearted.

4. *Justifying diversity under premise of 'diversity means better business results' sets the wrong foundation for diversity:* Lack of inherent deep commitment to diversity leads companies to chase superficial metrics.

5. *Principally, diversity needs no justification:* Diversity is as fundamental to society and business as right to vote. It's pointless to waste time and resources in building a business case for diversity, especially based on shaky arguments and misleading data implications.

Does Diversity Really Help Business?

Good leadership requires you to surround yourself with people of diverse perspectives who can disagree with you without fear of retaliation.

—Doris Kearns Goodwin

In the previous chapter, we argued that diversity is as fundamental as the right to vote. And yet, here we are, asking the next inevitable question: Is diversity always a good thing for a company? Admittedly, the latter seems to contradict the former. However, the paradox—of diversity being a fundamental aspect of how we work, and the question of its viability to business—is critical to the understanding of diversity beyond tokenism.

Let's consider the McKinsey's report *Why Diversity Matters*, published in January 2015, which starts with the line, 'We know intuitively that diversity matters.' At the outset, by no stretch of imagination, is it intuitive that 'diversity matters'. On the contrary, diversity at the workplace conjures up images of conflict and disagreement with people from different backgrounds—ethnic, cultural, style, thinking and education—arguing over different issues and struggling to build a consensus. Isn't it actually quite intuitive that if you've got a group of homogenous people who all think alike, it is far easier to reach a consensus? Having people with different perspectives, different experiences, different opinions and, perhaps, different working styles or expectations makes it so much more difficult to agree on issues. In addition, people from different ethnic or cultural backgrounds can have varying opinions concerning religion, lifestyle and politics that can lead to tension and conflict in a work environment. Therefore, the truth is that if diversity does indeed matter, it is extremely counter-intuitive. Any truth of life that is counter-intuitive needs to be explored and understood well. Without a deeper understanding, any change would either be faulty or rife with tokenism.

The next line in the McKinsey report, 'Diversity is probably a competitive differentiator that shifts market share towards more diverse companies over time', appears both sweeping and speculative. The use of the word 'probably' makes the whole statement a conjecture rather than a well-researched viewpoint, and a sweeping conclusion for diversity based on contrived logic can only strengthen the case of those who are opposed to it. Nowhere in the article is there any insight on either the causation or the exact mechanism through which diversity impacts business. Nailing down cause and effect so simplistically, in an arena where there are multiple variables at play and acting on one another recursively in a non-linear manner, is at best naïve and at worst misleading. In most such situations, because of the recursive nature of the relationship between the variables, it is even incorrect assigning labels such as 'cause' and 'effect'.

The argument of 'diversity creates business edge' is not limited to this report but used ad nauseam by diversity advocates. Hence, it is worth spending a minute longer on why it is important not to be hasty in assigning any kind of cause–effect relationship.

Take the example of Michael Homes, Professor of strategic management at the Florida State University, who, in an article in *The Conversation*, an online magazine, points out that 'although companies led by women or men took similar levels of risk, those with female CEOs generated smaller investor returns.' Now, it would be naïve to conclude that companies run by women tend to generate lower returns for shareholders. In the same article, Homes also points out that 'women who become CEOs are often appointed to companies that are in crisis or are performing poorly, as in the cases of Mary Barra at General Motors, Carly Fiorina at Hewlett Packard and Marissa Mayer at Yahoo!'[1] And therefore, it is more likely that the causation of lower returns is the nature of companies women are typically appointed to and not the inherent incompetence of women CEOs, as a casual reading of the article may have fallaciously concluded.

Popular literature on diversity and inclusion is full of unsubstantiated claims, often wrapped in impressive sounding empirical correlations and statements that sound politically correct. We have asked this question to many of the proponents of this theory as to why they thought diversity impacts business positively. Their responses were invariably inconsistent and full of contradictions—in fact, contradicting their own positions on other aspects of diversity. In less than five minutes, almost all of them were confounded and gave up. The shallowness of the discourse is quite striking. It is not that there are no genuine experts on this topic, but most of the real experts seem to have figured out that black and white

---

[1] https://theconversation.com/why-are-there-so-few-women-ceos-103212

perspectives on this theme, though they make for a good story, are completely invalid and unsubstantiated. Therefore, their views have not got the attention they deserve. All attention has been hijacked by those that have peddled simplistic and extreme points of view.

The obvious question is if diversity was so unambiguously beneficial, then why shouldn't companies quickly set, and achieve, diversity targets and not be further bothered by any of this discussion?

As we pointed out in the first chapter, Aileen Lee, in the same *TechCrunch* article in 2013, where she first used the term 'unicorn', observed that one of the findings of the comprehensive study of 39 unicorns was that there was very little diversity among founders in the Unicorn Club. Was it sheer coincidence that start-ups that had raced ahead to the aspirational finish line of 'unicorn' status had done so by consciously avoiding diversity, or was there more to this? Do start-ups with like-minded founders and early-stage employees tend to scale faster than the others, or is the lack of diversity pervasive across the start-up world which Aileen Lee, in her focused study on the 39 unicorns in the sample, did not spot? In which case was the lack of diversity among the unicorns no different from the rest of the start-ups that were not unicorns? And is it wrong for start-ups, and even mature companies, to consciously avoid diversity? Hold your horses for a few minutes and we'll come back to this towards the end of this chapter.

Over the years, the discourse on diversity has assumed moral overtones in which companies could not be seen to be even discussing whether diversity was good for their business, as we saw in Google's retaliation to Damore's memo. When Google sought feedback, did they expect everyone to wax eloquent on how far-sighted and liberal Google was with their programs on diversity? Did Google really expect that no difficult questions would be raised? As a result of this lack of openness to opinion and debate, many companies have gone down the slippery path of paying lip service to diversity by doing all the politically correct things like appointing chief diversity officers, creating a slate of diverse candidates for roles and having policies and goals on diversity. In most cases, these measures often tend to be superficial, instead of a long-term, well thought-through approach. They do not deeply reflect any fundamental beliefs. These highly publicized and cosmetic changes have become fashion statements that serve two broad purposes, namely, (a) makes your company look progressive and help avoid lawsuits and (b) communicate to the world at large that you are a socially responsible and ethical organization. These are sufficiently powerful reasons for companies to persist with this strategy even though they don't seem to genuinely alter anything on the ground or result in any of the financial benefits that McKinsey had called out in their two reports.

Glenn Llopis, founder of an acclaimed business strategy consulting firm named after himself, in an article dated 16 Jan 2017 in Forbes.com, says something that many other observers have also highlighted:

I find more companies using diversity and inclusion plans solely to get recognized on a top 100 diversity management list. We need to stop solving and looking for recognition and start thinking about and earning respect from the actual people in our workplaces and marketplaces.

This is not to deny that there are organizations that deeply understand why diversity matters and are committed to making this work. So, what is the truth? And therefore, the counter to McKinsey's report is, 'does diversity really matter?'

Diversity Is Neither Good Nor Bad

As the title of this book implies, it's important that diversity goes beyond tokenism, and we can ask honest questions without feeling compelled to be politically correct. David A. Kravitz, Professor of management at George Mason's School of Business, who has been researching the relationship between diversity and performance, says that 'Some diversity advocates claim that diversity is always good and some opponents claim that it's always bad.'[2] According to Kravitz, both these claims are naïve and inaccurate. Diversity in the workplace is far more complex than merely giving it epithets like 'good' and 'bad' and often has both positive and negative effects. A potential benefit is an increase in creativity, but potential challenges include an increase in conflicts and a breakdown in communication.

At a very high level, most experts on the topic do agree on the definition of a diverse workplace as one where people *do not just tolerate but accept and respect* people of different races, ethnicities, genders, ages, religions, disabilities and sexual orientations, as well as differences in personalities, skill sets, experiences and knowledge bases. However, in reality, diversity can mean different things to different organizations. The way a start-up views diversity could be very different from the way a large multinational company views diversity; the way a family business views diversity is very different from

---

[2] https://business.gmu.edu/news/862-the-good-and-bad-of-workplace-diversity/

the way a professionally managed company looks at diversity; and the way a company that operates in one country in Europe—or say within a small region India—views diversity would be very different from the way a company that is pan-Europe or pan-India views diversity. Therefore, the stage in the life cycle of an organization's evolution, the pattern of ownership and control, nature of the business and clientele, as well as the extent of geographic dispersion of its operations, among many other factors, influences the way a company views diversity.

If your company is operating only in Italy and serving Italian customers, it may not be out of place to hire people who have proficiency in the Italian language. So, job ads may specify that only those with a knowledge of Italian may apply. This is not to be seen as discrimination or going against the grain of diversity. If a job requires the candidate to work at night and the local law does not allow women to do a night shift or if the law and order conditions make it unsafe for women to commute at night, then it may be alright for a company to say in their job ad that only men may apply.

If your company is manufacturing products for say women, it is important to have people in the team who understand women, their preferences and buying patterns. In fact, one of the biggest pushes for diversity comes from this premise, which is, a company's sales force and product design teams should mirror their customer segments. A German company serving enterprise clients in North America should try and hire North Americans (predominantly) who understand North American buyers well and can connect with them culturally. By doing so, they are not going against the grain of diversity. Therefore, judging without understanding, or without having the complete picture, does not help.

Hence, assuming diversity always helps or always hurts is incorrect. It is important to understand the business context and structure before weaving in diversity.

In the next few sections, we'll take a look at some of the most common questions and themes in discussions relating to diversity.

The 'Not Like Us' Syndrome

One question that often pops up after a while, in any discussion on diversity, is aren't some type of people more suitable for some roles than the others? Would the head of analytics and data science in a company be considered guilty of a 'not like us' bias if they tend to pick people who are good at problem-solving and analytically oriented for roles in their team? If the culture in the team is to go out for a beer bash after a review meeting, would it be considered a 'not like us' bias if candidates open to late-evening outings are preferred, everything else being equal of course? If being polite and courteous towards peers is part of the company's values, would it be considered a 'not like us' bias if a candidate who is a bit rough at the edges and blunt in speech is not considered because of this?

These are important questions.

Diversity does not mean you would ignore the skills, educational qualifications and competencies that candidates need to possess to be effective in the role. Therefore, if an aptitude for numbers and analysis is a core skill that is essential for performing in a role, then only candidates who are good at it should make it to the shortlist.

Enthusiasm about the late-night beer bashes is not core to being able to perform in the role, though one could argue that bonding and a sense of team spirit is built in these outings. This is where the team should reconsider what constitutes bonding and figure out other better ways of bonding. Being more positively inclined towards a candidate who loves these late-night beer bashes over another candidate who is equally competent but not open to these outings is, in our opinion, certainly a case of a 'not like us' bias.

Now, coming to the last part about being respectful towards peers. This should frankly be a core expectation and anyone who is blatantly disrespectful does not make the cut. Here, of course, one needs to evaluate whether a particular candidate is being disrespectful or is merely outspoken and assertive. This is such a grey area and needs careful handling. If you turn down an applicant's candidature because they are disrespectful in their dealings, then it is the right thing to do, but if you turn down their candidature because they are outspoken and assertive, then it is a case of exhibiting a 'not like us' bias. In the last instance, there is a very thin line between being biased and being open. Most hiring managers may not even recognize that they are being biased because they may not understand the difference between being disrespectful, on the one hand, and being assertive or outspoken, on the other. It is here that intense training and coaching is helpful. However, only training without coaching is bound to fail. Training needs to be reinforced every day with the right signals, nudging and clarifying by the manager.

And finally, the most common question: 'If diversity is important, then does a company's culture not count for anything? Is it right or not for companies to insist on candidates being a culture fit? Should a company be open to a candidate even if the candidate is a poor culture fit? Shouldn't a company embrace people who bring in diverse cultural perspectives?

If culture fit is important, then doesn't it go against the grain of diversity?'

This brings us to a very fundamental point as to what is culture. If one answers this question thoughtfully, then this confusion would diminish significantly. Wrong notions on what culture exactly is tends to create cobwebs in the mind.

Edgar Schein, the demigod of organizational culture, says that culture manifests itself at three levels, namely, (a) artefacts, (b) espoused values and (c) the tacit stuff.

Artefacts are things like office décor, dress code, late-night meetings and get-togethers, beer on tap policies, etc. Espoused values are what the company specifically articulates such as customer centricity, agility, transparency, etc. Neither of these two actually represent the true culture of a company, though the espoused values at least indicate intent. It is not uncommon to see a company espouse customer centricity or, for that matter, any other value but, in reality, not be deeply committed to it. What truly represents a company culture are the kind of behaviours that are rewarded and recognized or penalized. It is the set of behaviours that are displayed every day by the leaders in the company. It is not what the leaders say but what they do that constitutes culture.

Culture fit is never about artefacts (the way a person dresses, or hairstyling, or openness to late-night parties). Unfortunately, culture fit sometimes gets misunderstood because hiring managers end up looking for a fit at the artefact level. Looking for a culture fit at an artefact level is an unambiguous sign of a 'not like us' bias. In fact, there is a specific term that is used to describe people who are like you and with whom you can get along because of similar interests, education, upbringing and experiences, namely, 'affinity bias'. The search for a culture fit should be at the level of espoused values and the tacit stuff.

Culture fit, as we just concluded, is often misconstrued because companies look for a fit at the artefact level. However, the question that still remains unanswered is—even if you look for a true culture fit at a values level, does it go against the grain of diversity? This is an important question and we'll try and answer that.

In our opinion, there are three types of companies:

1. Companies that have a limited understanding of their own culture and, hence, an inadequate understanding of what really constitutes a culture fit
2. Companies that have a good sense of their culture but are understated about it and don't necessarily deify it
3. Companies that publicize and glorify their culture

It is the third category of companies that have made culture seem like such a cool thing. From what we have seen, the aggressive pursuit of 'culture fit' by the third category of companies can sometimes become the flip side of intolerance. Companies that vociferously advertise their culture are also communicating a degree of intolerance. If you see carefully, you would discover that these companies mostly flaunt their artefacts and not the deep, underlying elements of what really constitutes culture. To an extent, these companies resemble cults, and cults have a tendency to augment and reinforce their identity with an almost authoritarian enforcement of the cult's beliefs and practices. And this goes against the grain of inclusion. We have addressed the nuances of culture fit and dissent in the chapter 'Dissent and Diversity'. Companies that have truly cracked the culture code are those in the second category. They truly get what culture is but do not use it to exclude like those in the third category. They take a balanced position and make culture truly work for them.

One of the biggest lessons in my career in managing cross-border, cross-cultural and globally distributed multi-ethnic teams has been about the importance of ignoring, or maybe even celebrating, the artefact-level differences but striving for commonality on the real culture stuff. In fact, genuine respect and appreciation for the artefact-level differences create stronger bonding and agreement around the core culture elements. In a cross-cultural context, by paying too much attention to the artefacts of style, your judgement would be coloured by what, in your culture, is considered a superior style. If you think a little carefully, you would figure out that culture is really about behaviours/styles that people believe make them successful. And beliefs about what behaviours/styles make people successful will differ by region and country. For instance, in some cultures, free, and even heated, debate is essential. In a different culture, people express disagreements more diplomatically. Therefore, by stereotyping and jumping to broader conclusions about individuals based on these stereotypes or even believing your style is superior is falling prey to the 'not like us' bias.

A melting pot, in the context of diversity, implies that individuals and groups surrender their individual identity and become a part of a larger identity. Giving up an identity is not an easy thing to do, so creating a melting pot is almost always about recruiting people who share a common identity. In contrast, a salad bowl implies an ability to preserve your distinct identity and yet be part of a larger group.

While the analogy sounds interesting and straightforward, it is never about a melting pot *or* a salad bowl. It is a bit of both. The identity at the artefact level is analogous to a salad bowl. Different artefacts can coexist in peace and with mutual respect. The identity at the level of espoused values and the tacit stuff is more analogous to a melting pot where everyone should strive to be similar.

Therefore, in many ways, this is the crux of diversity.

Affirmative Action versus Passive Support

Affirmative action has been a controversial thing, not just when it comes to diversity but in everything else too. Governments in several countries have taken steps to create a sort of level playing field for the historically disadvantaged groups by giving them special rights and benefits. The intent is to obviously compensate for the discrimination these groups have suffered in the past. The belief, and quite rightly so, is that in the absence of affirmative actions the gap would only continue to widen. The problem with affirmative action obviously is that individuals who belong to the majority groups have to pay for the creation of this level playing field by foregoing some benefits that would have otherwise been available to everyone equally.

When it comes to diversity, should companies take affirmative action? Does it mean that merit should be compromised, even if it is just a little bit, to accommodate a minority group? Should companies tweak their recruitment processes to achieve diversity targets? Should companies even go about setting diversity targets?

These are difficult questions but need to be addressed because they are on top of everyone's mind. Ignoring them or allowing people to come to their own conclusions can be damaging. It would be evident that there are no black and white answers.

For instance, one view could be that companies should just stay focused on genuinely creating a culture of 'inclusivity' and diversity would follow. This may sound logical but the 'diversity would follow' argument may not always be an entirely valid one, or even if diversity does follow, it would be an extremely slow process, and that could hurt a company that is trying to be a preferred choice for a diverse set of people. Reversing an overwhelming trend is close to impossible just through good intent. In reality, the trend gets accentuated and would worsen without affirmative action.

And here is why. For instance, women would not consider a company a great place to work just because it is open to gender diversity and is striving to build an 'inclusive' culture. They will want to see the proof of the pudding. Unless there is already a critical mass of women in the company, it may not be a workplace that is conducive for women yet. And if women perceive it that way, then the company loses out on a very large chunk of the talent pool. Therefore, it is important to get to that critical mass with some specific actions. And there is no need to dilute standards to achieve this goal. It would mean you need to cast your net a bit wider and have a position open for a little longer if need be to find the right candidate who not only meets the merit criteria but also advances the diversity goal. Willingness to have a position open for a little longer, especially in a high-growth organization, means willingness to undergo some short-term pain in exchange for achieving a long-term goal. One of the unambiguous signs of a good leader is the ability to convince the group to make this trade off.

Affirmative action serves two purposes, namely, (a) providing a few individuals from the disadvantaged group an opportunity to catch up with the rest and (b) creating a critical number of role models from the disadvantaged group to inspire the rest of the people in the disadvantaged group and giving them hope. Often the second objective is underrated and not understood well enough.

We have discussed affirmative action at some length and have actually strengthened the argument in its favour in the chapter 'Women in Senior Management'.

Let's now come to some interesting affirmative actions in the education space. Indian Institutes of Technology (IITs) and Indian Institutes of Management (IIMs) are India's most prestigious and premier educational institutions for technology and management, respectively and have, over the decades, received international acclaim and fame. These have been semi-government organizations for long and depended almost wholly on government grants because the tuition fees they charged until very recent times were nominal. These institutes were long-standing male bastions. When I (Hari) graduated from IIT Madras in 1986, there were only three girls in a batch of nearly 250. Of late, these institutes have taken affirmative action by lowering the cut-off scores in admission for the girls. We believe this was a bold move, and in some ways truly groundbreaking.

This brings us to an interesting, and controversial, question namely why were there only few girls in these institutes in the first place? Why didn't they fare as well as the boys in the highly competitive entrance tests? And therefore, were they not as competent as the boys? These are the kind of questions that Damore raised in his memo.

Our hypothesis is that there has been a vicious cycle at work here, and we have discussed the concept of a vicious cycle in this context in the chapter 'Women in Senior Management'. Girls have been nudged gently, and not so gently, towards certain professions, and engineering hasn't been one such profession. Traditionally, a job in engineering meant working on an oil rig, a factory, the high seas, a construction site or a workshop, and because of the relatively harsh working conditions and the exacting physical demands in these jobs, these were not considered suitable for women. However, over the years, engineering has evolved, and the job mix between the different branches of engineering has altered significantly. The digital explosion has resulted in a sudden surge in demand for those with expertise in coding, analytics, data sciences and the like. Therefore, most engineering graduates don't end up pursuing jobs they studied to take up. There are not sufficient number of jobs in say mechanical or electrical engineering in comparison with the number of students who graduate in these subjects every year. Therefore, most engineering graduates end up pursuing jobs in computer sciences, management and other unrelated fields. And these jobs are equally well suited for women. So, suddenly engineering is an attractive proposition for girls to take up. But some affirmative action is needed to provide the initial impetus before it can become self-sustaining. It's like priming a pump with an initial fill of fluid. The IITs have, therefore, done the right thing by providing this initial impetus.

Now let's come to a more fundamental point, which is, why does one need to even study engineering to take up these unrelated professions, especially management! Why waste four precious years of your life studying how to design turbines and transformers only to begin your career writing code at IBM or Infosys! Part of the reason, of course, is that it takes some time for 'supply' to recalibrate to a change in the 'demand' for skills. I graduated from IIM Calcutta in 1988, and engineering graduates constituted more than 80 per cent of my batch. Quite evidently, the selection process was heavily biased towards engineers, right from the written test (which was common across all the IIMs) to the interview process (each of the IIMs had its own criteria for this round). I still remember a quants professor, who was in my interview panel, asking me what's '"a" to the power of zero?' When I responded it was 'one', the delight on his face was palpable! If you have studied algebra and calculus, you would know that the answer is 'one'. Now, this is a nugget that is not of interest or relevance to anyone other than those pursuing pure mathematics. And most engineers have no clue as to why the answer is one! Knowledge of this is completely irrelevant to performing well in a management role. The subsequent curriculum, too, had a few mandatory courses in quants, some of which were quite advanced, particularly for those who came from a non-math background. Over the years, I discovered that success in management roles had a near-zero correlation with an engineering degree or a mastery over advanced statistics and operations research, both of which were imparted in liberal doses as part of the programme. None of the individuals who were selected into IIM Calcutta, on the basis of their flair for quants, seemed to recall an iota of what was taught in statistics in those two years even a year after graduation, forget being able to apply some of these principles as they scaled the ladder of management. Neither did they demonstrate any flair for numbers, which individuals from other backgrounds did not. So, the bias that favoured the boys in the engineering field continued in the field of management.

Therefore, the answer to the question whether these institutes had a preponderance of boys because boys were more suitable or competent is sheer nonsense. The vicious cycle and the myth of merit had colluded to create a false causation between inherent capability and the resulting imbalance.

Now coming back to affirmative action, we were speaking to Priti Parekh, Senior Managing Director at Morae Global. Priti has been a globetrotter and a successful executive who has been part of the executive teams in multiple companies. She has broken through the glass ceiling and is a highly respected name in the business process outsourcing industry. She was telling us that affirmative action goes well beyond hiring decisions. Proactively talking to women who are thinking of taking a career break and providing them with necessary support to extend their stay or making it easy for them to return to their career after a career break also constitute affirmative action. These actions in themselves could be quite therapeutic for women. She was telling us the story of Anushree Kokkalera, a brilliant 'quants' professional in her team, who was thinking of quitting so that she could devote some quality time to her young son. Priti spoke to her and asked her to take a short sabbatical instead and not cut off the umbilical cord with the firm. That's what she eventually did and made a quick comeback, and today she is the senior director of quants and data science at Moody's Analytics Knowledge Services.

While it is critical to create an inclusive workplace which acts as a strong foundation to launch diversity initiatives subsequently, it pays to also proactively take affirmative actions that do not dilute standards, and this can go a long way in quickly getting to the tipping point on diversity.

However, if implemented poorly, affirmative actions can result in a feeling of 'reverse discrimination', and if this feeling crosses a tipping point, it could result in a backlash. It is important that diversity initiatives be implemented softly and in an inclusive manner by getting everyone on board. We are not suggesting soft-pedalling on the implementation to appease a few naysayers. All we are suggesting is that the harder you push the naysayers, the more intransigent and more camouflaged their position becomes. Therefore, they need to be given time to reflect and see for themselves.

The next question is the trickiest of the lot, which is, should candidates belonging to a minority group be given an advantage when it comes to career advancement? Our view is that this is not necessary. It is important to just ensure that individuals from minority groups should be given equal access to any form of mentoring, formal or informal. And here is where an ombudsman like a chief diversity officer (CDO) comes into play. One of the roles of the CDO should be to ensure that internal cliques are nipped in the bud and mechanisms are in place to ensure that everyone has equal access to all kinds of resources including social.

First-hand Brush with Diversity

I have worked for six companies in my career:

- Three Indian companies with no international presence of any kind
- Three multinationals (start-ups that built international businesses, two of which were acquired—one by IBM, the other by Moody's and the third listed on National Association of Securities Dealers Automated Quotations [NASDAQ])

The average age of the management team at two of the three Indian companies was between 55–60 years and unsurprisingly was all male. There was no strong pipeline of women leaders and there were elements of an old-boys network. While one of these two companies paid lip service to diversity because it was a public company that was intensely focused on winning awards, the other did not have that compulsion. The outlook towards diversity at both these companies was patronizing. Many in these management teams had a limited exposure beyond their company or industry and hence their perspectives were narrow. In contrast, some individuals who were not part of the management teams in these two companies were more progressive with broader perspectives. Therefore, the idea that with age comes capability and a holistic understanding is a total myth. Any kind of stereotyping, you would soon figure out, is untrue.

The third Indian company, TaxiForSure, was run by very young founders and had the right mindset needed to build an inclusive climate and harness dissent. It wasn't just limited to the mindset, but this mindset translated to tangible outcomes like diversity in the management team across dimensions of gender, age and ethnicity, though the business did not demand this. This spoke of the founders' self-assurance and their sense of openness.

The three multinational companies had far more diverse leadership teams (in terms of gender, race and ethnicity), had a strong commitment towards creating a pipeline of women leaders and had a refined and sophisticated understanding of diversity. By their very construct, they were compelled to deal with it, and they handled it with panache. It is not that the two Indian companies were unethical or unfair. On the contrary, they were extremely fair in their business practices but were smug, patriarchal and set in their ways. For them, diversity was a new-age gimmick that some hoity-toity feminists had unleashed, something that was best quietly ignored. Any discussion on initiatives beyond training on unconscious bias was stonewalled. And the founders themselves never attended a session on unconscious bias. Not knowing that you don't know something, but presuming you know it, is the worst state to be in because it closes the doors to learning. And that is what exactly had happened.

Having seen diversity from close quarters in the three rapidly scaling start-ups, with globally distributed teams that were multicultural and multi-ethnic, I can say with confidence that it comes in shades of grey. Diversity in these organizations started off as a necessity forced by the geographical spread of the business, but over time, the benefits of diversity began to slowly emerge. Diversity didn't come without problems either. One had to put in conscious effort to make diversity work, and minor flare ups were common every once in a while. All these three organizations ended up being multicultural, multiracial and multi-ethnic because of business compulsions rather than as an outcome of trying to deliberately be multi-ethnic for the sake of being multi-ethnic. It is our belief that this is how diversity and inclusion take root in most companies—starting as a necessity. Very soon, wise leadership teams figure out that diversity is a potent weapon if leveraged well. And that is what I saw happen.

Two of these three companies were India-headquartered outsourcing firms with client-facing teams in the US and Europe and delivery teams in Asia and Latin America. The third company was headquartered in the US with an identical structure. The composition of the leadership team, to some extent, depends upon the numerical strength of the teams in different geographies and the origins and upbringing of the key executives.

Each of these was unique in terms of the extent of diversity across the company as a whole as well as in the leadership team. This is captured in the table below.

Name of Company	Diversity in Middle Management	Diversity in Executive Leadership
Daksh (acquired by IBM)	Ethnic diversity: Medium Gender diversity: High	Ethnic diversity: Medium Gender diversity: Medium
Virtusa (listed on NASDAQ)	Ethnic diversity: High Gender diversity: High	Ethnic diversity: High Gender diversity: Medium
Amba Research (acquired by by Moody's)	Ethnic diversity: High Gender diversity: High	Ethnic diversity: Medium Gender diversity: High

When a business compulsion forces a company to build and hire a diverse workforce, it inevitably begins to learn how to build capabilities that can make these diverse teams work together. Unless the leadership is extraordinarily inflexible and obstinate, it will begin to collectively learn the advantages of diversity. I have seen smart leaders, who had not experienced diversity in their past lives, quickly realize the power of an 'inclusive' leadership style. With some effort and nudging, they become quite adept at this. There are a few who struggle to lead in an environment where a business compulsion has made diversity inevitable. Such leaders need constant nudging, coaching and even a rap on the knuckles from time to time.

In all these three companies, ethnic and racial diversity was forced in varying degrees by the geographic structure of the business. Having an Indian expat lead a large team of Filipinos in Manila may be alright at the very beginning when you start operations in the Philippines, but it cannot be the default approach going forward. First, it is bound to create some undercurrents, however silent and trifling, in the local team; second, you would be missing out on a large pool of talented Filipino managers. Leaders who are sent out as expats need to have personally experienced multi-ethnic cultures and should have a degree of refinement. Absence of either will soon create serious issues.

Similarly, having a local American handle a large client in New York is far more likely to work than sending someone from Asia to manage the account. This is not to say that there should be no cross-border deployment of talent. On the contrary, as the multinational construct of the business intensifies, it actually makes sense to build a pool of leaders who are great cross-cultural leaders.

In all these three cases, ethnic diversity was forced by the geographical spread. Gender diversity simply helped access a larger pool of talent in each of the geographies.

Not all companies truly embrace diversity wholeheartedly. While some of them just end up tolerating diversity as a necessary evil that needs to be managed, a few others truly go beyond the bare necessity and try and make diversity work for them.

We think, everything else being the same, companies tend to become more committed to diversity when (a) the complexity and geographical spread of the business grows and (b) they go past the phase where they believe the organization will endure. And start-ups get to this phase of 'permanency' after an acquisition by a larger company or after becoming a public company.

My own experiences with each of these three companies (when they were still private companies) led me to believe that all three of them were very open to diversity of opinions and styles and were highly ethical companies committed to doing the right things. None of these companies had an explicit policy on diversity but intuitively understood what it meant and how it impacted the business, or rather why business imperatives made it so important to take a constructive approach to diversity. There was a degree of humility, openness to new learnings and a complete absence of 'not invented here' or 'not like us' syndromes in each of these three companies. As a result, they learned the nuances of diversity every day and got better at it. In my opinion, diversity became a powerful strategic lever in all these three companies.

One question that had occurred to me at the time was whether it was desirable to pursue diversity in ethnicity and/or culture even if there were no business compulsion? The answer to this question, I figured out, was that diversity in your employment practices should at least mirror (if not better) the diversity in the communities you serve or the talent pools you draw from. But diversity in thought process is more fundamental to a business than diversity in ethnicity, and therefore, for a company that may be operating in just Italy and has only Italian customers, it may not make a strong business case to pursue ethnic diversity but may still make sense to pursue diversity in thinking.

We'll now come back to the point we left incomplete early in this chapter on why the majority of the 39 unicorns in Aileen Lee's study were singularly non-diverse. Based on what we have seen, start-ups tend to take a more pragmatic approach to diversity than the large companies. The logic we believe is straightforward: Start-ups operate in a rapidly changing environment where response times are far more critical than arriving at well-debated and balanced views. When speed of response is so important, getting agreement on decisions and the way forward is far easier if the people involved are aligned and think somewhat alike. Where quick decision-making and rapid execution is a critical competitive advantage, diversity may not necessarily add value as much as it could when the time-frames for decision-making are a little longer and the organizational stability more assured. But beyond a point, it is our belief that this is a risky strategy even from a business perspective. Uber's culture of hustle and toxicity was non-inclusive on many dimensions including gender. It wasn't a safe place for women to work and this nearly brought the company down after Susan Fowler went public in a blog post. As the company becomes multifunctional and expands its operations geographically, an inability to embrace diversity can become fatal. 'Anti-diversity', if ever there was such a term, in our opinion, is a very short-term and high-risk strategy.

In conclusion: Sebastian Bailey, in an article titled 'Why Diversity Can Be Bad for Business (And Inclusion Is the Answer)' dated 20 May 2014 in Forbes.com, says that 'Extensive research shows that diversity alone is damaging for individuals and organizations: Research links difference alone to lower revenue, performance, employee morale and wellbeing, along with slower decision making, increased con-flict, absenteeism, missed opportunities and more (expensive) discrimination cases.'[3]

It is a well-understood fact that most initiatives that aim to change status quo, if implemented incorrectly, can actually put companies in a worse place than they already were at. And initiatives on diversity are no exception.

---

[3] https://www.forbes.com/sites/sebastianbailey/2014/05/20/why-we-should-prioritize-the-i-in-d-and-i/?sh=741b2f66600d

Diversity is bad when you don't have a clue as to why it is good, or do not understand what it takes to make it work! Diversity is bad when you pursue it to look good and win awards!

Companies that have made diversity work for them have done so through continuous commitment spanning several decades across multiple CEOs. The commitment starts at the board level, and diversity is often among the CEO's top three priorities in such companies. Monika Navandar, a global expert on diversity and inclusion in the workplace (D&I) and a former D&I leader at Johnson & Johnson, was telling us that you can figure out a company's commitment to D&I just by looking at a few hard and soft indicators: (a) the diversity in the management team of the company, (b) the rapidity of decline of women from entry level to senior management, (c) D&I friendly policies and, finally, (d) the quality of insights on D&I that you could glean through conversations with senior executives.

Therefore, pursue diversity only after you are convinced that it is good for your business and only after you can persuade 10 well-intentioned sceptics that it is a goal worth pursuing.

BIG IN THE CHAPTER IDEAS

1. *Popular literature on diversity is fraught with unsubstantiated claims and fallacious data implications:* Articles use interchangeably 'correlation' and 'causal relationship' between different aspects of diversity; even when a disclaimer is given, readers are likely to miss the fine print and draw incorrect conclusions.

2. *Companies take politically correct approach to diversity for short-sighted gains:* Highly publicized yet cosmetic diversity initiatives are geared towards avoiding lawsuits and being perceived as socially responsible and progressive.

3. *'Not like us' bias can hurt the cause of diversity:* Companies that focus too much on culture fit at the artefact level risk being intolerant.

4. *Affirmative action is necessary and not anti-meritocracy:* To bridge the gender gap, a critical mass of women professionals in key positions needs to be achieved. For this, a well-defined affirmative action is critical.

5. *Ethnic diversity is incumbent on nature of business; diversity in thinking is more fundamental:* Even multinationals may need to hire mostly locals for regional business, hence, be low on ethnic diversity. This could be a practical business need and not be frowned upon. However, they can still pursue the goals of achieving diversity in thinking.

Dissent and Diversity

We must not confuse dissent with disloyalty.

—Edward R. Murrow

Zappos, the poster boy of organizational culture, decided to adopt holacracy around 2013. What followed was, ironically, a my-way-or-the-highway situation. In early 2015, CEO Tony Hsieh gave an ultimatum to the employees, in a memo, to either align to the hierarchy-less structure or take 'the offer' and leave.[1] The attrition level of 2015 rose to 30 per cent ; however, the CEO did not seem too concerned by it.[2] Interestingly, the company has since 'quietly' backed out of the structure, which did not seem to have worked as well as expected.[3] What concerns us, in this case of Zappos, has nothing to do with the structure per se. Our interest lies in examining the fact that a decision to make teams more

---

[1] https://qz.com/370616/internal-memo-zappos-is-offering-severance-to-employees-who-arent-all-in-with-holacracy/

[2] https://www.theatlantic.com/business/archive/2016/01/zappos-holacracy-hierarchy/424173/

[3] https://qz.com/work/1776841/zappos-has-quietly-backed-away-from-holacracy/

self-managed had to be dealt with an iron hand. Hsieh shared in the memo that they had not made 'fast enough progress' and a 'rip-the-band-aid' approach was required to speed up the adoption.[4] What he said, in other words, is that they didn't have time to deal with dissent.

It's slightly odd that there's so much discussion around building diversity in organizations, yet so little conversation on how to deal with dissent. Differing points of view and ideas are inherent in the very definition of diversity. Disagreements are a natural consequence of those differences, requiring time and effort to resolve. It's nearly pointless to build diversity unless there is a conscious acceptance of dissent and defined processes to leverage it. Dissent suffers a bad reputation. It's considered negative, counterproductive and sign of a disgruntled employee. Contrary to popular belief, studies show that people express dissent out of a desire to solve problems at the workplace or protect the company from risks.[5] Dissent is simply a point of view that differs from the majority or officially held position.

Dissent, a Bitter Pill to Swallow

Dissent is not easy to deal with, both at a personal and organizational level. In his book *What Got You Here Won't Get You There,* Marshall Goldsmith talks about the habit of 'playing favourites', that is, the tendency to favour those who favour us. He observed that executives tend to reward those who

---

[4] https://www.washingtonpost.com/news/on-leadership/wp/2015/03/31/zappos-to-employees-get-behind-our-no-bosses-approach-or-leave-with-severance/

[5] http://www.dissentworks.com/uploads/1/1/4/9/11493526/introduction_to_communication_textbook_chapter_copy.pdf

give unconscious admiration to them while honest, forthright employees are at a disadvantage. This is despite those leaders principally disagreeing with the idea of 'sucking up'. In interest of the semantics in our context, we could consider praise as a form of agreement and criticism as a variation of dissent.

A study of the brain's posterior medial frontal cortex during disagreements[6] found that people tend to consider opinions that contradict their own as wrong, while having greater confidence in opinions that are aligned to what they think. It appears that human nature might be naturally wired against disagreements. Goldsmith's observations as an executive coach, about leaders favouring praise over criticism, points at the same direction. A google search on 'how to manage your boss' yields numerous search results. A recurring advice given for corporate success is that the 'boss is always right'. It appears that the word on the street as well, is that expressing dissent within organizations is not seen favourably.

Our challenge of dealing with dissent extends to organizations as well. Let's consider the case of James Damore being fired from Google upon publishing his views on why women can't code because of biology. His case is particularly significant because his views pertained to an issue in the realm of diversity. The point here is not whether Damore was right or wrong. In all probability, his conclusions about women were simplistic, backed by inadequate arguments. However, that inadequacy was just the same as anyone else's arguments at Google, arriving at any equally simplistic, though favourable, conclusion about women. Damore's memo in the very least was not inflammatory. Nor was it a mere statement of

---

[6] https://scroll.in/article/948042/the-science-behind-disagreements-or-why-we-cling-to-our-beliefs

opinions. He used evidence he thought would best support his arguments. We can at least concede that he was trying to have a reasoned debate, whether or not he succeeded in making his point. Damore even suggested how women could be supported better. Damore's firing is significant to our discussion, because upon close analysis of the facts, it appears that he wasn't fired so much for faulty arguments about women's biological capability to code as we might assume. His firing was because his argument was different from the official position taken by the organization. Further, Damore criticized Google for its politically correct monoculture. The memo was considered to be such a crisis that CEO Sundar Pichai cut short a vacation he was on and returned to deal with it, personally. Irrespective of any flaws in Damore's memo, the haste and zealousness with which he was fired is a standing testimony to the discomfort organizations have in general with dissent.

Dissent and Culture

While dissent is often not without consequences, fitting in, on the contrary, receives official endorsement from guardians of organizational culture. Before diversity appeared on the block, culture had been the Holy Grail of organizational development. It started receiving significant academic interest with Pettigrew's (1979) article, 'On Studying Organizational Cultures', in which he described organizational culture as an amalgamation of belief, identity, ritual and myth.[7] Ever since, businesses have looked for ways to define their culture and hire people who fit. A company like Zappos takes culture fit to the

---

[7] https://www.oxfordbibliographies.com/view/document/obo-978019
9846740/obo-9780199846740-0059.xml

next level, as something that can get you fired.[8] New hires at Zappos could be asked to leave at any point of a five-week training if they are not found to be a good fit to the culture. Zappos' business success story has often been told as a culture-success story. Admittedly, a start-up to billion-dollar company journey, where office floors teem with wacky expression of each employee's individuality, co-workers who are like friends and an unusual CEO who sports a Mohawk and lives in a trailer[9]—has all the bearings of a fascinating culture story. That is also what makes it relevant to the discussion on dissent in context of diversity. The point that culture fit might result in stifling diversity has been raised by many. However, the slippery semantics around 'cultural diversity' makes it difficult to nail the issue. Adam Grant asked Hsieh at a conference if too much emphasis on culture fit could mean hiring more White, bald dudes he could go have beer with. (The 'White bald dudes' description Grant gave was in reference to his own appearance.)[10] The question is particularly relevant for Zappos, because it actively emphasizes on the importance of employees getting along with each other and being inherently friendly by nature. In fact, it is not unusual for a Zappos employee to meet their future spouse at the workplace. Hsieh's response to the culture-stifles-diversity question was that diversity is built in the Zappos' core value, namely, 'create fun and a little bit of weirdness'. They believe everyone is weird and unique in their own way. However, interestingly, Zappos has a 10-point scale to measure potential candidates. Being close to '1' on the scale means the person is 'too strait-laced

---

[8] https://www.forbes.com/sites/csr/2010/11/23/at-zappos-getting-fired-for-not-contributing-to-company-culture/#1be3b4fb1b44

[9] https://www.youtube.com/watch?v=o6OLrBuCNAw

[10] https://knowledge.wharton.upenn.edu/article/zappos-tony-hsieh-holacracy-right-fit/

for Zappos'. This is where diversity gets lost in semantics. If everyone is weird in their own way, it should apply to a strait-laced person as well. However, such a person may not find a place in Zappos as an employee, because they are not weird, fun or friendly enough.

The point here isn't to criticize Zappos' culture. Their approach seems to have worked for them. The objective is to highlight that much of Zappos' success has been driven by the zealous pursuit of its 'culture of yes' and customer-friendly policies, rather than its much-popularized diversity. Without acknowledging this, we will risk committing the classic mistake of projecting a mere correlation as a causal relationship, as we've pointed out earlier in this book. Zappos' surface-diversity exists *alongside* its business success, instead of being the reason behind it. Zappos' business success is more the outcome of pursuing alignment rather than allowing diversity-driven dissent. In fact, any employee at Zappos can be fired for non-adherence to company values, which include 'being weird and creating fun', even if their work performance is up to the mark. Zappos is credited to be diverse in terms of the usual parameters of age, ethnicity and background. Yet, when it comes to style of functioning, it does not make space for differences and dissent. For example, customer service representatives are allowed to spend as much time as required to make the customer happy. They often talk of a call that went on for 10 hours. Would a process-oriented, 'strait-laced' manager, who feels customer delight can be delivered along with being efficient on call time and believes in checks and balances, find a place at Zappos? In the chapter 'Does Diversity Really Help Business?', we spoke about the risks of emphasizing too much on the artefact level of diversity in the name of culture fit. Hiring certain personality types might give a lot of hype to companies like Zappos. However, it might prevent hiring of employees, who actually align with the core values and goals but may have a different approach to doing things—which is the essence of diversity. Case in point is the strait-laced, process-oriented manager who could be as customer focused as any other Zappos employee but doesn't fit the profile and wouldn't be hired. As a result, alternative ways of achieving the same goals may not be explored. This is not about good or bad, right or wrong, as we often tend to view issues around culture, diversity and dissent. It is simply acknowledging facts as they are, without resorting to tokenism.

A term that gets thrown around by organizations that want to counter allegations of stifling diversity in pursuit of culture fit is 'cultural diversity'. It's another example of semantic jugglery around diversity. Taken at face value, it seems to suggest an openness towards differences. However, organizational culture in itself suggests certain homogeneity in beliefs and ways of being and doing. Therefore, 'culture diversity' is an oxymoron. What it often means is inclusion of varied demographic backgrounds. However, like in the case of Zappos, it may not mean that the organization accommodates differences in thoughts and opinions and thereby dissent. Culture fit can overpower these differences from cropping up. Margaret Heffernan, in her book *Wilful Blindness,* tells the story of an ex-Lehman trader, Brad Ruderman, who felt the compelling need to feel accepted in the highly competitive culture of the organization. Ruderman had done well in life and had already checked the boxes of owning a home and car. Ruderman accepted having transgressed the ethical lines of trading and even disregarding his client's best interests in order to meet his scoreboard requirements. Ruderman said it wasn't greed or need for money that was driving him. His sole motivation was to get accepted.

Business leaders may often fail to realize that culture fit fuels the compelling human need to belong. Definition of cultural norms and values could also be ambiguous and subject to interpretation. For example, what does 'being friendly' mean? It is not unheard of for quiet-natured employees, who may not be the quintessential lets-party-after-work type of people, to be tagged as 'boring'. Similarly, introverts, who prefer environments that aren't overstimulating, may be seen as unfriendly. Susan Cain, co-founder of Quiet Revolution, talks about how introverts are often prodded to 'come out of their shell' and how the bias against introverts can leave a deep psychic pain.[11] Another example of a vaguely defined cultural value is 'being a team player'. A supposed team player has to be mindful of toeing the line of agreeing with the team and being a cheerleader. Truth tellers and devil's advocates may be at the risk of not fitting in the assumed meaning of 'team player'. Cultural alignment may, knowingly or unknowingly, modify who the employee is as a person and how they behave in order to fit in, stifling dissent in the process.

This realization is gradually settling in, as organizations are trying to consciously move away from pursuing a strong culture fit. Patty McCord, the ex-chief talent officer of Netflix, describes Anthony Park[12] as a 'buttoned up guy' working at an Arizona Bank (*How to Hire*, Harvard Business Review). When Park got a job offer at Netflix, he was thrilled, yet wondered if he would fit into the company's high-powered culture. He wasn't much of a talker, but when he spoke, people listened. Park, despite being not the usual 'culture-fit', grew to a senior role. McCord sees this as a proof of organizations adapting to people's styles.

---

[11] Susan Cain, *Quiet: The Power of Introverts in a World That Can't Stop Talking* (Crown Publishing Group, 2012).

[12] https://hbr.org/2018/01/how-to-hire

It's important to understand why we are discussing culture in context of dissent and the relationship between the two. Culture provides the environment for dissent to be expressed or suppressed. We are not saying there's anything wrong with driving a clearly defined culture. We calling attention to the fact that dissent is neither easy to express nor accept. However, it is essential to running a business in the long term, especially given the market dynamics of our times. Therefore, what we *are* saying is that it is essential to acknowledge the role of culture as a catalyst or clog in the expression of dissent. As we see it, architects of organizational culture must weigh in the importance of dissent and make space for it, especially if the business is committed to diversity.

Dissent and Decision-making

In 2011, when Larry Page took the reins of Google as CEO, speedy decision-making was one of the things on his mind.[13] During a Google Zeitgeist Q&A, Page said, 'there are basically no companies with good slow decisions.' Upon taking charge, Page sent out a detailed email outlining the mechanics of decision-making, for example, every decision-oriented meeting was required to have one clear decision-maker, without whom the meeting shouldn't happen. Fast decision-making isn't just Google's priority. Jeff Bezos is a known advocate of high-velocity decision-making.[14] Amazon follows a disagree-and-commit policy, wherein employees or leaders may disagree but go ahead with the decision if someone is convinced about

---

[13] https://www.youtube.com/watch?v=srI6QYfi-HY
[14] https://www.forbes.com/sites/eriklarson/2018/09/24/how-jeff-bezos-uses-faster-better-decisions-to-keep-amazon-innovating/#589539957a65

it. Speed of decisions is prioritized over spending time to resolve the differences.

What's important to consider here is that choosing not to labour with dissent while taking decisions does not make either of these organizations autocratic. It is merely choosing what matters more to the business. Many professionals will give an arm and a leg to get an opportunity to work with Google. In Amazon's case, disagree-and-commit is not merely a top-down mandate. Jeff Bezos himself was not convinced about a certain[15] Amazon Studios Original. Nevertheless, he disagreed and committed to it because his team was convinced. What is also notable here is organizations like Google and Amazon are aware of the risks of bypassing dissent in a decision-making process. They rely on being able to course-correct or bet on the fact that overall wins will outweigh the failures in the final tally.

Studies have found diversity to be an enabler of better decisions. A study published in the *Journal of Personality and Social Psychology*[16] conducted mock jury trials, dividing 200 study participants into panels of six members. The panels were either all White members or a combination of four White and two Black participants. The panels were then shown video of a trial of a Black defendant and White victims and given the task of guessing if the defendant was guilty. It was found that diverse groups made fewer factual errors while considering the evidence as compared to homogeneous group.

---

[15] https://www.businessinsider.in/jeff-bezos-says-a-3-word-phrase-can-help-you-make-decisions-quickly-and-become-a-better-leader/articleshow/68397176.cms

[16] https://hbr.org/2016/11/why-diverse-teams-are-smarter

There has been lot of contemplation on whether Lehman Brothers could have met with a different business fate if they were 'Lehman Sisters' or 'Lehman Brothers & Sisters', metaphorically speaking. Many argue that diversity could have saved the day for the company, quoting studies that found traders with greater cultural and ethnic diversity, price assets with greater accuracy.[17] However, others are cautious to draw this conclusion, pointing at studies that show both men and women are likely to demonstrate increased risk-taking behaviours in presence of the opposite gender.[18] The research on the exact impact of diversity on decision-making, at this point in time, may be more indicative than conclusive. However, what we can discern from these studies is that presence of diversity alone may not guarantee better decision-making. In the study on mock trials on Black defendant and White victims using heterogenous and homogeneous jury panels, the reason for heterogenous panels to be more accurate was that they raised more facts and corrected errors during deliberation. In the study on heterogeneous trader teams making more accurate pricing decisions, reason behind better decisions was that diversity induced friction which further led to deliberations.[19] Hence, the clincher is that it's not diversity on its own but the dissent the emerges from it, which further drives critical discussion, is what leads to better decisions.

It's in this light that decision-making processes of organizations matter. Google and Amazon could be as diverse as they would like to be. However, diversity alone may not result in better

---

[17] https://www.pnas.org/content/early/2014/11/13/1407301111.abstract

[18] https://www.forbes.com/sites/timworstall/2014/03/29/of-course-the-crisis-would-have-been-different-if-lehman-brothers-had-been-lehman-sisters/#3bb16d3d7f9a

[19] https://www.pnas.org/content/111/52/18524.abstract

decisions, unless their processes are designed to harness the dissent resulting out of it. Annie Duke, in her book *Thinking in Bets,* opines that a productive group decision must be organized around scepticism. Further, she says that we need to be particularly sceptical about the information that agrees with us, because we may be inclined to accept it. John F. Kennedy's fateful decision on the Bay of Pigs is a case in point.[20] In 1961, America decided to allow about 1,500 Cuban exiles to invade the Bay of Pigs in Cuba. The group was supported by American military personnel on ground. The plan counted on other disillusioned Cubans to join the effort of overthrowing the then President Fidel Castro. However, the ploy failed, and the group was caught with many killed by Castro's military force. Casualties included several American soldiers and it was a public humiliation for the Kennedy administration. The question was, how did the top-50-odd military minds of America take this disastrous decision? After the event, Kennedy shared that five minutes into the event unfolding at Bay of Pigs, the decision-makers were dismayed on how they could have been 'so stupid'.[21] They realized that the flaws visible now should have been apparent at the time of decision-making. Kennedy shared[22] later that few people party to the decision told him that they were opposed to the decision from the beginning. However, there was no vocal opposition to the decision while it was being taken. Perhaps, groupthink[23] and a lack of formalized process of dissent prevented the naysayers from tabling their opposing views. The aftermath of Bay of Pigs led Kennedy to appoint his close aides, Robert Kennedy

---

[20] https://www.nj.com/business/2013/11/jfk_a_great_leader_learned_fro.html

[21] http://content.time.com/time/nation/article/0,8599,106537,00.html

[22] http://content.time.com/time/nation/article/0,8599,106537,00.html

[23] https://hbr.org/2013/11/how-john-f-kennedy-changed-decision-making

and Theodore Sorensen, as devil's advocates while deciding response to the placement of Soviet Missiles in Cuba.[24] Further, the National Security Council moved away from protocols of ranks and allowed for different perspectives, even those from lower-ranking officers who were closer to ground realities.[25] Ray Dalio, Founder of the investment management firm Bridgewater, had a Kennedy-like moment of reckoning of his own,[26] in the late 1970s. Dalio had predicted the debt crisis from his analysis of American banks' lending to emerging countries. His confidence went through the roof as his prediction came true and he was called to talk about this on leading platforms and even testify in the Congress. However, while his crisis prediction came true, the stock markets went up, and Dalio, who had bet too strongly on his prediction, lost everything to the point of having to borrow money for his personal expenses. This was a turning point in Dalio's decision-making style. He transitioned from saying, 'I'm right' to asking, 'How do I know I am right?'. Dalio started organizing his decision-making around scepticism by hiring the smartest people who disagreed with him. He built systems to ensure he heard those perspectives. At the core of that system is what Dalio calls 'radical transparency'.

Bridgewater records every conversation in the organization, makes it openly accessible and empowers people to express their opinions. Information sharing is another variable which merits a mention in the discussion of dissent. Not all organizations may prioritize speed of doing business over consensus-driven

---

[24] https://daily.jstor.org/how-the-bay-of-pigs-invasion-changed-jfk/
[25] https://www.theglobeandmail.com/report-on-business/why-banning-yes-men----or-women----can-improve-decisions/article18243574/
[26] https://www.ted.com/talks/ray_dalio_how_to_build_a_company_where_the_best_ideas_win/transcript?language=en#t-247707

decision-making, as we saw in the case of Google or Amazon. However, even without need for speed, organizations may struggle to harness dissent for the lack of adequate information sharing. To dissent in a meaningful way, access to information pertaining to the decision is necessary. This does not come naturally to all organizations, particularly those built on traditional hierarchies. When Ricardo Semler took to transforming Semco, from a hierarchical culture to a participative organization, in the early 1980s, one of the aspects he overhauled was sharing of information. Semco started the practice of leaving two seats empty in board meetings for any employee to walk in on first-come-first serve-basis.[27] This meant, that at times, even janitors got to vote on decisions and Semler felt that it kept the organization honest. When Semco wanted employees to decide their own salaries, a computer was placed in the cafeteria with all the information on company revenue, profits and benchmark salary data. Both Semco and Bridgewater adopted the principle of radical transparency to enable dissent, even if that level of information sharing is inherently uncomfortable. In his book, *Maverick,* Ricardo Semler says, 'A touch of civil disobedience is necessary to alert the organization that all is not right... we do our best to let them speak their mind even though they often become thorns in our side.'[28] Ray Dalio calls it radical truthfulness. Dalio says in his TED Talk that it's not unusual for an employee to write to him giving him a D– for not being well-prepared for a meeting. Allowing that level of truthfulness can feel like 'thorn on the side', especially to senior management who are not used to receiving criticism and contrarian points

[27] https://www.forbes.com/sites/kevinkruse/2016/08/29/the-big-company-that-has-no-rules/#4dcf67a756ad

[28] Ricardo Semler, Maverick: *The Success Story Behind the World's Most Unusual Workplace* (RHUK, 2001).

of view (i.e., dissent), especially from those junior to them. However, as Semler and Dalio realized, it was necessary to the fabric of the organizations they were trying to build.

Begin at the Beginning

A pro-diversity argument often made is that diversity enables organizations to survive uncertainty and ambiguity. The rationale for this argument is that unforeseen situations require unusual approaches, which is made possible by a diverse workforce. If this be the case, it's inherent in the very argument that organizations investing in diversity to be able to survive uncertainties must also be prepared to make space for dissent.

Not all organizations have the same *dissent appetite*; that is, a combination of *leadership's willingness* and *organizational readiness* to harness dissent. *Leadership's willingness* depends on the leader's own personality and values. It can be said without any prejudice that both Ricardo Semler and Ray Dalio have been unusually courageous in opening up to organizational dissent, in the manner they did. While that kind of boldness might not be every CEO's cup of tea, it's critical that leaders at least undertake an honest assessment of their personal attitude towards dissent. *Organizational readiness*, on the other hand, is a function of setting the right systems and processes to enable dissent. Ray Dalio has implemented a system of algorithmic decision-making at Bridgewater. One of the tools they use is called the Dot Collector, which collates everyone's perspective on any matter, stacks it up against what others are thinking and identifies principles of decisions along the way. Dalio believes in neither democracy nor autocracy of opinions. He uses a system of *idea meritocracy*, where an employee's opinion is weighed against their merits. Dalio's system of factoring in diverse points of view, even if not perfect, is definitely ahead of the curve. It's not necessary nor possible for all organizations to be at that state of readiness to begin with. Organizations are different. They are also at different stages of their journey. It's critical though for organizations to consciously define some processes, systems and principles to enable dissent based on their own context.

In Lewis Carroll's *Alice in Wonderland*, the white rabbit seeks the King's permission to read the unsigned letter, written allegedly by the Knave. 'Where shall I begin, please your Majesty?' the rabbit asks. The King replies gravely, 'Begin at the beginning. Go on till you come to the end; then stop.'[29] When organizations sign up for the diversity agenda, it's fallaciously assumed that diversity, on its own, results in outcomes such as being able to deal with uncertainty. Unless aspects such as dissent are nurtured, diversity left to itself may not yield its touted benefits. However, to enable dissent, organizations will need to dig deep into their very fundamentals. What are we here to achieve? What kind of people will we require for that? What kind of culture will work best for it? How prepared are we to deal with differing points of view? Do we have a system and process in place to harness those differing views? What is the leader's personal mindset around it? How open are we to sharing information? Often these questions get lost in translation as organizations pay lip service to them with rhetoric on 'cultural diversity', 'participative culture', etc. However, actual implementation of diversity, in a way that it yields business results, is a lot of hard work. Diversity is far from being an end in itself. It's one of those things where organizations will quite literally need to begin at the beginning.

---

[29] https://www.cs.cmu.edu/~rgs/alice-XII.html

BIG IN THE CHAPTER IDEAS

1. *Human nature and organizations are inherently wired against dissent:* We tend to agree with opinions that are aligned to ours and view contrarian points of view as incorrect. This continues within organizations as leadership and managerial behaviours, leading to discomfort with dissent at an organizational level.

2. *Culture can disable or enable dissent:* Culture fit seeks alignment, while diversity is about making space for differences. Unless culture architects incorporate dissent in a meaningful way, the goal of diversity will be lost in lip service and semantic jugglery such as 'cultural diversity'.

3. *Presence of diversity itself doesn't ensure decision-making is based on diverse opinions, unless process is designed to facilitate dissent:* Even seemingly diverse organizations may prioritize speedy decision-making over harnessing dissent. They rely on ability to course correct and bet on overall wins to be more than losses. However, for better decision-making, processes and practices of harnessing dissent have to be implemented.

4. *'Dissent appetite' is the combination of leadership's willingness and organizational readiness:* Leadership willingness is a factor of the leaders' personal values and mindset. Organizational readiness depends on organizational maturity, business context, systems and processes.

5. *Diversity can't deliver benefits unless dissent is consciously enabled:* Diversity is not an end in itself. Unless dissent, which is the outcomes of diversity, is enabled and leveraged through systems and processes, diversity cannot deliver results on its own.

Discrimination
and Diversity

*The thing that I fear discriminating against
is humor and truth.*

—Charles Bukowski

Serena Williams' penalty that cost her the 2018 US Open title
against Naomi Osaka, for calling the umpire a liar and thief,
opened floodgates of sexism accusations. While the umpire
was acting by the rule book, Williams cried foul that she was
being punished harshly only because she was a woman (while
male players got away with worse behaviour). That Williams
was returning after pregnancy into a highly competitive and
physically rigorous sport added to the heated debate. Critics
of the penalty felt it took away an opportunity from Williams
to create history. Interestingly, Novak Djokovic (a male tennis
player to state the obvious) got disqualified in the 2020 US Open
for accidentally injuring the line judge with a ball, hit in a fit of
frustration. Some expressed shock and disappointment, while
many said this was a long time coming with Djokovic's habit
of hitting the ball around in court. Both Williams and Djokovic
have had a history of being fined for aggressive court behaviour
and arguments with umpires. During the Williams incident,

those who claimed that men get away with worse behaviour did not shy away from finding elements of sexism in Djokovic's dismissal as well. This time, the criticism was for those who sympathized with Djokovic for being disqualified due to (what the Djokovic supporters argued) an accidental, unintentional hit. Images of Djokovic and Williams juxtaposed, appeared on social media, making it obvious that Djokovic was a White man, while Williams a Black woman. The picture such social media posts portrayed was that all the decisions and perceptions that Serena and her fans didn't agree with were being meted out to her because of sexism and racism.

To the facts of whether there is a gender bias in penalizing female players as compared to their male counterparts, the opinion is divided. Sexism theorists put out a list of bad behaviour by male players which weren't penalized as harshly. Others counter with instances where male players have been punished harshly and seemingly unfairly. Settling the debate is not our objective here. It's a complex debate to say the least, with many voices, perspectives, data and stakeholders. What we are interested in are some questions that such incidents beg to be raised, which will be useful in understanding discrimination in organizations, especially in context of diversity.

First, it's about arguments of the nature, 'men behave just as bad, they are not punished, women shouldn't be either.' It's a seemingly a fair point. However, does equality mean equal leeway in getting away with toxic behaviour? Or should we use this moment in history to challenge and correct the troublesome behaviours in the first place, whether demonstrated by men or women? Serena is often touted as one of the greatest players in history. Should her claim to equality be, *let me get away with screaming at the umpire as much as my male colleagues,* or could it be—*let me raise the bar of sportsmanship?* Or, *let me use my voice to question why players, both male and female, should abuse an umpire and break racquets at all; what example are we setting as role-models?* Would such an expectation from one of the greatest players tennis has ever seen, a woman, be akin to double standards and discrimination? Does challenging patriarchy and ensuring non-discrimination mean changing the questionable behaviours, or is it allowing women to participate and perpetrate the same behaviours as men? The moot question here is:

What is our definition of equality, and therefore, how do we interpret discrimination?

Second, while an individual person or organization should be held accountable for their own behaviours, can or should they be held accountable for, and be expected to rectify the wrongs of, historical, systemic or societal discrimination? Reportedly, Carlos Ramos, the umpire who officiated the Serena–Osaka match, is known for being strict to male players[1] as well. While he may not have gone out of the way to diffuse the situation during the fateful match, point is that his strictness wasn't limited to Serena Williams. Is it fair to expect him to take a decision based on the fact that Williams was making history with her post-maternity game, instead of the rules and his personal approach towards all players? If Ramos was found to have a pattern of being strict with women players more than men, there is a point of investigation. However, if that's not the case, is it fair to call him sexist, just because a larger gender bias exists in the world? The question staring at us is:

---

[1] https://www.nytimes.com/2018/09/09/sports/tennis/serena-williams-umpire-carlos-ramos-us-open.html

Should someone be held accountable for a larger systemic bias, beyond their own, specific behaviours?

Third, should we not differentiate between existence of a discriminatory behaviour and assigning any bias as the cause of that behaviour? One of the things Williams said to Ramos while protesting the penalty was, 'You are taking it away from me because I am a woman.' How does Williams know that it was *because of* her being a woman? Whether Ramos' decision was discriminatory is a matter of contention. However, let's assume for argument's sake that he was indeed harsher to Williams than he was to other players. This would mean that a discriminatory behaviour was demonstrated. However, how can we be sure that the reason behind that behaviour was a bias against women? Is there a basis to assume that about Ramos? Or does the fact that Serena is a woman automatically mean that any bias against her is *because* she is a woman? In the same year as the US Open incident, Serena got embroiled in another controversy, this time at the French Open. It was for a black, figure-hugging, custom-made catsuit inspired by the movie *Black Panther.* The suit was said to serve a medical purpose of helping Williams with her condition of blood clotting. The French authorities didn't take too well to the choice of costume. They said that things had gone too far and that the game and place needed to be respected. While Williams herself took a non-confrontational approach to the decision, saying she was not upset, the media and people raised a storm on familiar grounds of sexism and racism. Again, let's assume for argument's sake that the French Open authorities were demonstrating discriminatory behaviour towards Williams (though this wasn't any isolated incident of dress code defiance by players in history of the game). However, how can we be sure that the French Open authorities have something against her because she is a woman and Black? Why not consider that the bias could be towards her American in-your-face fashion expression which was overwhelming for the subtler French sensibilities? Or maybe, the bias was because of the fact that Serena stands out in her expression, at times bordering on defiance. History is fraught with examples of White men who have been prosecuted across all walks of life for challenging status quo. So perhaps, Williams' run-in with authorities was because of her being a dissenter, which may have little to do with her gender or colour. Hence, the question that begs to be asked is:

On what basis do we assign an '-ism' as being the root cause of a discriminatory behaviour?

Fourth, is the discourse around discrimination led by reason and facts or is it reactive, judgemental and, ironically, biased towards seeing bias? Caroline Wozniacki received bitter criticism for being a racist when she stuffed her garment to mimic Serena Williams' accentuated curves, during an exhibition match against Maria Sharapova.[2] Wozniacki was touted as a White woman trying to make fun of a Black female's body type. This is despite the fact that players mimicking each other to entertain the crowd is a well-known practice in tennis. For example, Novak Djokovic has often done impressions of Nadal, Federer and even female players like Maria Sharapova and Serena Williams. Both Djokovic and Andy Roddick have stuffed towels into their clothing to mimic Williams in the past. Djokovic had sported a blonde wig on court to imitate Sharapova. These acts are meant to be in good humour and not considered either racist or sexist. Williams herself

---

[2] https://www.nbcnews.com/news/other/was-it-racist-caroline-wozniacki-imitates-serena-williams-stirs-controversy-v15845710

dismissed claims that Caroline Wozniacki's act was racist. Now, let's say Serena Williams was ranked 350 in the world. No one, perhaps, would have bothered to mimic her, despite her gender and race still being what it is. It might be argued that her colleagues choose her because she is significant and famous. It comes with the territory. However, given the strong reactions on social media, one wonders if any humour involving Serena Williams or a woman or Black or any minority is necessarily an act of 'ism'. Does it make for a better story to project Serena Williams as a *target of racism*, being a Black woman, instead of seeing her as a *subject of significance*, being a super achiever? The final question to be asked here is:

Is the narrative on discrimination driven by a reasoned voice, or are we drowning ourselves in reactive noise?

Our interest here isn't to mull over whether or not certain behaviour was discriminatory, racist or sexist. Our interest lies in exploring the underlying thought processes that dictate our opinion, reaction and action on discrimination. We seek to explore questions that are key to cutting through the noise and finding a sustainable way for businesses to deal with discrimination.

Discrimination Is the Very Basis of Management

This idea might seem preposterous on the face of it. However, a close look into how organizations discriminate at every stage will establish that far from being preposterous, this is actually a fact we all accept and live by.

In many job posts, we find organizations outrightly mention 'Tier I (or Ivy League) schools/colleges only', denying anyone outside the bucket to even try. That's discrimination. But it's also a hiring strategy which is considered normal. For example, top investment banks only hire the top students of top colleges. Others don't even get a chance to try. Who is to say that someone with a lower score in those top colleges or one studying in a lower-rung college will not make a top investment banker? The movie *The Pursuit of Happiness* portrays the life of a Wall Street legend, Chris Gardner. As a medical-device salesperson, Gardner did not remotely fit the profile of an investment banker but went on to break all stereotypes. Compensation is another form of discrimination. A premier college graduate is offered a higher pay than his colleague from a lower-rung college for the same job. That's discrimination. And it's not only accepted but also becomes the reason for millions of youngsters and their parents aspiring to make it into these premier colleges. The entire performance management system is an official exercise in identifying and discriminating among people at different levels of performance as defined by the organization. Businesses discriminate among customers as well. Be it airlines or banks, select customers get to stand on the red carpet, get quick service, while others wait in long queues. Coinage of the word 'cattle class' for economy airline tickets represents more than just the seat size. There have been discussions on algorithmic pricing of cab services, and how it might charge customers more based on neighbourhoods and factors like your phone battery running low.[3] Giving preferential treatment to customers based on their lifetime value of business is an established business practice.

---

[3] https://www.forbes.com/sites/nicolemartin1/2019/03/30/uber-charges-more-if-they-think-youre-willing-to-pay-more/#7771bce97365

One might argue that these are examples of 'differentiation', more than 'discrimination'. There's only a fine line between the two in many cases. The start-up world is rife with murmurs of entrepreneurs anguished about investors having a pedigree bias; that an IIT-ian or the like may find initial funding easier than someone outside the Ivy League. In inside conversations, many investors may agree to it, their rationale being that the initial bet is made on the entrepreneur. They opine that while pedigree may not be the only decider, it's considered a proxy indicator for capability and ability to go through the grind. To some, this may seem like a case of differentiation. To others, it may be education-based discrimination. Giving differential treatment to customers based on their buying capacity could be termed as economic discrimination by some. Getting lost in semantics is both futile and non-productive to our goal.

What's necessary is to acknowledge the principle that while discrimination has become a bad word, it's the very algorithm by which people, whether employees or customers, are managed. The corollary to this principle is that equality cannot or should not be expected of organizations given the nature of business. This brings us to the concept of *fairness*, which is often used inaccurately to mean *equality*. Both are not the same things. Organizations are increasingly being put in the dock for seeking to hire certain demographic profiles, pay differentially, etc. In other words, they are expected to practise 'equality'. Differentiating between the need for organizations to be equal, as opposed to being fair, becomes critical. *We cannot expect organizations to be equal. But we can expect them to be fair.* And here lies the key to dealing with discrimination in organizations:

Organizations cannot be non-discriminatory. What they must strive for is to discriminate using fair and transparent principles.

What's Your Family Situation?

Many, if not most, women professionals have been asked a variation of the question 'so what's your family situation like?' I have faced this question once in an interview, when as a single woman I was asked in the manner of friendly small talk on what my plans of getting married were. Such questions decidedly feel anything from mildly annoying, intrusive to downright offensive. Most importantly, these questions are considered discriminatory and even banned by law in many countries. Why do interviewers ask women candidates this question in the first place? Is there bias against hiring female employees? I have witnessed this bias first-hand, when the leader of a technology team told me he would avoid hiring a female team member at a certain point in time. We might immediately want to crucify such managers at the altar of discrimination. Except that this manager was no woman-hater, nor did he think any less of a woman-engineer's capability. His team was handling a high-pressure project and was thinly staffed. There was a hiring freeze and additional staff was not being approved. He feared a situation where his female team member might need to go on a maternity leave, which as a norm typically gets extended to a 9–12 months duration. The organization wouldn't allow him an additional headcount, backfill or temporary staff for that duration. Also, the organization was not a top payer in the segment. The team needed a specific skill-set and any rehire, if approved, would've been a long process. The manager was not being discriminatory. He was just trying to find means to deliver outcomes expected of him within organizational constraints and was considering the additional work pressure on his already over-worked team members. Admittedly, the solution was not the best one and it put women at a disadvantage. However, this case demonstrates the need to *separate the existence of a discriminatory behaviour per se from the reason behind it.* Rushing to assign the root-cause to an '-ism', without a deep dive into the problem, leads businesses to focus on shaming and penalizing such erring managers instead of finding solutions to the actual problem. Shaming employees who bring up uncomfortable questions does not ensure non-discrimination. It only serves to disguise it. HR practitioners in candid off-the-record conversations will tell you, hiring managers find indirect ways to gauge the personal situation of a female applicant in such high-pressure, project-based roles. Even though HR is aware of the bias, often it's difficult to pin down such behaviours as the candidate's rejection is assigned to a different and 'officially acceptable' reason.

One of the gaps in legislations and policies that prohibit discriminatory behaviours, such as discriminatory interview questions, is the failure to recognize business scenarios and cultural context. The intention behind such prohibitions is laudable. It's just that prohibitions alone might be ineffective and insufficient. When Zomato announced period leave for its employees, Barkha Dutt, a well-known journalist and self-confessed feminist, came out against it strongly.[4] In her tweet, she spoke of women aspiring to fight wars and fly planes. She has spoken of her own struggle during reporting a war, where she did not have access to sanitary pads, her bag having been shelled, and managed with toilet paper.[5] With due respect to the challenges Dutt overcame to deliver the commendable reporting on Kargil War, her stance on this issue demonstrates the fallacious equality-for-all argument. Dutt was criticized by several women for typecasting all women

[4] https://www.huffingtonpost.in/entry/period-leave-twitter-debate_in_5f34eb 20c5b64cc99fe26cc8
[5] https://twitter.com/bdutt/status/1293176636662116352?lang=en

as wanting the same things in life. Many women may want period leaves and not all women want to fly planes or go to war. Somewhere the narrative on women empowerment, which runs in parallel to rhetoric on diversity, has confused between giving women a choice and deciding that all women necessarily want to make the same choices. Sheryl Sandberg's appeal to lean in notwithstanding, many women may still want to make the choice to 'lean out' and raise children. There is no right, wrong, good or bad to it. Similarly, a woman may quit her job to accompany her husband to a different country if it serves the latter's career interests. Is it okay for women to have to compromise on their career, *if they don't wish to*? Of course not. However, fact remains that many women *still* do make that choice, either willingly or unwillingly. Understanding the context of any discriminatory behavior is necessary. In case of the 'what's your family situation' question posed to women, the statistics of women choosing to take a back seat, acts as the context. We need not agree with it, but we need to acknowledge it if we are to find real solutions. Diversity enthusiasts might quip, 'so what if women have traditionally made choices that put their careers on the backseat—that doesn't justify asking such discriminatory questions.' They are right. Like we said earlier, seeking to understand and acknowledge the reason behind a discriminatory behavior is not the same as accepting the behavior. We'd also like to clarify that our point is not to say misogynistic beliefs don't exist. For example, a Reddit user,[6] who identified himself as a tech-company founder, commented that he did not hire women because they don't come with as strong technical backgrounds as men. Also, that California had 'ridiculous maternity leave laws' which made female applicant 'quite undesirable'. The

---

[6] https://www.dailydot.com/irl/silicon-valley-ceo-stripper-party-sexism/

founder's original query on the thread was whether he could host an in-office stripper party without getting into legal issues. Here, the founder has admitted to his thought process, which we can safely say is deeply misogynistic. From his language and tone, it did not seem like he saw it as a temporary business challenge for which he was willing to find a solution. In this case, it was expressed as a strongly held belief about female employees. The perspectives we are sharing in this section are for cases where discriminatory behaviours are driven by context. Building a deeper understanding of those contexts will open doors to real solutions that go beyond merely prohibiting and punishing a behaviour.

The prevalence of women candidates being asked prying questions about their family situation comes from the context of stereotypical gender roles of men being breadwinners and women being caretakers. Those stereotypes are changing but only gradually. On the one hand, the act of asking the question to only women, not men, wrongly assumes that all women who start a family or get married will go easy on their jobs. On the other hand, prohibiting such questions overlooks the reality of gender roles that still exist in society. Maybe there is another solution. Organizations could look into their manpower planning and allow for temporary replacements in case of women on maternity leave. Also, most organizations are far from granting paternity leaves, which will go a long way in removing leave-related taboo associated with women. Businesses could also look for constructive interpretation of legal frameworks and see if a better question can be asked. What if managers could be allowed and trained to have a transparent discussion on their concerns. What if, instead of asking, 'What is your family situation?' to women, they could ask, 'Is there anything about your personal situation in the next 2 years, that could foreseeably require you to avoid a high-pressure job role?' Such a discussion could be had with *both* men and women.

Our core points in this example are, first, that demonizing a discriminatory behaviour neither tackles unfair discrimination nor enables diversity. People simply find a way around to do it secretly. Second, it's important to accept that discrimination, in principle, is the basis of doing business and we must make allowance for it. For example, if any candidate man or woman, is assessed as not being equipped to handle a high-pressure job (because of having a child or for any other reason), businesses must have the leeway to make that discriminatory choice as a part of business requirement, as long as the principles are fair, transparent and applied uniformly without prejudice to any demographic profile. Finally, consequent to privilege is also responsibility. If allowance is to be made for organizations to discriminate fairly as a part of doing business, then they must also be committed to going beyond the easy route of deploying policies that prohibit certain behaviours. Instead, they must consider investing time and energy to enable difficult conversations and finding sustainable solutions to address the very root cause of discriminatory behaviours.

Equal Opportunity Employer

A post appeared on my social media feed, and people seemed to be commenting angrily on it. An HR influencer had shared a job advertisement by some small Indian organization asking for 'male only' candidates. The influencer called the ad shameful and discriminatory. Everyone else fumed and followed suit. I remember looking up the post to search the company, having felt sorry for the public desecration and curious to know why they wanted a 'male only' for the job. It turned out to be a small, unknown firm registered on the professional networking site. This firm wasn't the only one advertising such jobs. A search on Google shows many such listings. In fact, there are many 'female wanted only' jobs as well. Some only want female tele-callers, while others want only males for field jobs. But why do such jobs exist? Is it the outcome of some mala fide sexist mindset? Are we equally outraged about 'only women can apply' jobs? On the other hand, the businesses that call themselves 'equal opportunity employers' in job advertisements—what does it signify? Are they 'equal' in true sense of the word? And should all businesses be expected to become equal opportunity employers?

The Cisco case has brought caste discrimination back into public and policy discourse.[7] At the time this book was being written, Cisco had been sued by the California Department of Fair Employment and Housing on behalf of a Cisco employee, in the US, who claimed to have been discriminated against for the reason that he belongs to the lower caste Dalit community. Arguments have been thrown by both sides; those who want this case to pave the way for legal recognition of caste, alongside race, in the USA, as a cause for discrimination; and those who feel that the issue has been blown out of proportion. Similar advocacy has happened in the UK as well where, until this point in time, the government has refused to enact a law specifically recognizing caste discrimination. Strong lobbies, both advocating and resisting these changes lead to a fundamental question, that is, why should it matter whether or not law specifically mentions a certain category of discrimination (such as caste in this case)? Organization policies and processes should take care of any form of

---

[7] https://www.firstpost.com/world/case-against-cisco-systems-caste-discrimination-slips-through-cracks-in-legal-system-that-only-sees-black-and-white-8736631.html

discrimination whether or not the law specifies it. The push for legislation might be indicative of the fact that organizations are playing it safe and just ticking boxes the law requires them to. It's in this light that we can examine the aspect of organizations calling themselves equal-opportunity employers.

Although equal opportunity employment laws may vary across countries, the core framework remains to protect defined minorities and prohibit discrimination based on specified criteria such as colour, gender, race, etc. For an organization to call itself 'equal opportunity employer', they simply need to comply with the law, and not necessarily be equal in a true sense of the word. For example, organizations could be strongholds of alumni of certain educational institutions or ex-employees of specific organizations. This is usually an outcome of the leader having a bias towards hiring incumbents from his alma-mater or ex-organizations for all key roles in the leadership. This by default means wilful discrimination towards anyone who does not fit the profile. Yet such an organization might end up labelling itself as an equal opportunity employer since it didn't discriminate on a basis defined by law.

On the other hand, there are those 'male only', 'female only' job advertisements which may actually be in conflict with the law. The businesses posting these, the jobs themselves and the associated pay are usually too small for anyone to pursue it legally. However, they might provide us the pretext to understand why all businesses cannot be expected to be equal-opportunity employers, at least not all at once. There are multiple issues at hand. Many of these 'male only' jobs are for field jobs or for something like a graveyard shift. Laws often require organizations to make adequate safety arrangements for women especially if they need to work late.

This could mean arranging for conveyance, security guard to escort female employees or such measures. Finding decent accommodation in remote areas could be a challenge, if the job involves travel. Businesses cannot claim lack of funds as a reason for lapses in these. Feminists might retort that women are fighting wars and working in remote areas today, and they are right. What we must understand here is that irrespective of a woman's willingness to take the risk, the law will hold the company accountable if an untoward incident happens. When organizations decide against women employees either openly or covertly, they are acting out of cognizance of their legal liabilities. Unlike Fortune 500 companies, they may not even have deep pockets to manage the legality or launch a PR campaign to clear their name.

The other set of challenges organizations face are around ensuring appropriate behaviour for safety from harassment in general and sexual harassment in particular. Not all organizations are Microsoft or Tatas. There is an entire small- and medium-scale industry employing millions, which may lack the awareness and maturity, even at leadership level, on how to handle these matters and try to steer away from hiring men or women for certain goals Some of these male- or female-only jobs could also be the result of gender stereotyping; for example, women make better receptionists and HR, while men can do better sales. This is further evidence of the lack of organizational and leadership maturity. Quality resources and expertise available to them, in preparing the organization, are also limited as most D&I experts prefer to focus on the Fortune 500 category. We'll remind the readers here that this is not to justify the admittedly skewed rationale of these businesses. The discussion is to understand the mindset and why legislation alone cannot ensure that organizations will become 'equal opportunity' immediately.

Start-ups are another category of businesses that may have unique situations, where their foremost goal is business survival and getting work done, usually at breakneck speed. They are always in a constant state of flux with limited bandwidth to focus on long-term organization building. Yet, many of these organizations scale up to large employee bases. However, can the expectations from a 1,000-employee strong 3-year old start-up on equal opportunity be the same as that from a 1,000-employee strong 10-year old organization? An equally important question to ask is what kind of governmental and bureaucratic support need to be extended to help businesses become equal-opportunity employers? In some of the organizational anecdotes we heard, trans-people having undergone a sex reassignment surgery face significant hurdles in getting the gender changed in all the government documents. The process was both tedious and embarrassing. The stigma faced in these situations is hardly spoken about. What kind of awareness and sensitizations have been done in these sectors? Unless there is a commitment to create a seamless and holistic support system across legal processes, expert support and large-scale awareness, expecting all organizations to be equal employers, without consideration to the nature of business and organizational maturity, is naïve, impractical and to some extent unfair.

We are not suggesting that all of these can be put in place overnight. The point of critique here is that there has been no visible attempt to approach the matter systematically, involving all stakeholders and ensuring there is a shared accountability. Discriminatory mindset is a deep-rooted social problem. However, the mantle to resolve this widespread problem falls largely on businesses. For example, organizations often have to conduct 'diversity sensitization workshops' meant to help people understand the 'right behaviours' towards women, lesbian, gay, bisexual, transgender, queer, intersexed, asexual (LGBTQIA) community, etc. These are the most fundamental aspects of human conduct in a social set-up. How come there is no thrust on schools and colleges to create this sensitization when human minds are in their formative stages? While these sensitization workshops have been normalized, one cannot miss the irony of 30-, 40- or 50-year olds having to be taught fundamentals of human interaction, what is appropriate and what is not. How come, even at a ripe age, the best of us struggle to expand and explain L-G-B-T-Q-I-A and need a workshop to help us understand it? It is also well-established fact that attitude and mindset are some of the most difficult human attributes to change. It's almost as if organizations are having to start on the back foot, leaving them constrained with time and energy to focus on long-term solutions. This is not shifting of blame. It is just saying that *unless the accountability is shared by other sub-systems such as education, it will be naïve to expect that businesses can get anywhere close to becoming non-discriminating, equal employers.* One of the metrics taken as an indicator of lack of diversity and consequent presence of some discrimination are demographic ratios of the organization's headcount. However, what about the skew in demographics in the actual talent pool from where hiring happens? The expectation from businesses is to have a demographic balance that reflects the societal demographics ratio. For example, engineering companies may consider the ideal scenario to have nearly 50 per cent of their automobile engineers as women, or X per cent as LGBTQ or some other minority group. A basic question is—if all companies aspire to achieve the ideal balance, is the commensurate talent pool available? This leads to the next question—why isn't there enough discussion on how the education system can enable this? We are not talking of efforts being made by handful of Ivy

Leagues, who are in the news. Just like not all businesses are Microsoft and Tatas, not all educational institutes are Harvard and Stanford. If we are to really achieve equal opportunity in the workforce, the conversation has to include lower-ranking educational institutes as much as it must consider the practical reality of smaller businesses and start-ups.

Off the record, managers will talk about how they want to 'stay away from trouble' of hiring women, LGBTQ and other protected minorities. They'll never say it in the open for the obvious reason of not wanting to be badgered. We are not willing to listen to such points of view, and take a default position of contempt for such talk. However, unless we open up the conversation, organizations will be equal-opportunity employers only on paper. *Laws only serve a limited purpose for a limited time. True equality opportunity and non-discrimination will come from understanding why managers and leaders covertly consider it 'trouble' to hire minorities that the laws seek to protect.*

- Is it because they don't feel adequately equipped to handle various situations (e.g., lack of clarity on what it means to have a transgender team member)?
- Is it because they think it will take more time and effort? Is it because they want to avoid the shaming that happens 'if anything goes wrong' (i.e., people are more cautious in areas dictated by laws and seek to avoid it)?
- Is it a mindset that wasn't taken care of during formative years (actual bias)?

This is the proverbial elephant in the room that no one wants to address. These concerns manifest as murmurs, water cooler conversations and hushed grudging voices fearful of backlash from diversity openly. These problems may not be to our liking. But these are real problems which need solutions beyond tokenism. The government has taken a simplistic approach. While they have passed legislations, very little has been done to role model the change in terms of implementing a non-discriminatory culture in government departments and public sector under-takings (PSUs). Businesses, especially the ones who have the resources and muscle to make a real difference, are taking the easy way out by simply checking boxes. The phenomenon of 'woke-washing', that is, organizations building an image of being non-discriminatory in their marketing communications, while doing very little meaningful work on ground, is evidence of that.[8] Unilever CEO, Alan Jope spoke about it at the 2019 Cannes Lions International Festival of Creativity.[9] Champions of diversity, too, have largely limited themselves to sensitization workshop, protests and shaming, not pushing themselves to go deeper into the problem and find sustainable solutions. There hasn't been adequate lobbying for laws that provide a practical way for businesses to bring about a change in mindset, keeping business challenges in mind. Backlinks haven't been established with K–12 and higher education systems through industry–academia collaborations. There haven't been serious efforts to create enough skill set to build non-discriminatory organizations. The path to becoming actual discrimination-free, equal-opportunity employers is neither linear nor simplistic. It must begin with the understanding that *discrimination at workplace is not an agenda to serve as fodder for rallying and rhetoric. It is a*

---

[8] https://hbr.org/2020/07/woke-washing-your-company-wont-cut-it
[9] https://www.unilever.com/news/press-releases/2019/unilever-ceo-warns-advertisers-that-woke-washing-threatens-industry-credibility.html

problem of the most complex nature, which requires hard-core, practical, on-ground problem-solving.

Fifty Shades of Black, White and Brown

Dove released (and later withdrew) an ad where a black woman changes shades to finally become white.[10] Social media went ballistic over derogatory implications about the black skin colour. Never mind that the brown lady, who also turns into white, found no mention in the black-white rhetoric. In 2020 USA presidential election race, Kamala Harris, the Democratic running mate, was a purple cow of sorts, being a woman of a multiracial lineage (Black Jamaican from her father's side and Brown Indian from her mother's side). Her representation in the press makes for interesting observations. Harris has largely been projected as a Black woman candidate, despite the fact that she was raised mostly by her Indian mother[11] and is closer to her 'Brown roots'. On the other hand, she has been criticized for talking about her Brown roots, love for dosas and appeal to *chittis* (Tamilian word of endearment for aunt), in an alleged attempt to appease Indian–American voters. It appears that whether in Harris' candidature or the Dove ad aftermath—choice of colour in the rhetoric is more than just incidental. Perhaps it is for this reason that East Asians debate whether using yellow as their colour-word (because brown doesn't quite describe them) hurts or harms their case.[12] #BlackLivesMatter raged around the world following

---

[10] https://www.theguardian.com/world/2017/oct/08/dove-apologises-for-ad-showing-black-woman-turning-into-white-one

[11] https://theprint.in/opinion/being-indian/hinduphobia-kamala-harris-identity-liability-black-us-media/480293/

[12] https://www.npr.org/sections/codeswitch/2018/09/27/647989652/if-we-called-ourselves-yellow

the police brutality on George Floyd. Soon #AllLivesMatter appeared on the horizon, only to be bitterly criticized, for taking away from the specific struggles of Blacks.[13] Videos appeared on social media of people showing that while all lives matter, the problems of Blacks are worse than what others face, and hence, one should not use #AllLivesMatter. In these arguments, the comparison was between privilege of Whites and struggles of Blacks. However, globally, there could be many other groups who have suffered just as much discrimination and felt as wronged as the Blacks—which is why #AllLivesMatter may have felt more relatable. We are not so much interested in the specifics of the representation of Kamala Harris as Black or Brown, or the choice of hashtag for George Floyd or the selective black outrage on the Dove ad in context of our discussion. However, these incidents lead us to questions that could unearth principles of dealing with discrimination at workplace, that is:

- Does every group need a separate movement, separate laws, separate representation in organizations to combat discrimination?
- Or should organizations deal with discrimination with fair and uniform process and keep it relevant to the actual facts of the issue?
- Does the discrimination against 'a Black', 'a woman', 'a heterosexual', 'a backward class', etc., hold more weightage than discrimination faced by an employee who doesn't belong to these groups—that is, do #AllEmployeesMatter when it comes to tackling discrimination at workplace?

[13] https://www.hindustantimes.com/art-and-culture/all-lives-matter-here-s-why-sara-ali-khan-kareena-kapoor-khan-and-tamannah-bhatia-s-instagram-posts-are-tone-deaf/story-Bs0Dn0UL3kGPvl7JdnBG0O.html

I was meeting a friend after a long time. Both of us are entre-preneurs, building our respective start-ups. Somewhere during our discussion, he said, 'I am scared if I ever have to lay-off my female team members. You (reference to me) can fire a woman, as a woman, no one will tell you anything. But I am a man. I can be charged with harassment.' This friend is no meek person. Yet, he seemed genuinely apprehensive of having to fire 'a woman' for business reasons. He is probably right. If any controversy did happen, the focus may be less on the specifics of the case but on the fact that 'a woman' was fired. 'A woman' comes codified with the centuries of wrong that have been done against women. When the phrase 'a woman' is invoked (as opposed to the specific person in question), the accused is not guilty to the extent of the actual action (let's say there *was a* wrongful act); the accused bears the weight of historic wrongs codified in those words of 'a woman', 'a Black', 'a lower caste', etc. For example, when the Cisco case became public knowledge, articles on historic caste discrimina-tion and traumas of lower castes flooded the internet. In com-parison, only a small number of articles mentioned the actual case facts of the alleged discrimination of job responsibilities and promotion, as have been raised by the plaintiff. Very few articles informed that Cisco had conducted internal investi-gations and did not find discrimination to have happened.[14] We don't intend to comment on whether discrimination hap-pened or not, and if the cause of discrimination was caste bias. We don't have access to any first-hand information and there-fore are not qualified to take a view. The matter is in court, and only they can decide. Nor are we saying that there hasn't been a painful history of caste discrimination in India. What

---

[14] https://www.news18.com/news/india/cisco-case-tip-of-iceberg-us-based-dalits-worry-over-export-of-indian-caste-system-2698369.html

we are pointing out here is the nature of public discussion, which focused very little on the specific incident but almost entirely on the fact that the complainant was 'a Dalit' and the manager is someone from 'a higher class'. Take the instance when Member of Parliament and author Shashi Tharoor criticized Indian demonetization, creating a pun on the then Miss World (2017), Manushi Chhillar. He said the government did not realize the dominance of Indian money and even the Indian chhillar can win Miss World ('chhillar' sounds similar to the Hindi word for penny)[15]. Tharoor was pulled up for it, on twitter, by notable individuals and even the National Commission for Women. Humour can be tricky. While to some his comment was witty wordplay, others didn't find it funny—which is alright. Tharoor's mistake, if any, could be that of cracking a bad joke. His offense would be to Manushi Chhillar alone. Coincidentally, Chillar gave a light-hearted response to it. However, Tharoor got blamed at a national level for sexism because his joke was on 'a woman'. He was said to have insulted 'a daughter of India and state of Haryana'. It was reminiscent of Wozniacki trying to mimic Serena Williams. At best, Wozniacki could be blamed for a poor imitation, and her offense would be to her fellow player, Williams. But the former was said to have made fun of 'a Black woman's body type' as 'a White woman'. Her offense was escalated to racism and she was held in contempt of an entire race. It is this approach that makes managers and people like my entrepreneur friend feel apprehensive of working with protected groups. Perhaps they know that if there is an issue, their wrong would not be against a specific Jane or John Doe, but against the loaded code

---

[15] https://www.firstpost.com/india/shashi-tharoor-faces-twitter-backlash-for-joke-on-manushi-chhillar-ncw-asks-if-will-call-his-own-daughter-chillar-4217971.html

of 'a someone'. Acknowledging this might feel uncomfortable to many, and denial may be our instinctive response. However, like we said earlier, seeking to understand the cause does not mean accepting the behaviour. However, understanding the context is necessary to solving it. Let us then consider what is being called *reverse discrimination.*

The phrase (reverse discrimination) is silly, if you come to think of it. What does it even mean; because any discrimination is discrimination, isn't it? Yet the fact that such a phrase exists is evidence of this—'a someone' coding. The discourse around discrimination at workplace implicitly refers to minorities and historically discriminated-against groups. We don't really think of discrimination as something a man, an upper-caste person, White or a straight person can face. Hence, *reverse discrimination* had to be coined to represent the possible discrimination of non-minorities. Even more difficult is to imagine that a woman, a Black a lower-caste person, an LGBT person or the like can be the perpetrator of discrimination. Priyanka Chopra Jonas, in her interview to Brian Rose,[16] shared that she was bullied when she was at a high school in Boston. She was called 'Brownie' and 'curry', among other things, which affected her impressionable teenage mind and made her return to India. While one might imagine her 'racist bully' to be a mean White girl, Chopra has shared that her bully was in fact an African American girl. Interestingly, while there are articles talking of this racism in Chopra's life, they seldom talk about her bully. Would those articles have been written the same way, if Chopra was bullied by the stereotypical 'White supremacist'? An African American bully doesn't fit the code. It will be politically incorrect to mention it.

---

[16] https://www.youtube.com/watch?v=gb7wDd2wB28

The publication will risk being called racist and pulled up for spreading stereotypes against Blacks. However, if the bully was a White, highlighting it would be akin to raising one's voice. A typical counterargument one hears is, 'But there are many more Whites bullying Blacks than other way around.' And that is *precisely* the point we have been making; that is, we decide our attitude towards an incident of discrimination and how enraged we are going to be about it, based on historical context of discrimination against 'a someone', rather than the actual facts of the case. While politicians may have vote-bank agenda, media may bear allegiance to a narrative, and Twitterati take joy in expressing themselves without having to face any consequence of what they write—*can businesses afford to deal with discrimination the same way?*

Businesses have a business to run—products to sell, customers to serve and employees to pay. They cannot afford to cower down to the pressure of taking one-sided approach to discrimination. Yet, businesses have played to the gallery, succumbed to the noise and tokenism, instead of putting serious industry-level thought to how they can effectively deal with the situation. Google's rushed firing of engineer James Damore for holding a politically incorrect view, with Sundar Pichai cancelling his personal leave to do the needful, without considering the route of dialogue or seeking to understand, is a classic example of approach taken by businesses. Organizations seem to want to take the path of least resistance—or perhaps least effort. However, it's only a matter of time before the murmurs grow louder and the unrest becomes visible in organizations. Naysayers may see 'fairness for all' approach, as a dilution of historic discrimination—just like #AllLivesMatter was seen to dilute #BlackLivesMatter. However, the only sustainable way to remove the discrimination that indeed *has been meted out* over centuries is to deal with the mindset of discrimination by looking at facts and their root cause. The way to remove discrimination is *not to lay grounds for a new kind of discrimination*. As more women or minorities come to leadership positions, will they be held accountable for discriminating behaviour? If we are not careful, in another few decades, that is where we will head. The problem of discrimination will remain, only the roles of who bullies whom will change. *Organizations have a moral imperative, even more than a legal one, to remove discrimination. However, businesses* **cannot afford to deal with discrimination discriminately,** *depending on where someone is on the skin-colour shade card or gender and sexuality continuum.* Understandably, the argument from diversity advocates will be that, right now, we are far from getting justice for the protected groups, to even be talking about this. That is again, *precisely* what the point is. Discrimination cannot be a matter of sequencing who gets respite before whom. It cannot be about trying to fix one problem, while laying grounds for another. It needs tackling the very root cause of discriminatory behaviour, which coincidentally means a lot more work for organizations—the reason why they may have shied away from it in the first place, choosing tokenism over sustainable solutions.

Equal Pay for Equal Work...
Is Not the Solution

This brings us to the critical question—what about the inequity that exists today? How do we ignore the fact that certain sections of the society are lagging behind? How do we bridge the gap? Take the example of pay parity between men and women. During a leadership summit,[17] two leading actors of India, Akshay Kumar and Kareena Kapoor, were asked about

---

[17] https://www.youtube.com/watch?v=VWsZQzWmo14

gender pay disparity in Bollywood. Kapoor said she would like to get paid as much as Kumar. The latter said he was actually a partner to the producer in their current movie together. Further, he offered Kapoor the opportunity to be a 50 per cent partner in the next movie, not seeking remuneration for her acting, but taking half of what the movie made at the box office. What this conversation reveals is that pay gap is not merely a gender-bias issue, and the solution is not as simple as paying women more. A case in point is Grand Slam prize money for male and female tennis players. Over the years, major Grand Slams have transitioned to equal prize money for male and female players.[18] However, the debate is far from over. Male players have continued to argue their reasons of why they should get paid more than their female counterparts. Novak Djokovic said,[19] 'Women should fight for what they think they deserve and we should fight for what we think we deserve.' Arguments, in general, include longer match time and audience pull of male players, etc. Of course, these arguments get countered as the debate continues—with both sides using examples that suit their point. Leading female players like Serena Williams and Martina Navratilova have said that women athletes should play 5-set matches.[20] Apart from prize money, disparity in other areas such as media coverage of male and female players continue to be discussed. The debates are raging in every sector. A sexism debate in start-up world is why a small fraction of venture funding goes to female founders as compared to male founders. There are multiple arguments

---

[18] http://news.bbc.co.uk/sport2/hi/tennis/6385295.stm

[19] https://www.theguardian.com/sport/2016/mar/21/novak-djokovic-indian-wells-equal-prize-money-tennis

[20] https://www.thetimes.co.uk/article/women-should-play-five-sets-at-wimbledon-says-navratilova-jh9m0fh0n

on both sides. Those claiming sexism say, investors have a bias against women founders. Others say that women present themselves conservatively during pitches while men exaggerate their qualities. Recently, funds specifically focusing on female founders have cropped up. However, is that a sustainable solution? How do we deal with this never-ending debate, in every sector?

First and foremost, we need to define the context of such debates, clearly. Are we talking in strict business terms or from the perspective of larger social good? For a business context, we need to consider business parameters. For example, some opine female founders should not have to change themselves to get investment, but investors should meet them half way. From a utopian, equal and just-society point of view, that makes sense. However, putting oneself in an investor's shoes, from strict business point of view, one will invest money based on expected returns. Hence, the long-term solution in the business context will be to understand and resolve what keeps female founders behind while seeking investment, instead of setting up special funds, to 'meet them halfway'. We are not saying some additional efforts are negative. Our point is that, in a business context, the root causes of discriminatory practices need to be addressed, taking a practical view instead of expecting utopian scenarios.

Another key aspect to consider while dealing with discrimination in remuneration, etc., is that the decision variables are not shared transparently. Whether it is actor's pay or chief experience officer (CXO) salary or tennis players' earnings—the parameter should be defined and made public by decision-making authorities. Allocation of courts is a major issue in Grand Slam tournaments, leading to gender debates on who should get to play in major courts. What if the organizing team were to make their criteria officially known? What if media houses were required to publish how they decide the coverage of male and female matches? What if producers of movies were to announce their criteria of deciding the pay of male and female actors? What if organizations were to share their compensation formula? What if investors had to be transparent about their funding decisions? What if organizations needed to state their rejection and selection parameters clearly? For example, if organizations were to share transparently that they will pay anyone returning from a break less than others, with reasons. Or if media houses were to publish their internal assessment of ratings of players based on which they decided to cover player A twice as much as player B. Or investors were to say upfront that they did not fund a female entrepreneur because they thought she would not be as available to work, as they would expect her to be. This radical truthfulness will lead to multiple outcomes. The very need to publish their decision parameters will put greater accountability on decision-makers to examine whether they have defined clear, fair criteria and have a systematic decision process in place. Making the criteria public also helps in fruitful discussions, instead of endless rhetoric. For example, if it is transparently shared and widely understood that any actor who takes a share of profits as a pay-out model, instead of a fixed compensation, has a chance of earning more, the discussion will move beyond 'why male actors get paid more than female actors'. If it is declared that viewership of a match is a criterion for player earning, a pay-out model can be re-looked at and applied uniformly to male and female players. If indeed women entrepreneurs are consistently found to be underplaying business plans, we can further look into whether a change is required in how women entrepreneurs pitch; or whether an unconscious bias is at play in the investors' mind, which needs to be addressed; or, a third possibility of male entrepreneurs consistently over-playing business plans. The idea of such radical transparency might seem uncomfortable to begin with. However, if we can build the appetite to both tell and hear the truth, it can lead to fact finding and real solutions.

A study by a Wharton professor[21] of two large stockbrokers found that saleswomen were earning less than salesmen, despite a system of merit pay, because they were being given smaller accounts with lesser commission and lesser support in terms of staff, mentors and amenities. Here the wage gap was not the problem. It was a symptom of the real problem (i.e., women not being entrusted with more challenging accounts). Hence, merely levelling-the-pay cannot be a solution in this case. Why was the account allocation as such? Was there an actual bias at play? Was there a genuine capability gap? Or some other challenge? If the company had an obligation to be transparent about the principles it used to allocate accounts to male and female employees (just like tennis authorities were to share their principle of allocating courts), the company would be forced to be accountable. They would be compelled to address the actual root cause. In short, the solution to discrimination needs to begin with defining and sharing of decision parameters, and the uniform application of it, to all stakeholders. Such radical transparency can make many in position of authority jittery. But transparency is what can drive accountability and fairness.

The final piece of reducing the gap caused by historic discrimination is capability development including government–industry–academia collaboration. In the last few years, there has been

---

[21] https://hbr.org/2013/09/women-in-the-workplace-a-research-roundup

a thrust for companies to have a gender balance in their boards. This has led to many notable appointments of female CXOs, which is well and good. One also comes across lot of articles on the 'need to promote more women'. However, if there is an overall shortage of women at senior roles, is mere promotion going to help? What happens after the existing talent pool has been tapped? The rest of the companies will either struggle or, worse, have to compromise on the candidate. This might be an 'ouch' observation, but let's look at it with clinical objectivity. We have categorically stated in the chapter 'Women in Senior Management' that there is no basis to speculations that female board members are in any way less capable than male board members. Hence, our point here is not in the least to suggest women leaders are lacking in anyway. It is simply that there needs to be real investment in increasing the talent pool of women to bridge the wide gap that exists because of historic discrimination. Merely *promoting* women (and other protected groups) will not help in the long run; however, *preparing* them will. There is only so much female-founder-specific funding that can happen. But helping them learn new behaviours necessary for the domain is what will put them on equal footing with male founders, on a larger scale. There are disgruntled murmurs in organizations that affirmative action is another kind of discrimination and means a 'compromise on meritocracy'. We have refuted these faulty arguments in the book. However, if affirmative action does not include capability building at a war footing, naysayers will be proven right in the long run, hurting the cause of diversity and anti-discrimination.

We acknowledge that the aforementioned is a delicate argument to make and can be easily misunderstood to be downplaying the pay gap. If aspects of diversity were so straightforward, it wouldn't be fraught with tokenism in the first place. By suggesting that we need to focus more on preparing women better, rather than on maxims such as equal-pay-equal-work, is not to refute the gap. In fact, if anything, the pay gap leads to social inequality, much beyond organizational discrimination. Gender equality in society cannot be achieved, unless women are financially at par with men, for which the pay gap has to be levelled. What we are saying is that we cannot limit ourselves to it. Instead, we need to aggressively build the capability of women at all levels so that they can make different career choices and silence all excuses that have been made earlier to justify the gap. Even further, focusing on pay-for-outcome means women need not only limit themselves to the goal of getting paid equal to men but aspire to get paid more.

Businesses don't exist in isolation; they are a part of society. One aspect that does not get spoken about often is discriminatory behaviours by customers themselves.[22] The society, in general, who might be outraged with any organizational discrimination on Twitter, could be the same people demonstrating bias in their behaviour while seeking a product and service. This dichotomous behaviour is the final reason why businesses cannot take the approach of tackling discrimination based on public opinion, which can be fraught with double standards. Organizations will be unable to sustain the piecemeal, incident-based and issue-specific approach to discrimination. The solution has to be about fair principles, applied to everyone. Hence, if Kareena Kapoor can take more business risk than Akshay Kumar, and if Serena Williams' matches get sold out faster than Djokovic's, then they should

---

[22] https://scholarship.law.duke.edu/cgi/viewcontent.cgi?article=6083&context=faculty_scholarship

claim to get paid, not just equally, but even more than their male counterparts. Much in the same way, if they don't, they should be okay to not get paid as much. The alternative to discrimination isn't so much as *equal pay for equal work*. True equity, especially in high-stake roles, will come from *equal pay for equal outcomes*.

With Truth and Humour...

Charles Bukowski's *Tales of Ordinary Madness* (1983),[23] a collection of short stories, did not go down well with the public library in Nijmegen. The book was banned from the library based on a complaint from a local reader calling it discriminatory, among other things. Bukowski, a man of his convictions, wrote back a letter to the library. He said (in his letter), he wrote badly about homosexuals, Blacks or women because these were whom he met, and that he has seen both the light and darkness in life, and if he only wrote about the former, he would be a liar. He pointed out that there were many bad White men, and if he wrote about them, no one would complain. He questioned if he must point out that there are good Blacks, homosexuals and women. For those who were criticizing his work, he said that they overlooked the sections of his work which entailed love and joy, and that they were taught to look only one way, when many ways exist. It was in this letter that Bukowski said, 'The thing that I fear discriminating against is humor and truth.'

It is true that centuries of oppression have suffocated the souls of men and women around the world on basis of their birth, colour, gender and nationality. It is true that there exist men and women who consider themselves superior and

---

[23] https://lettersofnote.com/2011/10/18/may-we-all-get-better-together/

others inferior, deserving of lesser dignity, opportunities and ambition. It goes without saying that these are wrongs that must be made right. It is also true that somewhere real solutions are not being worked upon in the noise and din. The history of discrimination should serve as a lesson and give us reason to resolve this problem with missionary zeal. And for this precise reason, we must be willing to look beyond tokenism to end the vicious cycle of discrimination, the path to which is neither straightforward nor easy. Corporation are a part of the society and they carry the mantle as much as on governments, institutions and individuals of the civil society.

Sometimes, the best way to define a word is to identify it's opposite. The foundation of discrimination is bias. Bias is a *distorted perception of facts*, about one's worth, one's status and entitlement as a human, in comparison to another. Therefore, the opposite of discrimination is not equality. *The opposite of discrimination is truth—seeing things as they are.* And a truly diverse and discrimination-free organization which fulfils business goals along with upholding human values will need leaders who have the wisdom to evaluate every situation by the truth of it, little humour to see through the brouhaha and, must we add, the commitment to do whatever it takes.

BIG IN THE CHAPTER
IDEAS

1. *Discrimination is the basis of management:* Businesses function on the core principle of differential selection, reward, engagement of employees and customers based on parameters. Fundamentally, businesses cannot be expected to treat everyone as equal. However, they can be expected to be fair.

2. *Separate a discriminatory behavior from the -ism behind it:* Every discriminatory behavior may not be the result of racism or sexism, etc. It is important to understand the context behind a behavior, to find practical solutions.

3. *'Equal-opportunity employer' needs to go beyond legal compliance:* Businesses cannot limit themselves to checking the legal box of 'equal opportunity' employer, but seek to solve on-ground roadblocks to creating truly non-discriminatory organizations.

4. *We can't deal with discrimination based on minority identities alone:* Reactive, incident-based, public-pressure-driven interventions focused on certain minorities cannot effectively end discrimination. Emphasis should be on fair and transparent principles being defined and applied to everyone uniformly.

5. *Equal work-equal pay isn't sufficient to bridge the gender gap:* Identify reasons behind pay gap and invest resources in resolving the root cause.

Equal, Not Same

For I am born to tame you, Kate,
And bring you from a wild Kate to a Kate
Comfortable as other household Kates.

—Shakespeare's *Taming of the Shrew*

Katherine is rich, witty, doesn't want to marry and lashes out at suitors, especially the ones less qualified. She is seen as a 'shrew', berated for her sharp tongue, rather than praised for her sharp wit. Naturally then, she must be reined in to become an obedient wife. To this end, her husband subjects Katherine to hunger and thirst, till she learns to call the sun the moon—if her husband so commands. *Taming of the Shrew* is one of the most controversial plays of Shakespeare. While some accuse Shakespeare of misogyny, others defend him saying he was only depicting the prevalent mindset of that time. Irrespective of whether Shakespeare was depicting societal misogyny or being a misogynist himself, the play points at uncomfortable realities of the role and perception of women around the world, irrespective of cultures. Even more importantly, we must note that these attitudes are not just imposed upon women by an external 'society' but often accepted by women themselves, as status quo of who they are, what they can become and how they must live life.

As we increasingly talk about gender equality, in the society and workplaces, many debates, big or small, continue to rage. Should women get a special period leave? Should we have gender-neutral restrooms? Should women's sports have the same duration as men's? Are men and women wired differently to be more or less suited for specific jobs? Should a man offer his seat, in a crowded conference room, to a female colleague standing next to him? These make for heated debates in office, at water coolers and online, and the answers are far from being straightforward. It's simply not an either–or, this to that, me and you, us versus them. Hence, first, as we try to find practical and fair ways to navigate these questions of gender diversity, an attempt must be made to understand and acknowledge the societal and cultural contexts. Second, as the authors realize, while readers of this book might be urban, educated, social media-savvy individuals, the conversation of diversity cannot be limited to the woke population alone, as it quite often is. While enquiring deeper into hardwired mindsets and behaviours, we must bear in mind that different sections of society across the world are transitioning to the new status quo at different paces. Some have moved faster and feel frustrated at the world not keeping pace with their notion of equality. There are others who still want to hold on the existing status quo as something which they may not necessarily agree with but definitely feel more comfortably familiar with. Finally, the most important aspect of this exploration is to not look at any of contexts with the binary lens of *good* and *bad*, or *agree* and *disagree,* as we might be tempted to. It's the very nature of contexts to be situational rather than absolute. Seeking to understand the context of behaviours does not imply accepting or agreeing with them. It merely gives us a better canvas to take a reasoned approach to diversity. Hence, it will serve us best to detach ourselves from our opinions and emotions temporarily and look at the context with dispassionate objectivity.

Lajja

As the story of Ramayana goes, when Lakshmana was faced with the difficult choice of either guarding his sister-in-law, queen Sita, or rushing into the jungle to find his brother and king-in-exile Rama, he did what he thought would help him fulfil both his duties. Using his skills, Lakshmana drew a protective line around the hut, instructing Sita to stay inside it, while he ran to help Rama who appeared to have run into danger. Ravana, who had plotted to draw Rama and Lakshmana away from the hut, couldn't get to Sita because of that line. It was only when Sita was lured out of the circle of protection could Ravana abduct her, as he had planned to. Lakshman Rekha (*rekha* means 'line' in Hindi) continues to be known several centuries later, not just as part of lore, but a metaphorical reminder for women to operate within limits and rules set for them. Joan of Arc, the French peasant girl who dressed like a boy and led French troops in war as a teenager, is unmistakably one of the most remarkable women in history. Now officially recognized as a saint, Joan of Arc was ironically burned alive in punishment for many transgressions she was charged for, including dressing as a boy and practising witchcraft. Her trial record noted[1] that by dressing as a boy she had 'broken bounds of modesty... forgetting all female decency'. Joan's counterargument to the judges, that it was a practical choice of clothing while around men and that she had been molested in prison when she dressed like a woman, fell on deaf ears. The trial further recorded that if her guilt were to be proven, there would be no choice but to condemn her to 'purifying flames'. Joan of Arc was captured by the English while fighting for the French.

---

[1] https://www.history.com/news/joan-arc-burned-stake

The fact that she would be prosecuted as a prisoner of war, might be expected, if not accepted. However, it's the nature of charges against her which is telling of the moral code that a woman is expected to live within. In the Victorian era, a sign of well-bred women was wearing strictly coded clothing such as corsets and crinoline. Corsets were known to cause breathing difficulties, internal bleeding and digestion issues due to the extreme tightness of the clothing. Crinolines, made of steel hoops to give a flare to gowns, have been the reason of deaths of thousands of women as it caused the garment to catch fire.[2] Despite the well-known perils of this clothing, the women defying the established dress code came to be called 'loose women', implications being both literal and figurative. 'Witch hunt' studies show that women constituted majority of those persecuted as witches across centuries. While lot of these witch hunts had a religious background, the heavy gender skew, as per scholars, could be possibly ascribed to the belief that women are more fallible to weakness[3] than men. Lakshman Rekha and witch hunt are not comparable. In fact, they are on the *opposite sides* of the *same continuum*. Lakshman Rekha was drawn for protection and safeguard of Sita. Witch hunt was a tool of restraint and control. Hence, they are *opposites*. Yet they are two opposites of the *same continuum* where key aspects of a woman's life, whether positively or negatively, gets decided by men. Either men are unable to trust other men to be assured about the safety of women they care for, as in the case of abduction by Ravana. Or men cannot trust themselves to uphold moral standards, and therefore, the moral-code mantle must be borne by woman alone. Take the case of the

---

[2] https://historydaily.org/crinoline-victorian-fashion
[3] https://theconversation.com/most-witches-are-women-because-witch-hunts-were-all-about-persecuting-the-powerless-125427

1864 Contagious Diseases Act in the UK to stop the spread of sexually transmitted diseases. The law required 'suspected' prostitutes to submit to medical examination and be held in a hospital if found infected.[4] The gaping misogyny of the law, which led to protests, was that it only required women to be inspected. The law was especially targeted at sex workers, the women, while putting no onus on their clientele, the men, who were the ones voluntarily seeking the services.

The mindset that women must demonstrate higher moral standards while men take liberties has seeped deep into the psyche of our civilizations across cultures. The behaviours have been codified and normalized over centuries of hardwiring. *Lajja* (pronounced as luh-ja in Hindi and Urdu; or loh-jja in Bengali) means a few things. Sometimes, it refers to being shy; at times, it means shame. With slight variation across cultures, girls are raised to be coy—from speaking softly, walking gently to veiling their face. Girls are constantly reminded to walk with smaller strides, keep their bodies contained and feet together. In contrast, boys are seldom monitored on these matters in their growing years. The painful 'parallel feet' (i.e., women crossing one leg over the other such that it sticks straight and parallel to the other leg) has been popularized as the 'sexiest posture' for women to sit in. Whether a girl attends an elite 'finishing school' or gets nudged by older women at home, containing one's body movement is something every girl is nagged about, irrespective of social status. It's interesting to note that the science of body language correlates occupying larger space to exerting greater power. Stretching to occupy more space is the typical body language of men and the very opposite of what women are routinely conditioned to demonstrate—making

---

[4] https://www.jstor.org/stable/4048453?seq=1

it the very design of things for women to be in low-power positions as compared to men. The restraint on women is not just physical but also psychological, manifesting as need to seek approval and validation. This runs deep in the minds of even those women who may believe they have broken free. Is it okay if I like being a homemaker? Is it okay if I am careerist? Is it okay if I want to quit my job to raise my children? Is it okay if I hire a nanny? Is it okay if I don't cook and order out? Should I raise my hand in the meeting, do I know enough? Should I ask for a raise? Anyone who is privy to conversation among women on WhatsApp groups or in-person discussions will be sorely aware of these questions. Women constantly feel the need to be told, 'it's okay'—which is the invisible psychological *lajja* at play—the tendency to hold oneself back, to question one's ability and await someone's approval. Shame, the other meaning of *lajja*, has been the universal tool of choice to keep women in their place. In due time, women seem to have developed a capacity to auto-generate shame for themselves and their kind, whether it's a woman who goes all out after her career, or one who chooses a more domestic life of playing the good wife and mother. Author Chetan Bhagat had posted a comment endorsing his wife being a career woman who does not make *pulkas* (Indian flatbread) for him and that he was okay with it.[5] The note raised a storm on social media sparking debates between the career woman and homemaker, each side taking potshots at the other. Another comment seemingly representing the 'other side' of stay-at-home mothers by celebrity Mira Rajput[6] did not yield any different outcomes.

---

[5] https://www.implicitly.me/nothing/personal/house-wife-or-working-wife-you-decide-dont-let-chetan-bhagat-decide/

[6] https://movies.ndtv.com/bollywood/shahid-kapoor-on-mira-rajputs-puppy-comment-she-was-speaking-for-a-section-of-women-1670150

(Bhagat and Rajput's comments were unrelated and made at different points in time.) Rajput said that she couldn't spend merely an hour with her daughter and leave, because her child was not a puppy and what was the point of having a child in that case. This comment again led working women and stay-at-home mothers to lock horns on social media. The moot points here are: (a) irrespective of their life or career choice, women find themselves seeking to debate, justify, validate their choices, (b) women experience shame for their choice, which feeds the need to hear someone say 'it's okay', (c) women not only experience shame, but resort to shaming other women, perhaps as a means for psychological release and (d) similar discussion on men's life choices, seeking validation and shame, are conspicuous by its absence.

While shame is the stick used to keep women in place, the proverbial carrot lies in store for those who manage to be obedient and agreeable. Katherine, the wild shrew, does not only get tamed by her husband at the end of the play, she also surpasses other maids in becoming the most obedient wife. Being agreeable is a quality often expected of women at workplaces—an expectation that most women have submitted to, whether knowingly or unknowingly (including the best among us, who upon reading this, might even be shaking their head in denial, at this time). Few years ago, Sheryl Sandberg launched a campaign called 'Ban Bossy', where she was championing the discontinuation of using 'bossy' for girls, which discouraged them from taking up leadership position, for the fear of being less likeable. In an interview,[7] Sandberg said that *even she,* the author of *Lean In,* when named one of the most powerful women in the world, kept asking friends

---

[7] https://abcnews.go.com/US/sheryl-sandberg-launches-ban-bossy-campaign-empower-girls/story?id=22819181

to not post about the announcement on social media. There are three aspects to observe from Sandberg's own instinctive response to the power she wielded. First, that women exerting authority *are indeed* seen as aggressive and less agreeable. Second, being agreeable or liked *matters* to women. Third, as Sandberg points out, many girls call other girls bossy; which means it's not just men, but *women themselves who propagate these stereotypes*, knowingly or unknowingly. However, the problem is not limited to the above and has an element of paradox. Sandberg's 'Ban Bossy' was both hailed and criticized. The critics[8] of it argued that the movement may compel women to conform to established culture of masculine domination and aggression. Indeed, women playing down their femininity to fit into the 'boys' club', as they climb the organizational hierarchy, is not unheard of. There has been a parallel rhetoric of accepting women as they are, in their feminine selves, in leadership roles. Both Sandberg and her critics are right in their own way. Some women can exert authority better, while others are naturally more agreeable— just in the same way different roles need different levels of authority and agreeability. However, narratives that project either authoritative or agreeable as more important qualities than the other, outside the context of a job requirement, compelling women to wear a persona that isn't true to who they are, is like the Victorian corset playing out all over again.

The organizational cost of *lajja* could be high and, worse, hidden. It is known in common experience that women hold themselves back from making a point in the meetings, if they aren't completely sure about it. Men, on the contrary, are known to take a chance and present it anyway. Women may

---

[8] https://time.com/21498/i-dont-give-a-if-you-call-me-bossy/

hesitate to rock the boat, challenge a status quo or ask for a role, raise or promotion which is rightfully theirs, for the fear of being seen as aggressive. In one of my organizational roles, I was given the responsibility of organizing a live customer discussion for a conference. It was the first time something like this was being done. Since key customers were to be called on stage and the situation was expected to be dynamic, it required good stakeholder management. I had managed this event end-to-end, from reaching out to the customers, communicating with them, managing the logistics and discussion facilitation. It was a pre-lunch session. As would be appropriate, we had invited the customers to join us for lunch. I learnt, to my disappointment and shock, that while a cross section of the organization had been invited to join the customers for lunch, I was left out of the list. Invitees included business leaders and even my peers in the support function. I was confused, if it was a (gross) oversight in the thick of things, because I could think of no other reason why I would be kept out. When I raised this to the function head, his first reaction was to question me, for asking to be at the lunch as something of an overreach on my part. His reaction in turn did not make any logical sense to me. It was quite literally the asking-for-a-seat-at-the-table moment for me. I was crystal clear that as the core facilitator of the event not only was it a courtesy to invite me, but also as the product manager of the very product under discussion, it was necessary for me to get the opportunity to build rapport with the customer, in an informal setting. I was sure that, given my role, I needed to be there, much more than many others, who were on the list purely because of their designation. The function head relented, but not without me feeling a generous dose of embarrassment and self-doubt for having asked. For some strange reason, in that moment, I felt like Oliver Twist who dared ask for just that ladle of extra porridge, which should have been served to him anyway. Shaming of women for speaking logically and asking fairly, even for the smallest thing, is a hard reality. And it's not just the women who miss out, but also the organization which loses out on valid perspectives, ideas and rock-the-boat counterpoints which are critical to business. While the fallouts of *lajja*, in its various manifestations, have been the subject of research, we are inclined to view it from the perspective of how women lose out in their careers because of these behaviours. However, there is an equivalent albeit hidden cost of these hardwired mindsets to the business itself, in terms of capable women employees holding themselves back. Unless the latter costs are measured and highlighted, our response might remain limited to standard diversity-sensitization workshops that merely scratch the surface of what must otherwise be a pressing business priority.

The Good Wife...Mother...Melony Musk

In Mahabharat, queen Draupadi was disrobed in an open court by her brother-in-law. Following the incident, an epic war was waged by her five husbands to avenge the blasphemy. What's ironical is that the very reason of Draupadi's public humiliation was her being offered as a wager in a dice game, by the oldest of her five husbands—Yudhishthira. Known as the Dharma Raj, that is, an expert in right and wrong, Yudhishthira was enticed into the game by his cousins, the Kauravas and their uncle Shakuni (the latter known to carry a set of bewitched dices). Irrespective of the deceit by Kauravas, Yudhishthira's actions, especially given his knowledge of dharma, have been a subject of debate. Many opine that the incident cannot be viewed from simplistic lens of the rules of contemporary times and that apart from being a husband and brother, he was also the king (Yudhishthira bet his brothers in the same game as well). Indeed, we will not attempt to draw any simplistic conclusions lacking context. Let's take this incident, isolated from anything else in the story, to just demonstrate just one point: *that a woman's identity, role and destiny, in society, in most cases, if not all, has been relative to men.* She is 'a wife', 'a mother', 'a daughter', 'a daughter-in-law' before she is a person in her own right. Therefore, her decisions, the course of her life and expectations of her are in connection to those roles more than being dependent on herself as an individual. Draupadi got dragged and paid a personal price in a situation which had nothing to do with her, simply because she was the 'wife'. This is true across different time periods and cultures.

In the 1700s, When Austria and France had to end seven years of war and start a new alliance,[9] the monarchs of Austria are said to have 'offered' the hand of their 14-year old daughter, Marie Antoinette, in marriage to future King Louis XVI. They were married by proxy in Vienna a few years later, as the future king and queen had never met. The later infamous life of Antoinette notwithstanding, hers is again a story of women, being a cog in the larger scheme of things. If Antoinette had not been used as a means to seal the deal, who is to say how her life would have turned out. How a woman fares in her personal life roles, as mothers, wives, daughters, etc., seems to be as important and, sometimes, more so than how she fairs in her professional role. American sitcom *The Good Wife* is based on the story of a philandering States attorney caught in a Clinton-styled scandal, who later rises to the level of a governor and a presidential candidate. His

---

[9] https://www.history.com/topics/france/marie-antoinette

wife is forced to stick by his side in every campaign, often against her conviction, to give the picture of a forgiving wife and happy family. The popularity of the sitcom is an indicator of the reality that semblance of a traditional perfect family ('semblance' being the operative word) is important to even American voters, considered 'cool, progressive, modern' by the rest of the world. More importantly, as in the case of real life Bill and Hillary Clinton, the onus falls on the woman, much more than the man, to save the day and keep up societal traditions. One wonders if Hillary Clinton had taken a different decision when Bill Clinton was embroiled in the Monica Lewinsky issue, would she be, 'the wife who left her husband'? How would it affect her perception in the society and her own political candidature, despite her husband being the person who actually erred?

Take the case of Melony Musk. She doesn't exist for real. But let's say she did. Let's say she was the top techo-preneur of our times, trying to colonize Mars, changing the landscape of renewable energy and finding technology to upload human brain to AI. Let's also say she got married and divorced thrice and had a spate of relationships. She has five children from her past marriages, all through surrogacy (because Melony Musk, given the nature of her work, cannot spend five years of her life bearing children). She also had a sixth child recently the same way, this time out of wedlock. Of course, she loves her children, but clearly, she personally cannot be around to take care of them. How much content traffic would her personal life drive? What kind of a person is she to keep having children but never find the time to raise them? What does the spate of relationships say about her? If she ever failed in her ambitious ventures, would it be her professional failures alone, or would they be compounded by the nature of her personal life? Of course, Melony Musk is a not-so-subtle allusion to Elon Musk, who is an incredible mind by all measures. We don't bat an eyelid about his personal life the way it is, and never see it as a reflection on his professional capabilities and rightly so. But hand on heart, would it be the same for Melony Musk, if she existed, even at that level of genius and achievement?

Women are almost always described in terms of their personal roles, either entirely or at least in part. Jacinda Ardern, hailed for her terrific leadership of New Zealand amidst COVID-19, gun killing and many other challenging situations, is described in a lot of places as the woman who led with a baby in her arms. Whether it is Indra Nooyi or Sheryl Sandberg, 'how they manage family' and nature of relationships with their spouses and children is a point of curiosity. This is not so much the case with male executives. The mention of 'my beautiful wife' may come up in thank you speeches and events, but a discussion of spouse and children, and even less their parents, is not considered necessary to complete the identity of a male professional. Satya Nadella's description of his experience as a father, in the book *Hit Refresh*, is one of the rare exceptions of a successful male executive talking about family as an integral part of his evolution, beyond just an ornamental addition to their decorated accomplishments. However, for women professionals, their personal roles are not just good to talk but need to talk, without which we find it difficult to complete the picture of a woman in our minds, irrespective of their level of achievement. This is not just an external societal standard but just like *lajja*, a status quo that women perpetuate themselves knowingly or unknowingly. Women professionals, too, attach themselves to their personal roles and talk about it a lot more than male counterparts. For example, off late, one observes many women writing 'mother' on their LinkedIn headline (a professional networking site), alongside other qualifications and achievements. This entanglement of personal and professional roles has fallouts we don't necessarily realize. For example, when we hail a Jacinda Ardern's 'great leader with a baby' story, perhaps it's to convey—'she is a mother, yet she achieved so much.' However, we may be missing the corollary implication of it. If a woman's achievement is, in some way, more significant because she is a mother, it would follow that her achievement would be somewhat less significant or special if she wasn't playing any of the traditional roles (or was failing in them). Herein lies two risks. First, the woman 'professional as a mother' rhetoric alienates increasing number of single women and married-without-children women. As a single woman, I can personally admit to feeling disconnected in 'women in XYZ' profession kind of forums and groups, where the discussion is focused on motherhood and balancing home and work, instead of specific professional and domain challenges. Scholars of gender inequality,[10] during their research on explaining the factors that held women back at workplaces, found that people put forth observations based on the assumption that *all women are mothers*. This might mean overlooking why single or childless women lose out in the corporate rung, without the typical family commitments of women with children. The second fallout of the heavy emphasis on women professionals' personal roles is the added pressure and judgement of how they fare in those. Scholars found that women who succeeded professionally and held strongly to their professional identities were often described as bad mothers and 'horrible' women, which influences the

---

[10] https://hbr.org/2020/03/whats-really-holding-women-back

mindset of junior women about their choice between career and homes.

Some sections of diversity practitioners opine that hiring women who are successful as mothers and wives into leadership roles will help break the mindset that women have to choose between the two. The argument is flawed. First, bringing more women into leadership itself requires time and effort. It's not simply a matter of giving more promotions, but first creating that pipeline of female leaders in senior management— where the drops-outs are most visible. Second, how does one 'get more women who are married and mothers into leadership' without creating a new bias against women who don't fit that description? This approach creates more problems than it solves. It's understandable and required that there be conversation and action on making it easier for mothers to return to work and grow in their career. However, most organizations have limited their efforts to just that. As we see it, while it's necessary to create these support systems, a long-term shift is required in allowing women's professional identity to exist independent of their personal roles, in a way similar to men. It's important that we recognize Melony Musk's successes and failures for what they are professionally; with her marriage, children—presence or lack of both, being of no consequence to her work. And the change begins with how women see and describe themselves.

Sampann

One of the words associated with women in the Indian tradition is *sarv gunn sampann* (pronounced *ser-vuh goon sum-punn*), that is, being complete with all qualities. In Bengali traditions, a girl is expected to know everything from *jooto-shelai* (pronounced *joo-toh sheh-laa-ee)* to *Chondi path'* (pronounced *Chon-dee paath*), that is, from mending a shoe to chanting an ancient, complex incantation for Goddess Durga. This represents the range of skills a girl must build. This is akin to the positive stereotype of women being 'good multitaskers', having to wear multiple hats in life. Perhaps it's also symbolic of a woman's hardwiring to *be it all, do it all* and *have it all.*

Sometime ago, Arianna Huffington popularized #StyleRepeats, wherein she advocated women to be comfortable with repeating outfits and, in general, being comfortable with their appearance instead of spending a disproportionate amount of time on looking good instead of more important pursuits. She highlighted how this gave men a competitive advantage, who did not seem to be spending as much time worrying about clothes.[11] Before Huffington, Mark Zuckerberg was in news for his repeats of grey T-shirts, so that he has one less thing to decide on during the day. However, Zuckerberg, unlike Huffington, was not role modelling for men or starting a movement but simply going about his business. The point of interest here is not whether wearing the same coloured T-shirt every day leads one to achieve more significant things in life. It's to note that appearing attractive is an added responsibility of women in a way it isn't for men; perhaps the reason why changing this for women requires a special movement— which for men is not a big deal. An accomplished woman must be attractive as well. But a successful man can pass off looking any way. The contrast remains consistent even when we reverse the situation. What is the equivalent masculine phrase for 'beauty with brains'? None that comes to the mind immediately. 'Handsome with brains' doesn't seem to be much of a requirement. What is the masculine for 'bimbo'?

---

[11] https://thriveglobal.com/stories/arianna-huffington-style-gap-expectations-costly-women/

There appears to exist a word called 'himbo', which is not even remotely as famous as bimbo. The vocabulary to call out women with 'shallow beauty' is far more active than that for good-looking men. So, this way or that way, women have a taller bill to fit than men. Smart women must be attractive. Attractive women must be smart. Women are expected to be more *sampann* than men. Perhaps it is for this reason that Huffington felt the need to call it out categorically and send a message to women that it's okay to not always be insanely worried about what one wore. The challenge for women is not only spending more time to make themselves presentable while their male colleague could be comfortable looking obnoxious. Sometimes, it's the reverse mental strain to try and look 'natural' to not be criticized for wearing make-up, as we pointed out in the chapter 'Bias Is Pervasive'.

Another manifestation of *sampann*, is how much we women fret, mull and talk over where are we on the have-it-all scale—a career, husband, kids. The have-it-all rhetoric feels like these are a list of *trophies* one must have to feel complete, rather than *life choices* which would naturally vary across different women. Therefore, for a woman who managed to do well in her career, with a loving husband and kids by her side, can gleefully talk about being 'blessed to have it all'. However, a woman who does well in her career, but divorced or married with no kids or single, ruefully feels the lack of the have-it-all medallion (same as the woman who has a loving family but no career). I was once talking to a friend who is a mother to a toddler. She is professionally qualified (and driven) and married to her classmate. However, after motherhood, it was her professional life that went topsy-turvy lot more than her husband's, despite both being on the same capability and qualification footing. In a candid moment, I asked her if at times she felt it would have been easier to focus on her business had she chosen to not be a mother (or be one so early). It was not her response but the manner of response that is very telling of the expectations women set themselves up for, and a hesitation to acknowledge it. She said 'Yes... sometimes (with great reluctance, her throat almost not allowing those words to escape her mouth)... but you know... when I look at the child's face... like how can I think of this?' In comparison, there was another classmate I was conversing with about taking career risks, and he said it would be difficult for him to quit his job as he had fallen into the 'house trap' and 'child trap' (i.e., he had purchased a house and had a child). This is not to cast any aspersions whatsoever on the latter's role as a dad, but just to contrast the relative sense of comfort or discomfort of women and men in trying to 'do it all'. Both my classmates were struggling in their own ways, not being able to do what they wanted to; but there was a difference in the ease with which they would acknowledge it. It appears that for women it's important to be it all, in a way it isn't for men.

In the book,[12] *The Confidence Code*, authors Katty Kay and Claire Shipman refer to studies which found that women tend to apply to jobs when they feel 100 per cent prepared, as compared to men who will take a chance if they felt they were 60 per cent ready. It's perhaps the same tendency when women don't raise a point in meetings unless they are completely assured of it, as opposed to men who will give it a try even when they are partially sure. Kay and Shipman propose various reasons for this limiting behaviour of women that stands in stark contrast to that of men. One of the things they talk about is the tendency of women to be perfectionists, which leads them to fear failure. Shipman, in a talk on the

---

[12] https://www.theatlantic.com/magazine/archive/2014/05/the-confidence-gap/359815/

same subject at Google,[13] draws correlation to the fact that girls outperform boys in school and that may lead them to fear risking failure later. One of the reasons behind gender pay gap, apart from the much touted 'pregnancy penalty', is also that women don't negotiate as much, starting with college placements. The tendency continues across other scenarios such as asking for a pay raise or promotion. Even in the start-up world, one of the reasons attributed to why female founders find less funding than male founders, is that they tend to under-project business plans. All of these behaviours of women are typically pinned to factors such as risk-taking behaviours, negotiation skills and confidence. However, here's where it gets interesting.

Let's take *negotiation skills*. There is so much rhetoric on women not negotiating enough for salaries and hikes. However, in a whole lot of interpersonal situations and product-purchasing scenarios, women are touted to be solid negotiators. With respect to *risk-taking*, research by a team of psychologists[14] from University of Exeter and University of Melbourne, found that women can be just as risk-taking, or even more so, as compared to men when the traditional macho measures of risk-taking (such as walking on tight-rope across the Grand Canyon or high-stake poker game) were replaced with other criteria. In such scenarios, women were rated to be as high risk-takers as men. Finally, let's consider *confidence*. Kay and Shipman's focus was on building confidence for girls, so that they could go out of their comfort zone. They conducted polls to find that girls tend to lose confidence by puberty. We might take the polls as merely indicative, as we have argued earlier in this book, on the need to be cautious about making

---

[13] https://www.youtube.com/watch?v=6Dvdl5UP8zw
[14] https://www.sciencedaily.com/releases/2017/10/171005102626.htm

conclusions from one-off studies, especially pertaining to cause and effect. Hence, overall, there is no harm investing in confidence-building, risk-taking and negotiation skills for women. However, assigning those as *definitive causes* for women getting left behind in certain areas, based on either contradictory research or non-confirmatory polls, could be misleading. More importantly, it may prevent us from considering other factors of gender behaviours and identifying gaps.

The framework of *sampann* is worth being investigated as subject of research by social and behavioural psychologists as a plausible cause of self-restricting behaviours of women. Kay and Shipman, while discussing their book, put forth their theory about the tendency of women to be perfectionists and how that comes in the way of taking risks. Interestingly, there is lot of contemporary literature propagating the theory that women tend to be perfectionists. However, we hardly came across any robust research that could substantiate this. For example, in one of the articles, a study was quoted to support the theory. When we followed the reference, it was found that the study only pertained to women feeling pressured to look (perfectly) good[15] and didn't say anything about perfectionism per se. Hence, 'women are perfectionists' is at best a conjecture, which is getting used to explain many behaviours such as fear of failure, risk-taking, etc. Since the premise of perfectionism of women itself is unproven, the correlations are also fallacious. In fact, in my own experience as a woman, and the many women I have interacted with across my life, there is no reason for me to believe that women are necessarily perfectionists. However, what I *have* observed

---

[15] https://www.theparentingpartnership.com/raising-girls-self-esteem-and-the-curse-of-perfectionism

as a pattern among women, is the tendency to do more and be more and the commensurate guilt when that 'more' cannot be achieved. This is why, we feel, *sampann* is a much better premise to investigate than perfectionism. *Sampann* is not the same as being a perfectionist. The latter is more about achieving a certain gold standard of quality. *Sampann* is more akin to being complete in all qualities, fulfilling multiple roles. The premise of *sampann* in the context of Indian traditions, mentioned at the beginning of this section, is actually towards the end of raising women as well-rounded human beings, capable of shouldering a range of responsibilities. Despite all the negatives we discussed around a woman's social and environmental circumstances (e.g., *lajja*), *sampann*, in a strange way, actually positively discriminates women in preparing them for the vagaries of life, more than men. Women have been found to be more resilient of the two genders, with greater survival rate in tough situations as compared to men. Perhaps, somewhere in teaching women *jooto shelai* to *Chondi path,* we are betting more on them, to cope with difficult situations, than men. However, as the world evolves at a breakneck speed with changing gender roles, what it means to be *sampann* needs to be re-calibrated. Perhaps, *that* is the help and conversation that women need. This brings us to another significant point.

Sampann is quality of a complete individual—*whole*, as opposed to being *perfect*. As the world becomes more fluid, being *sampann*, that is, building a wide range of skills, ability to multitask, is critical, not just for *women* but also *men*. It's important for young boys to start learning household chores, caregiving and other roles that their younger sisters do. As Gloria Steinem said, 'We've begun to raise daughters more like sons... but few have the courage to raise our sons more like our daughters.' While women can get help in not allowing *sampann* to manifest as a feeling of inadequacy, it might just help for men to build in some healthy self-doubt, as they learn to juggle more roles than they traditionally have. It will be good if women start projecting their business plans to investors with a bit more elan, just like it will help for men to question their assumptions about their projections. To restore the balance in society and workplaces, the goal cannot be to make women less *sampann* but to make men become a little more of it.

Equal, Not Same

Sometime in 2017, I had an article draft saved on LinkedIn. It was titled 'Men and Women Are Equal, Not Same'. This was long before I realized the idea could grow into a book, or that I was destined, in the near future, to meet a like-minded co-author who would brave putting forth these ideas with me. At that time, everywhere I looked, it appeared that we were often confusing the fact that both genders deserved equal opportunities with the myth that both genders were necessarily clones of each other. 'Equal, not same' seemed like a profound idea that time and also a straightforward one. In 2020, when the social media debate on Zomato's period leave was rife, a hashtag trended on Twitter namely #EqualNotIdentical. It appears that in the last few years, the distinction between *equality* and *sameness* of genders has entered our collective consciousness. However, my own thought on it has undergone a change since 2017. I still look at it as a significant idea. Differentiating what it means to achieve equality versus whitewashing all men and women into one indistinguishable whole is critical in the pursuit of diversity and inclusion. However, I no longer think the idea is straightforward. It's complex and perhaps even complicated. 'Equal, not same' cannot define the complex dynamics of gender equality, unless both *equal* and *same* are qualified.

Let's begin with qualifying 'equal'. In one of retreats I attended, the participants were playing an early morning game of dodgeball. Both teams were mixed-gender groups of men and women of all ages. Few players (men) of the other team shouted, 'Target those three girls.' I immediately protested, 'That's unfair,' thinking not too highly of those players in my mind. However, upon reflecting about this incident later, I realized that it was not misogyny at all. As players, we always identify the strongest and weakest members of the opposing team and strategize accordingly. In this match, the weakest players happened to be 'those three girls'. If you are in the game, the rules apply to you the same way as others. Equality is always more desirable when it means getting equal privilege, opportunities and status as another gender, social class, etc. However, we never talk about equality as much when it comes to equal responsibility, penalty and consequences, which is the uncomfortable side of equality. In other words, the question is—when we say *men and women are equal,* are we prepared for *absolute equality?*

At this point in history, because the gender status quo is significantly skewed, our focus is largely on bringing women up to speed and bridging the gap. Some readers might question, at this juncture, if conversation is to suggest that 'women have it easy' in anyway (i.e., does mentioning that women need to take equal accountability somewhere implies that women don't do so already). The answer is an emphatic *no*. That's the reason this is a difficult aspect of equality to discuss. Talking about equal rules for women is to risk being seen as suggesting that women are not already held equally responsible or somewhere seek privilege. As many women will say, 'If anything we have to work double to be considered at par with men.' *Absolute equality* does not negate any of that. Allow us the benefit of doubt for a few moments, as we make the point. There are many committed women, who have braved odds and made sacrifices to break the glass ceiling. We talk proudly about them. There is another category, we never speak about, loudly, though they are topics of water-cooler, hush-hush, closed-circle discussions. I have heard many mentions of how difficult it is to lay off a female employee for performance issues for the fear of being charged for harassment. Admittedly, there is a larger problem in corporates of all sizes, on how performance is managed and feedback given to any employee, whether man or woman. Lack of empathy, transparency and general professionalism in organization gets mentioned on social media routinely. Also, there are organizations where women bear the brunt of negative perceptions. For example, a female employee may not be seen as a primary breadwinner of the family, impacting how pay-raise and lay-off decisions are taken. And those biases must be addressed. What we are saying is that, in addition, the unspoken apprehension around holding any female employee accountable, *where it exists,* must also be addressed through difficult conversations, clear communication and transparent and fair processes. In fact, this principle applies to all scenarios involving protected groups. We have discussed this principle in the chapter 'Discrimination and Diversity'. I was talking to a senior from college who mentioned being frustrated with debates that men have on affirmative action being discriminatory in some way. These are closed groups of top B-school alumni placed in senior roles in organizations. There is an undercurrent which is both strong and prevalent among those in positions of influence in organizations. These professionals are forced to give lip service to affirmative action on various forums, but in person, they have different convictions. We cannot afford to brush the matter aside. In fact, one of the biggest failures of D&I efforts, in its current version, has been to not engage these differing points of view in a dialogue. We have mentioned the Google's firing of James Damore many times in this book, as a sore reminder of the above. Incorporating the context of *absolute equality* in processes and policies is critical in addressing the apprehensions of naysayers.

There's another side to *equal*, as we see in case of the *women card,* the infamous token of female privilege. In one of the apartments I lived in, once, there was a furious discussion on a major remodelling being done in one of the flats. There was terrible noise for months, and everyone was complaining. Finally, the apartment association swung into action when one of the owners threatened to rake up female harassment and go to one of the NGOs, because his octogenarian mother-in-law was getting disturbed. I google the NGO. The kind of 'harassment' they dealt with was domestic violence and the like. Not only would the NGO have never stepped into this matter, the issue, while troublesome, had nothing to do with women per se. However, the point is, a *man* used the *woman card,* and it worked. Women racking up the 'because I am a woman' argument are often accused of using the woman card. However, think of it this way. Any card—woman card, minority card, caste card, race card—exists only because it's required. If the societal and organizational systems were fair and equitable, one would not need to use any cards. A *card* in some way is symbolic of the fact that a gap exists. The card's role is to bridge that gap. Sometimes it's a necessary evil. Therefore, sometimes, being *equal* is about having *equity,* requiring special privileges to be given for a specific goal, for a specified time. Affirmative action, which we discussed in the chapter 'Does Diversity Really Help Business', is about building *equity*. It could also be in form of reserved seats on buses and trains or allowing an additional period leave to women. When used wrongly, as in the case of this gentleman in the name of his mother-in-law, a card becomes an abuse of privilege, which we must watch out for. But communicating the concept of equity, which necessitates special privileges, for a specified period of time, is another necessity that D&I initiatives miss. In fact, communicating privileges and their boundaries clearly, instead of making them available covertly and selectively, is what defines the difference between a structured, goal-driven affirmative action versus reverse discrimination, unhealthy preferential treatment and the like.

Hence, *equal* in 'equal, not same' can be in context of both *absolute equality* and *equity*. Defining the context is necessary because, sometimes, one is confused for the other. When a woman cries fowl for facing the same consequence as her male colleague for non-performance, it is failing to recognize *absolute equality*. When male colleagues criticize a transparent, well-defined affirmative action as discrimination, they are accusing a valid step towards *equity*. Discerning this difference is necessary to create a fair, level playing ground for everyone.

Now let's qualify 'same'. We can begin by asking which entities are we referring to as *same*? 'Men' and 'women'—isn't that what we are discussing? Gender status quo is far more complex than that, and the discussion cannot be limited to men-and-women equation.

First, not all women are same. There are hairline cracks that we foresee will emerge as a clear fault lines in near future, among women themselves. There is a section of women who are evolving out of their hardwiring and outgrowing their stereotypes much faster than others. That's one divide which is most prominent across generations of women. This is what manifests as YouTube channels of millennial mothers mocking their own mothers' generation for dedicating their whole lives to raising children. Or young girls shaming 'aunties' publicly on social media, who in turn shamed them in person for being skimpily dressed. The other fault line is between women of the same generation with different ideologies. Some think a career is essential to define the identity of women, while others want the freedom to choose a domestic life and not be judged for it. Another divide is between married women with children and those without children or single women. Challenges of mothers dominate every conversation on women's forums, often sidelining the needs of women who have made different life choices.

Second, men and women are not the only stakeholders in the discussion on sameness of genders. That 'gender is a continuum' is an understanding that's growing steadily. We are sorely aware of the limitation of this book, discussing perspectives from the binary perspective of just men and women. It is not for the lack of will but the lack of human experience and understanding of the multitude of gender identities. This lack of understanding is also a demonstration of the need to deepen conversations on contexts of employees across the entire gender continuum. Even J. K. Rowling[16] erred in this matter when she raised an issue with a magazine which used the phrase, 'people who menstruate'. Rowling was irked by the fact that 'women' were generally being referred to as 'people'. She missed (or was perhaps unaware, like many of us) that many trans-people got periods or experienced PMS-like syndrome. Similarly, the Zomato period leave debate was also

---

[16] https://timesofindia.indiatimes.com/home/sunday-times/yes-some-men-bleed-why-jk-rowling-is-wrong-that-only-women-get-periods/articleshow/76363810.cms

only from the point of view of women. Hence, *same* in 'equal not same' needn't assume that all women are same as other women, or that the discussion is limited to binary identities of men and women.

Finally, let's address the most glaring gap in the entire discussion of equality and sameness of men and women—that is, *the very absence of men*. In the chapter 'An Ideological Echo Chamber', we argued that the difference between men and women are most likely the outcome of differences in culture and societal context than biological differences. Hence, understanding the historic context of how women have lived, made choices and expressed themselves is necessary. However, as gender status quo continues to evolve, how can the discussion be limited to only how women are changing, without a commensurate discussion on men? In fact, it's interesting that men themselves have chosen to be passive bystanders to the story of 'changing of gender roles', which, by definition, must include men as well. Perhaps this is because both men and women fallaciously see this shift in gender dynamics as a change for women, but none for men. It's like one gentleman wrote on a professional networking site, during the initial lock-down days, that women should be cut some slack at workplace as their workload at home has increased. It was a kind comment on the face of it and got kudos from many on the network. I decided to remind him that both men and women can be excused, to be able to share the household work equally.

There is so much talk on women taking up careers but very little on how men will contribute to household chores. In the chapter 'Women in Senior Management', we argued that men must be allowed paternity leaves, so that they can contribute equally to raising children. There is so much discussion on women's hormonal and biological upheavals, but no mention of male menopause. Women have become vocal about their needs at workplaces, men have limited themselves to talk about gender equality from only women's perspectives—either under pressure or goodwill. However, men themselves aren't speaking much about how they see their own roles changing, their emotion and experience about it. Even at the societal level, there is discussion on how girls can be raised differently, to rewire the cultural and environmental factors that set women back. However, there is very little focus on how boys need to be rewired. The dynamics of gender are changing, and men cannot be spectators to what they must be equal partners in. What is equal and what is same will evolve so much that a new chapter will need to be written soon in future. But before we get there, men will need to begin their own journey of change. As it turns out, perhaps another implication of *equal, not same*, is that as women grow, men cannot possibly expect things to remain the same for them. Maybe boys can no longer be boys.

BIG IN THE CHAPTER IDEAS

1. *Women feeling compelled to act likeable is not only women's problem but a business problem:* Measure the 'cost to business' of women holding themselves back at workplace.

2. Sampann *may be a better framework than perfectionism:* Women tend to be 'Sampann' (complete in all roles), resulting in have-it-all, do-it-all goals, causing feelings of inadequacy. This could be a better research hypothesis than saying, women lack confidence because they are necessarily perfectionists.

3. *Shaming is a hard-wired tool of choice to keep women in check:* Women not only get shamed by men but also routinely shame themselves and each other.

4. *De-link narrative on women professionals with their personal roles as mother and wife:* It alienates women who are not mothers or married, and unduly attaches the identity of all professional women to success in their personal roles.

5. *Women needn't have it all, nor do it all:* Don't merely enable women to balance home and work, enable men to contribute to household and caregiving responsibilities.

6. *Men and women are not same, neither are women and women:* Discussions need to be deeper and more deliberate, recognizing the groups within groups.

7. *Boys can no longer be boys:* Conversation on gender equality must include how men's roles and behaviours evolve at work and home.

Women in Senior Management

*Women meet more resistance,
and more isolation as they move up the ranks.
Article after article, interview after interview reveals
why—it's the impact of subtle, implicit bias.*

—Lynda Decker, President and
Creative Director, Decker Design

Why are there so few women leaders in senior management? The last three decades has seen huge progress in the education of women and their entry into corporate jobs. Almost the same number of women graduate every year today as the men, and academic performance at school and college level is at par, if not superior. Why is it that despite being present in almost equal numbers as the men at an entry level, the number of women at senior management continues to be abysmally low?

Catalyst is a global non-profit that works with companies to help build workplaces that work for women and helps organizations to accelerate progress for women at work. As per their research, India, South Korea and Japan have the lowest representation of women in management globally. In 2019, women held only 8 per cent of management roles and were only 2 per cent of CEOs in India. In 2019, in the USA, women represented 48 per cent of the workforce at the entry level and this tapered off to 21 per cent in the 'C' suite, with only 7 per cent as CEOs. The percentages were almost identical in Europe. In Canada, in 2020, women constituted only 7 per cent of the named executive officers in the top 100 publicly traded companies, though the entry-level percentage is comparable to the rest of the Western world.[1] Women are outnumbered in leadership roles across sectors. This palpable gap at the leadership level is a cause for serious concern. It is critical that we understand the reasons that are keeping women from advancing in their careers and do something about it.

A story from Indian history elegantly highlights some of the challenges a woman faces in rising to the top in a predominantly male arena. It also brings out how exceedingly reluctant society is to accept a woman leader at the very top and how much it is ingrained in our culture to resist female authority. The forces at work to keep women out of powerful jobs are complex and devious at the same time. The story also brings out how women can create lasting impact if they are able to shatter the glass ceiling and get to the top. The parallels with the struggle of women in today's corporate world are quite striking. What is equally striking, and worrisome, is that these challenges continue to manifest in an almost identical fashion even after more than 200 years. The story also highlights a leadership style that is a perfect blend of the feminine and the masculine and the role it played in creating peace, harmony and prosperity.

---

[1] https://www.catalyst.org/research/women-in-management/

Strong but Gentle Queen of Indore

Mandu is a beautiful heritage site on the Malwa plateau in Central India. Indore is the nearest airport and a popular base for the tourists visiting Mandu and Maheshwar. Located on the southern edge of the Malwa plateau, at an average altitude of 550 metres, Indore has the highest elevation among all the major cities of Central India. Home to an IIT and an IIM, it is a city dotted with educational institutions. Indore has history, art, culture and mythology etched all over. At the entrance to Indore's Devi Ahilyabai Holkar International Airport is a huge statue of the queen (Ahilyabai) herself.

Ahilyabai Holkar's rise to power makes for a fascinating study. She is not one of India's better-known historic figures, but the beauty and diversity of any country can only be discovered through the lives and stories of those who have not found a prominent place in the annals of history. History is strangely dominated by wars and conquests. Rulers who prevented wars and forged peace just find a passing mention. If we had to rewrite the history books, they would be full of stories of people like Ahilyabai.

Ahilyabai Holkar ruled Central India for 28 years during one of the stormiest periods of India's history. Anyone even remotely familiar with Indian history would have heard of the three battles of Panipat and even committed the dates to memory. However, for those not as familiar, each of the three battles fought on the plains of Panipat, less than 100 kilometres to the north of Delhi, were crucial turning points in Indian history. In the Third Battle of Panipat, that had been fought just six years before Ahilyabai was crowned, the Marathas—who were the dominant power of the era—had been defeated by a coalition led by the Afghan ruler Ahmad

Shah Abdali. Indore, over which the Holkars' ruled, was a tributary state of the Marathas and had supplied men and materials for the Battle of Panipat. After the defeat of the Marathas in this battle, India was in a state of flux and many rulers were jockeying for power. Yet Ahilyabai's reign, in its entirety, was largely peaceful.

Ahilyabai was the perfect balance between driving reform, on the one hand, and respecting tradition, on the other. Being a woman, she had played the balancing act more adroitly than a man in her role may have had to. When her husband died, she refused to commit 'sati' by immolating herself on her husband's pyre. For those not familiar with the custom of 'sati', it was a historical practice found chiefly among the Hindus in which a widow sacrificed herself by sitting atop her deceased husband's funeral pyre. Led by the then British Governor-General of India, Lord William Bentinck, this practice was outlawed in 1829, though it took a while to be erased from popular custom. Ahilyabai was fortunate to have had the support of her father-in-law in refusing to undergo 'sati'. On the death of her husband, she did not stake a claim to the throne. That would have been seen as too ambitious and may have faced with severe resistance that could have resulted in a palace coup. In deference to tradition, she allowed her young son to ascend the throne. He ruled for 12 years under her tutelage. It was only when her son died that she staked her claim to rule. Many in Central India still opposed this. They were unwilling to accept a woman as a ruler, but she won over the army chief. This proved to be a very smart move. With the army behind her, she petitioned the Peshwa in Pune, who was the emperor of Central and Western India, to rule.

After assuming power, she reinstated some of her rivals who had administrative skills in key roles, much like what Barack

Obama did when he appointed rival Hillary Clinton as the USA secretary of state in his first term as president. This was despite the fact that the fight for the Democratic Party's nomination had seen Obama and Hillary locked in a no holds barred bitter battle. Realizing the challenges of her times in getting society to wholeheartedly support a woman ruler and that too a widow, Ahilyabai adopted a very enlightened and mature style of leadership. During her reign, relations with neighbouring states were friendly and all disputes were resolved amicably, making it a win-win for all. Trade and commerce flourished, and art and religious tolerance were at an all-time high. She was the epitome of a leader who instinctively and, by design, did things that prevented a crisis. Some anonymous person had once said: 'Nothing is as strong as gentleness and nothing is as gentle as real strength.' This held true for Ahilyabai. Her leadership style represented a fine blend of masculine and feminine qualities.

The terms *feminine* and *masculine* don't mean *women* and *men*. They represent qualities of femininity and masculinity more than the physical gender. Therefore, some men do possess a few feminine traits and vice versa. A powerful feminine trait that Ahilyabai brought to her leadership was about creating a very caring government. She promoted the softer aspects of art and culture that brought out the best human qualities in society. She dealt with the militant tribes on her borders by understanding their economic compulsions and by providing solutions for those. She also realized that religion and religious tolerance were essential elements for creating lasting peace and she went out of her way to promote these. Indore and Maheshwar (the capital of her empire) are full of artwork and paintings that depict her religious side. We believe that her religious side was carefully cultivated to increase the legitimacy of her rule and get support from the citizens. Her masterstroke was in carrying out administrative duties in the name of the local deity, Lord Shiva (part of the Hindu trinity of Brahma, Shiva and Vishnu), which got her greater acceptance in a highly patriarchal society. This was essential for her to keep her critics and opponents at bay and avoid giving them a handle to whip up any resistance to her rule. At the same time, she was not averse to doing whatever it took to assume power, which was hers by right. She also demonstrated some of the other masculine traits that were essential to her ascendancy to the throne and, subsequently, held her empire together. She built forts and created a well-disciplined army that acted as a deterrent to anyone attempting any misadventure.

Ahilyabai's story offers critical cues to reconsidering our image of a woman leader. As more women rise to leadership positions, we unconsciously expect them to step into the existing leadership culture which is not just male dominated but also predominantly masculine. In such a scenario, while inclusion goals can be fulfilled by getting more females per se, diversity goal of adding new dimensions to the existing leadership approach will remain unfulfilled. The other extreme is the narrative of females being all-feminine, which may not be conducive to a leadership role which will require some elements of masculine traits. Ahilyabai Holkar's story gives us the framework to understand leadership styles in terms of masculine and feminine qualities, as we induct more women into the upper echelons of organizations, towards meaningful diversity.

At the Root of This Imbalance

Based on what we have seen and the conversations we have had, we believe there are three broad heads under which we can find an explanation for why there are so few women in top management.

- *Home and family:* Women carry the burden.
- *Stereotyping and bias:* Leadership is a man's job.
- *Vicious cycle at play:* If things are bad, and if left to themselves, they usually get worse. In other words, an uneven playfield gets even more uneven with time.

We'll take each of these in turn and dive deep.

Home and Family

Women end up bearing disproportionate share of the responsibility for home and the family. This is the biggest reason why women begin to drop out of employment after starting in equal numbers as the men. Maternity is immutable, but we strongly believe that as long as the woman continues to bear the burden for the home front beyond giving birth to a child, the problem of insufficient women in top management is inevitable. Even if we fix everything else, but leave this one thing unresolved, we cannot expect any significant change in the current situation. If this mindset does not undergo a change, and we will go on to argue that women are partly responsible for driving this change in mindset, then we may perhaps have to live with the reality that women, with a few exceptions, will never have serious careers. They will continue to have equal access to education and will excel in it as much as the men, they will continue to supplement income for the family, continue to work on and off to avoid total ennui, but excepting for the few odd cases, they will never get to top-management jobs.

The stereotyping that women are caregivers and men are breadwinners is so deep, so widespread and so timeless that changing this is almost as difficult as reversing climate change or solving the problem of world hunger. There is no end to 'caregiving' for the simple reason that a human child needs care for at least 18 years, after which aging parents begin needing attention. Therefore, unless support systems are strong and equitable, it would be the woman who has to always give up her career or take her career lightly. Some of the more ambitious women juggle their different responsibilities by putting in superhuman effort, but invariably, it begins to take a toll and is unsustainable. It's not without reason that only women get asked this question, 'Can you have it all?' No man is ever asked this question. The implicit bias in this question is twofold: First, women have a responsibility for managing the home front that men don't have, and second, women should feel privileged to be given the exclusive right to manage the home front.

In some cultures, the pressure on a woman to take her caregiving role very seriously is immense, and any career ambition that comes in the way is viewed as inconsiderate and misguided. Under these circumstances, interestingly, it is the other women in her family (mother, mother-in-law) and network who can be her biggest critics. These cultures also have a tendency of looking down upon husbands who periodically allow their careers to take a backseat to allow their wives to advance in their careers. This is not to imply that there are no exceptions. On the contrary, in almost all cases where women have had a successful and fulfilling career, anywhere in the world, the support from family and networks has been one of the biggest reasons behind the success. We have discussed these hardwired stereotypes in the chapter 'Equal, Not Same'.

The biggest leg of this support system is the attitude of the husband and his willingness to offer his wife a fair shot at her career by shouldering responsibilities at home. Shouldering responsibilities at home is not just about providing moral support but a willingness to take six months of paternity leave after the woman exhausts her maternity leave. It is about agreeing to make sacrifices by turn when it comes to relocations related to career advancement and not expecting the wife to always follow the husband. Therefore, it appears that under the current social set-up, the nearly biggest determinant of a woman's career success is the choice she makes about her life partner and the quality of some of the subsequent conversations she engages in, with him, at the key points in her career. It is a cringeworthy thought, living in the times of women empowerment, that a woman's career is dependent on the husband's support, whether her support to the husband is taken for granted. However, social systems and mindsets take a very long time to change. Women can accelerate that shift in status quo by making more conscious choices about: whether they marry, when they marry, who they marry and under what terms they marry.

One could argue that a family should try and optimize their combined income by allowing the partner who is naturally more ambitious and better placed in terms of competence for career advancement to take the lead. For example, if the husband is earning more, or in a more senior job, the wife gives up her job to accompany him to another country and try finding a job there. No harm in this kind of thinking as long as the assessment is fair and there is an equal chance for the woman to take the lead and the decision is mutual. Although we must point out an inherent problem with this widely taken and seemingly practical approach. Typically (if not always), in the current social system, 'men marry down' and 'women marry up' in terms of success and social strata. Also, conventionally the husband is older than the wife, imply-ing if both are working, the husband is likely to be in a more advanced stage of his career. Therefore, in many situations, the husband's salary and position will be higher and safeguarded for the family's interests, applying the principle we mentioned earlier. Further, assuming the wife's job pays lesser, it may still be valuable to her ambition, identity, self-worth and financial independence. Therefore, we will need to again loop back to the point on women making very conscious choices about their marriage and having clear conversations with their partner. This is until we are able to change as a society.

Companies have a role to play too. Just offering six months of maternity leave is not sufficient to help women advance in their careers. If companies are sincere, they must allow 'fathers' to take paternity leave of six months, anytime when the child is, say, between 6–18 months, to shoulder their responsibilities at home. Organizations could take a call on whether this needs to be a fully paid leave or partially paid leave. Despite the facility, a man may or may not take six months off to enable his wife to return to her career. This is where the woman needs to assert herself and have that crucial conversation with her husband.

Because women have the burden of caregiving, they are not available for the kind of networking and male bonding that happens outside office. Inability to participate in these networking events tends to make women feel guilty and internalize the responsibility for not fitting in. This guilt manifests itself in different ways—deferential behaviour, loss of confidence, lack of assertiveness in fighting for what is due to them and trying to keep everyone happy. Over time, this becomes a self-fulfilling prophecy by reinforcing the stereotype that women are not decisive, assertive or ambitious. Similarly, being penalized for taking breaks by the recruiters, who have somehow created a social stigma around career breaks of any kind, creates a loss of confidence. They tend to settle for less both in terms of compensation and role. With so many disincentives for taking a legitimate break, the woman is forced to wonder if it is worth all this trouble to make a comeback. Women who have fought these odds, made a comeback and rose to the top have invariably demonstrated a never-give-up attitude, a deep self-belief, have had moral support from family and friends, have had role models they have looked up to for inspiration and some thick skin to shrug off the uncharitable comments and biases.

Stereotyping and Bias

Stereotyping is rampant and one of the roadblocks in women's ascent to higher offices. In the chapter titled 'Bias Is Pervasive', we discuss some of the common unconscious gender biases. The biggest stereotyping is what we just talked about, namely, 'women are caregivers and their primary role is at home.' The corollary of that is 'men are bread earners whose primary role is outside the home.' We discussed some of this in the last section.

Women at work tend to be judged a lot more on appearance, dress sense, looks and style of communication far more than men. Shachi Irde, a former executive director at Catalyst India and a thought leader on diversity, told us that because women are judged on looks and what they wear, what they say (which should be the focus) gets lost and needs amplification to just be heard. It is not uncommon for a woman to be judged by the style and height of her heels, the colour of the lipstick, the perfume she wears, her hair styling and the quality of the suit or saree. Men who have not been part of set-ups where ambitious women were competing with alpha males may find it difficult to understand this phenomenon and could think that this is all being made up.

A woman aged between 25 and 35 years of age is at risk because she could go the family way anytime. A woman who is above 40 years of age is at risk because she could have aging parents and in-laws at home who need care. At no stage can she be trusted with responsibility. When a woman is soft-spoken, she is too woman like, and when she is aggressive, she is not sufficiently woman like. As a result, women have always had an identity crisis at work. When a woman gets married, her pay need not be competitive because there is a second source of income for the family, but when a man gets married, he needs to be paid more because he has additional responsibilities.

In corporate (and other) award ceremonies, women often end up escorting guests to the podium and passing on the prizes to the guest to be handed over to the winners. Women also end up planning office parties and doing a lot of work behind the scenes. 70 per cent of all human resources (HR) teams are staffed by women, and HR, in many companies, is seen as the office equivalent of the home front or family! Did you ever wonder why the theme of every other conference of HR professionals is 'getting a seat at the table'? When I (Hari) moved into HR after 11 years in engineering, this was a bit of an enigma. No other bunch of professionals ever had to repeatedly keep discussing what they needed to do to get a seat at the table. They *had* a seat at the table! It took me some years to understand that it was because HR was staffed largely by women, and because what they did was considered 'house work', they were never given a permanent place in the hallowed portal of top management. Even in the medical profession where women are present in large numbers, heads of departments in hospitals are dominated by men.

Vicious Cycle at Play

It is quite evident that there are several forces at play that keep women from getting to top-management jobs. The odds are heavily stacked against them. That some of them get to these jobs, despite the immense constraints, is in itself a wonder. We already have a small number of women in top-management jobs, but the belief of a vast majority of us is that this is insufficient, and we need to have many more of them in these jobs. This is possible only if there is a strong pipeline at all levels and conditions that make it easy to create and sustain the pipeline. There is a vicious cycle at play here. A vicious cycle can be seen as a sequence of reciprocal cause and effect in which two or more elements intensify and aggravate each other, leading inexorably to a worsening of the situation. For instance, a debtor being caught in a vicious cycle could mean that he is in prison because he couldn't repay a debt and he can't repay a debt as long as he is in prison. In the context of women in leadership, it really means that there are very women in leadership roles because of insufficient role models and there are insufficient role models because there are so few women in leadership roles. The idea of a vicious cycle exists elsewhere too. For instance, a vicious cycle led the continuous worsening of conditions for 'Dalits' in pre-independent India. To break a vicious cycle, some affirmative action is essential, and in the context of the Dalits, the constitution of India provided for some reservation in government jobs and in government-supported educational institutions. Besides affirmative action, several more fundamental steps need to be taken to correct the playing field which, while the vicious cycle is in play, is heavily tilted against the victims of the cycle.

Proponents of diversity have suggested several steps to aid women in their careers—providing mentors, development opportunities, counselling and flexible working being some of them. Many of these interventions are often centred around women being advised and provided help to adapt to a male-dominated environment, rather than changing the male-dominated environment. While some see these as steps in the right direction, we believe they are tactical, incremental and will not change the game in a significant way. And above all, they don't create a 'level playing field'. They just help individual women navigate an unfair playing field a little better. Therefore, even if they succeed, the success is not sustainable because the women end up losing their authenticity, giving up their femininity and resembling the men. From what we have heard from women who have experienced these programs first-hand, we believe they don't even have a marginal impact. It just ends up locking these women into a trap of hope and activity.

As long as women continue to be in the minority, interesting and complex woman–woman dynamics also tend to play out that continue to keep women disadvantaged. For instance, we have seen women employees who have learnt to handle male managers by subtly, and even unconsciously, playing on the natural man–woman affinity. Such women employees usually find it difficult to work for women managers because this approach would just not fly with women managers. If women in top management are a very small minority, they may not make any move that threatens their position and that includes being unsupportive of other women. Like any minority member admitted to a majority elite group, they tend to display the behaviours of the majority group even more strongly than the members of the majority group. They try and fit in by discussing all the male topics, being a part of smoking groups and avoiding any discussion around challenges they may be facing as they juggle home and work, being more manlike than the men themselves. They further their own career by seeking patronage and helping preserve status quo. In such a workplace, it is unlikely that the relationships between women would be collaborative and mutually supportive; instead adversarial relationships are more likely the norm. And finally, a single woman in top management may not support moves that seek to get other women into top management. This could manifest itself in the form of her finding ways to keep high-potential women leaders away from the rest of the management team. Therefore, it is even more important to get to a critical mass of women quickly into senior management to overcome some of these dynamics.

We need to therefore prioritize, take some bold steps and go beyond tokenism. No major change has been achieved by incrementalism and soft-pedalling. So, what are some of these bold steps?

We'll start with the analogy of 'organization culture'. Culture is always driven top–down. Nothing else works. If the 5–10 senior-most leaders in an organization live and breathe the culture, the rest of the organization would soon follow suit. If the 5–10 senior-most leaders do not live and breathe the culture, everything else you may do to drive the culture is superficial, ineffective and counts as tokenism. By the same logic, changes to drive diversity need to start from the top. And we are not suggesting changing the attitude of a bunch of male leaders at the top. That would be amounting to soft-pedalling and tokenism. We are suggesting forcing gender diversity at the top.

A 'tipping point' is defined as the point at which a series of small changes or incidents becomes significant enough to cause a larger, more important change. Until a tipping point is reached, progress tends to be slow and sedate. We believe it is important to create this tipping point in the diversity movement. We have no doubt that the best chance (and even that is not guaranteed for several reasons) at getting to a tipping point is having a critical mass of women at the top. Nothing else would do.

Strong affirmative action is a way to get there. The biggest argument against affirmative action is that it creates reverse discrimination and brands the beneficiaries as 'quota candidates'. The argument is that 'quotas' don't create the right kind of diversity. But as a starting point, is any kind of diversity not better than no diversity at all? It is natural to brand any affirmative action as a wrong approach. The alternative that critics of affirmative action often suggest is 'change the mindsets of people'! Mindsets haven't changed for centuries! And the issue we have with an approach that can be summarized by 'the problem is with mindsets and therefore it's important to change mindsets' is that this cannot be a universal prescription for every problem in this world.

The human mind normally applies a faulty logic (unconsciously and consciously) when evaluating two alternatives. Let's say we evaluate two alternatives as possible solutions to a particular problem. Each of the two alternatives, say 'A' and 'B', have their own sets of pros and cons. Alternative 'A' is quota-led diversity at the top and alternative 'B' is no diversity at all. Let's assume that, in balance, alternative 'A' is the better of the two and you pick that for implementation. Obviously, the negative aspects of alternative 'A' would soon begin to manifest and those who were opposed to alternative 'A' would use it to argue that it was a bad choice and that 'B' would have been a better choice! The way to deal with these folks is to go back and place the pros and cons of both the alternatives side by side and then have a discussion. Similarly, the way to deal with those who are opposed to strong affirmative action because it could create reverse discrimination is to discuss which is the lesser of the two evils, or ask them for concrete steps that can change gender parity in top management in a relatively short time frame.

Be that as it may, we think it is time to bite the bullet and take strong steps. A percentage of board seats in companies must be reserved for women, and companies cannot be allowed to get away for non-compliance by paying a fine. There should be more serious consequences. Someone was telling us that many women candidates who have been appointed to boards because of company law guidelines are subpar. We have no doubt that many men on boards are subpar too, and all-male boards have presided over many a catastrophic failure in governance. The board of Enron comprised many notable personalities, all men of course. The board of Satyam was no less illustrious—Krishna Palepu (Professor of strategy and *governance* at Harvard Business School), Rammohan Rao (Dean ISB), Vinod Dham (father of the Pentium chip), T. R. Prasad (a cabinet secretary at one time) just to name a few. In both these companies, the boards were intimately involved in aiding and abetting the fraud either through incompetence or through active collusion. Memories are short and many of these individuals still strut around. Many board seats are occupied by ambitious males and ambition is often equated with competence. Nothing makes for a more lethal mix than unbridled ambition and greed. This mix has given rise to destructive and dysfunctional behaviours. Behaviours that led to someone of Rajat Gupta's (of the McKinsey fame) repute doing prison time! Was Rajat Gupta not subpar? Are you 'par' if you are clever, avaricious and unethical? This attempt to brand women board members as subpar is nothing more than a clever use of the 'anecdotal evidence fallacy' to launch a smear campaign that would stymie the move by the company law board that insists on having women on the boards.

Finally, it's important to make the same allowance for women to fail in their journey as leaders, while driving ambitious goals and taking organizational risks—as much their male colleagues. It will be unfair to not allow women leaders the possibility of failure that comes with the territory of being a leader—without it casting aspersions on women's capability to be leaders. In the chapter 'Equal, Not Same' we mentioned the prevalent perception that women don't take as many risks as men. While we argued in the chapter that there is contradicting research on it, for a second let's assume that perception to be true, for argument's sake. Risk-taking involves failure in its very definition. Is it not unfair to expect women to take risks, while not making allowance for them to fail without being called incompetent, unlike their male counterparts? As the first set of women break the glass ceiling, we might be inclined to have all eyes on them, watching every win and failure. We must be cognizant of not holding women leaders to unrealistic standards compared to male leaders in the same position, in a bid to get them to prove their worth.

Given the weak pipeline of women leaders today, having even a single woman in top management is a very powerful signal that a company can send to the talent pool, in particular, and to the world, at large. Getting a woman into top management is a strong, and reasonably unambiguous, signal that the company is sincere in its diversity drive.

Male-dominated Workplaces

We have used this phrase at multiple places, and therefore, it's important to clarify what this means.

On 19 February 2017, Susan Fowler, a software engineer at Uber, wrote a blog post in which she described in a fair amount of detail the sexual harassment she had to suffer at Uber. In the post, she recounted how the company's HR refused to punish her former manager, who had propositioned her for sex. She also described other gory details about the prevailing toxic culture in the company. Silicon Valley was revered by the rest of the world as an innovation factory. However, the many skeletons in the cupboard including the widely prevalent bro culture at Silicon Valley was a well-kept secret. This blog post spilled the muck into the open.

Sarah Benstead, in an article titled 'Bro Culture and Why It's an Issue for Startups' on 18 October 2018 in breathehr.com, describes a 'bro culture' as one that prioritizes young macho men with obnoxious and toxic behaviour above all else. The average 'bro' tends to be a hustling guy who places winning and success above respect for others. 'Bros' operate in an environment of excessive partying and bullying with harassment of colleagues being the everyday norm. She goes on to say that, typically, start-ups with a 'bro culture' encourage excessive partying as a motivating tool and the office is generally a toxic pot of gossip and negative chatter. The 'bro culture' is not unique to the Western world. Several start-ups in India too have been accused of a bro culture. Many women have told us that they have not been comfortable in these cultures where a bunch of aggressive alpha-male leaders take important decisions outside of office hours during late-night beer bashes. Women often find it difficult to participate in these decision-making forums because of safety issues or because they have children to look after at home. Some women cope by outwardly trying to be a part of this culture, but it begins to take a toll.

Psychologists believe that bros can be good at hustle, breaking the rules and driving outcomes without a care for the means. Since most start-ups aim to scale rapidly and quickly hit the proverbial jackpot, they tend to nurture the bro culture or at least turn a blind eye to it. Often, this can get you some quick wins, and for the outside world without visibility into the inner workings, this start-up can come across as the paragon of a conquering hero. Until someone like a Susan Fowler chooses to break the silence or an innocent child in the crowd blurts out that the emperor is wearing nothing at all, and the cry is then taken up by others.

Following the uproar in the aftermath of the blog post, the mercurial founder-CEO of Uber, Travis Kalanick was eventually fired.

This is one type of a male-dominated workplace or culture. There can be another type where there is no hustle, no late-night parties and very little explicit aggression. However, the leadership is dominated by men at all levels and there are very few women. The organization operates with stereotypes about women (consciously or unconsciously) and has a paternalistic culture, where a woman would be supported as long as she 'complies' with the norms, has male patronage and is not particularly ambitious.

Every Dark Cloud Has a Silver Lining

The most mature, insightful, balanced and holistic conversations I have had on the topic of diversity and women's rights have been with my daughter. She has never taken one-sided, biased or untenable positions, which made these conversations fulfilling and full of learning.

When she decided to pursue engineering after high school and had to pick a branch, her choice was mechanical engineering. This was because kinetics and dynamics had interested her deeply in physics when she was in high school, and mechanical engineering was a natural choice. I tried to subtly dissuade her since I thought that may not be the best choice for a girl, given the likelihood that she would be one of the very few girls in her batch, and also based on the choice of jobs that would follow her graduation. But she was undeterred. Her response was, 'If I'm the only girl in class, or on the shop floor, I would stand out and get all the help, support and attention. And I can make this work in my favour.'

If, as a working woman who is serious about her career, you are being forced to bear the brunt of caregiving at home and this is coming in the way of your career advancement, you need to deal with it. There is no point complaining about it to anyone. And who can you complain about this to? If every time there is a parent–teacher meeting, you are the one attending, every time your parents or in-laws fall sick and you are the one taking them to the hospital, every time you are the one quitting your job when your husband decides to relocate, then it is time you discuss this with the family. In fact, women making these choices consistently leads to stereotypes about hiring women professionals, which may seem like discrimination but is a reflection of the social reality. We have discussed how organizations can find solutions in the chapter 'Discrimination and Diversity'. However, organizational interventions cannot change hardwired social norms, unless women, at least the ones who are educated and empowered, take the lead.

All of us are individuals at one level, trying to adapt and make the best of the circumstances that have been handed down to us, and this adaptation is a combination of accepting things that you cannot change, with equanimity, and doing something about things you can change. At another level, we are all agents of change. As change agents, we need to feel a sense of righteous indignation that things are not what they should be, and from this righteous indignation emerges the motivation to bring about change. You can contribute to this change by altering your own personal circumstances or helping bring about change in society at large.

BIG IN THE CHAPTER IDEAS

1. *Women leaders needn't fit into stereotype of male and female leaders:* A balance of masculine and feminine leadership traits is a better framework to use while inducting more women into leadership ranks.

2. *Women need to push for change in their traditional gender role of being primary caretakers:* It begins with conscious choice around marriage and having crucial conversations with one's partner. Organizations need to support with policies such as paternity leave.

3. *'Women as caretakers' stereotype permeates organizations:* Women are staffed majorly in functions deemed equivalent of caretaking roles within organizations such as HR and even subtle behaviours such women being the ones to gift flowers to guests and light lamps.

4. *Women may feel inhibited in helping other women when in minority:* First few to break the glass ceiling, they might feel compelled to fit in, maintain status quo and hesitate to show affinity with other women. It's necessary to help reach a critical mass of women in leadership roles to overcome the dynamics.

5. *Claims of female board members being subpar are meaningless:* There are enough subpar male board members that corporates have tolerated and celebrated. Casting aspersion on capability of female board members lacks sense. Companies should be penalized beyond fines for not meeting gender balance on boards. Women leaders, in general, must have the same leeway to fail as male leaders in the course of taking risks and pursuing ambitious organizational roles.

#MeToo

Men sexually harassed because they could.
Women are talking today because,
in this new era, we finally can.

—Salma Hayek,
'Harvey Weinstein Is My Monster Too'

Let me start with three instances, involving three different sets of people, at three different points in time.

Instance 1: 'According to you, what percentage of sexual harassment scenarios are a result of misunderstanding verses deliberate?'. I had posed this question to a group of managers of both genders in a sexual harassment workshop I was facilitating. The question was based on a frequent quip I had heard about 'misunderstandings'. I had a hunch about what I would discover but couldn't be sure. All the female managers felt 100 per cent of sexual harassment was deliberate. Almost all male managers felt 50–90 per cent of sexual harassment was a result of misunderstanding. The divide in the room could not have been starker.

Instance 2: 'My relative was in a senior HR role in a well-known organization, where the practice head was charged with sexual harassment by a junior. The police had come to arrest the practice head at office, but he (the relation in HR) successfully managed to help him avert the arrest' a senior business leader once told me, with an unmistakable hint of reassurance in his voice that sexual harassment complaints can be managed.

Instance 3: 'Can I talk to you for a minute?' A male student stopped to speak with me at the end of a session on gender sensitization I was conducting at a B-school.

'I have a friend who went into depression because a girl accused him of sexual harassment. How is all this sexual harassment awareness going to ensure that women don't misuse it to harass men?' he asked me, visibly agitated.

'What do you think should be done?' I asked him back.

'The law should be looked into.' He said.

'Who should get the law changed, since getting this version of the law itself took so many years?' I asked him again.

'I don't know, maybe you people working in this area?' he replied.

'Since you clearly feel so strongly about it, are you willing to file a PIL or something?' I asked.

The conversation ended quickly after that.

'I will someday if I have the time,' he muttered as he hurried towards the door.

These three instances represent some of the core issues around tackling sexual harassment at workplaces, both prevention and redressal. The foremost challenge is that a shared understanding of what constitutes sexual harassment is grossly missing. In general, people are aware of scenarios of blatant sexual harassment. However, for innumerable scenarios which need to be seen in context, there are widespread discrepancies in understanding. Symptoms of this missing shared understanding are misgivings, questions and fear such as:

- I am now scared to give compliments to my female colleague.
- I now need to be careful about cracking a joke, aren't we all adults?
- I ask my secretary to be around while talking to a female student.

This gap in understanding is not only because of a superficial understanding of sexual harassment in general, but it's also the outcome of how 'sexual harassment workshops' are designed. Typical workshops focus on cut and dry awareness of law and straightforward scenarios and ignore addressing mindset and deeper understanding of principles of inter-gender communication. Also, strangely, often these workshops are delivered to separate audiences of men-only and women-only employees, as if the matter were too embarrassing for all employees to discuss under one roof. Worst is putting an e-learning course on it, followed by a quiz—which employees are mandated to take, offering an easy way out for administrators to tick the box of meeting statutory requirements. The question here is:

What does a shared understanding of sexual harassment look like? Why do gaps exist despite existing training? How do we plug them?

The second challenge is that the investigation process undertaken by sexual harassment committees, under the Prevention of Sexual Harassment (POSH) Act 2013, continue to be a black box for employees. For those in HR reading this and nodding their head in denial at this time, thinking 'we have done all the mandatory communications,' try asking a few employees, at random, the following questions, for a reality check.

1. If you face any sexual harassment, who will you report it to?

   (Most likely response will be 'HR'. While in a real scenario, HR will direct them to the POSH committee, but the response itself is indicative of the lack of awareness of the POSH committee.)

2. Can you name any two non-HR members of the POSH committee?

   (Most employees will draw a blank, or resort to guesswork.)

3. Where will you find more information on the company's sexual harassment policy?

   (Again, the response is likely to be, 'I'll ask HR' or guesswork like 'maybe company website'.)

The above questions are not even difficult. They are the *most* basic questions, which most employees would fail to answer. If we go a little deeper and check for awareness on how the investigation works, the findings would probably be worse. Take, for example, questions such as: *How is the investigation conducted? What is the timeline within which you can expect the investigation to be completed? Will the accused be informed of the complaint? What is the nature of punishment that the committee can decide? What about people indulging in gossip about the case—can there be action against them as well?* The truth is that most employees fail to even distinguish between HR and the POSH committee. We will not attempt to educate the readers on the process here. Our interest lies in exploring the (a) reasons behind gaps in awareness even in some of the basic aspects of redressal, despite all the 'mandatory training' and (b) the consequences of the gap. The latter leads employees to make assumptions and develop misconceptions. It also results in a general lack of trust in the investigation process and the nagging question: 'If the accused is a senior person, can he influence the process?' Unless employees are fully aware and reassured of an impartial and confidential investigation process, redressal mechanisms will only be seen as an eyewash. The question that needs addressing here is:

How do we create and communicate a sexual harassment redressal process that is robust, credible, fair and fast?

Another pressing issue is the role and conduct of HR and leadership, which is not discussed enough. How often has anyone witnessed a CEO and his executive team sit through a 'sexual harassment awareness session', alongside other employees? It makes one wonder:

- Is the leadership team above it all?
- Are they not responsible for role modelling the right behaviours?
- What message does it send to the employees and managers, if the leaders behave as if they are too busy or too important to attend these sessions?
- Isn't the leadership team, comprising of people in positions of power, not at the risk of actually committing a sexual harassment offense, as has been reported in many cases?

Exploring the role of HR leads to equally interesting questions.

- How often is the HR team given training on how to handle complaints, maintain discretion, conduct investigation, document evidence and communicate complex messages?

  Ironically, while HR is busy organizing trainings for everyone else, their own capability building is often missed out. It is assumed that anyone working in HR already knows all of this—which couldn't be further from truth. B-schools may teach the law, but they hardly train students on these skills. Also, all B-schools don't teach the same things. I have witnessed scores of HR professionals, even at senior levels, regularly tasked with handling such situations, but ill-equipped to do so.

- How do we ensure that the investigation process is not compromised, given HR's low-power position in organizations, in general, especially when the accused is a high-performing powerful business leader?

  This is one of the most debated aspects of redressal of sexual harassment in organizations globally. There have been many reported anecdotes when HR heads have failed, either lacking the moral courage, or incapacitated by organizational power structure, to initiate investigation into rampant harassment.

- How do we monitor the conduct of HR itself, in maintaining sanctity of processes, discretion of information, not enabling or being party to sexual harassment?

  Unfortunately, there are cases when HR heads and directors themselves are perpetuators of sexual harassment and are not pulled up for it. One can only imagine the state of prevention and redressal of harassment in such organizations.

The moot question in all of these is:

What is the required conduct and capability of business leaders and HR team in both redressal and prevention of sexual harassment in organizations?

The final issue to look at is: Whose business is prevention and redressal of sexual harassment? Despite paying lip service to the issue, candid conversations with business leaders reveal that most of them have a basic discomfort with the matter, like walking on eggshells. Many are secretly very apprehensive of not digging too deep, for the fear of what might come out. Business leaders are happy outsourcing the matter to their HR team, to do what is the bare minimum required by law. For as long as there are 'no complaints', everyone is happy playing the emperor's clothes. This attitude percolates down the organization and everyone finds it convenient to dilute the gravity of the situation with blanket statements like, 'but men also get harassed' and 'women do it for publicity' without being willing to delve deep into understanding the issue. Various surveys have shown that anywhere between 30 to 80 per cent of women face sexual harassment at workplace. Even if we take the lowest number, that is, 30 per cent for the purpose of our discussion, that is one in every three women. How come so many women face harassment, and yet there are so few complaints? Perhaps the reason behind it is the general hands-off mindset around safety, from leaders to managers to employees, that is, 'it's not my problem.' It was the same mindset with which the student (a 'future manager'), we referred to in *Instance 3* at the beginning of the chapter, wanted the convenience of pointing at issues in POSH, without taking responsibility of being a part of the solution. He too thought MeToo was 'not my problem'.

Hence the question to explore is:

How do we create an urgency around safety and make it a shared goal within organizations?

Sexual harassment always existed as an issue. #MeToo made it famous. As we see it #MeToo is not a movement, neither is it a solution. #MeToo is merely a symptom of a grave problem that has gone unchecked within organizations for far too long. #MeToo is symbolic of the tokenism with which leaders have dealt with safety in general and sexual harassment in particular, without resolving which, talking about diversity, is naïve at best and hypocrisy at worst.

(Amy, Anne, Alisha, Andy, Axel, Anthony are all fictitious names used in anecdotes in the following sections. The anecdotes are either real incidents that we are aware of through conversations [the ones with aliases] or reported in media or have experienced personally.)

Harassment Is a Continuum

Let us consider the following situations:

Situation 1: Amy works at a corporate office and is responsible for customer engagement. She is on a visit to customer locations in India accompanied by the local sales team. The locations are remote and require travel by road. The sales team and Amy shared a good rapport. Though there were three men, one driver besides herself in the car, she was completely comfortable. Since it would be a 10-hour drive, the team was ready with music and food. It promised to be an enjoyable drive. Amy had interacted with the team earlier, though this was the first time she was taking such a road trip with them. They treated her with respect. One hour into the drive, the men took out their bottles of 'soft drinks' that looked like cola. Listening to their conversation, Amy learnt that these were bottles of cola spiked with alcohol. It was apparently a usual practice to carry drinks on such road trips. Amy spoke to them upfront and said she wasn't comfortable with them drinking during the trip. They tried telling her it would be okay, but Amy was firm. They gave in, though not cheerfully, Amy being from the head office. Rest of the trip went on uneventfully.

Situation 2: Alisha was visiting a client along with a local customer service representative, Andy. The client meeting went on till late, and they could not find conveyance to go back. While Alisha was trying to work things out, Andy sought to take lift from a teenager (a minor girl) leaving in the direction they were heading. She was the daughter of someone at the client's office (whom Alisha and Andy did not know). The teenager was alone with her driver. By the time Alisha realized what was happening, Andy was already in the car. Alisha reluctantly joined him, uncomfortable about getting into a car with a teenage girl they didn't know, given how quickly this could become an issue. Andy even started conversing with the teenager on where she studied, how old she was and where she lived. Alisha cringed and tried to divert the conversation to general topics such as her favourite subjects. When it was time for them to get off, Alisha thanked the girl and advised her to never let strangers into the car. Alisha returned to work and reported the incident to the function head. He shrugged and didn't do anything about it.

Situation 3: Anthony is a senior manager. Once, multiple teams were on an offsite. It would be Anne's last trip with the team, as she was moving out of the organization. She was Anthony's colleague from another team. On the last day, Anne was saying her goodbyes to everyone. In the process, she was hugging a few of her female colleagues. Anthony saw this and said, 'I need a hug.' Anne wasn't comfortable with the request, because she was not on 'hugging terms' with this colleague, even though they shared a good rapport otherwise. She avoided the situation for a while but eventually relented to a few seconds of 'group hug' with few other colleagues. Anthony and Anne are Indians.

When the *New York Times* best-selling poet Rupi Kaur was asked about a controversial #MeToo case during an interview,[1] it led to an interesting point on the need for the right language, more words and correct nomenclature to describe sexual harassment. There are umpteen situations at workplace, which are clearly problematic or offensive, yet the word 'sexual harassment' or simply 'harassment' doesn't feel right. This is what leads to lot of contention, when one party expresses feeling offended using the word 'sexual harassment' (for the lack of a more accurate word), while onlookers feel like it's an overreaction and calling it 'sexual harassment' is a bit too much.

Another challenge is the fact that sexual harassment is, at times, used as a blanket term to describe a multitude of issues such as sexism, misogyny and bullying. All forms of harassment are problematic and need to be dealt with. But not all harassment is sexual harassment. Within organizations, grievances may be dealt with under different policies depending on the nature of harassment. The procedures specified under the POSH Act in India applies specifically to what is defined as sexual harassment. Other forms of harassment maybe dealt with under disciplinary and other such policies. What is important, and often missed out, is ensuring that organization has policies and frameworks to deal with different kinds of

---

[1] https://www.youtube.com/watch?v=6JU47Wurtr4

grievances and they are communicated to all employees clearly. This pertains to redressal.

Now let's talk about prevention. In the incidents of Amy, Alisha and Anne, nothing went wrong, per se, but could have. More importantly, each scenario involved a behaviour that could be problematic in future. Amy should never have had to ask her colleagues to not drink in the car on an official trip, especially when a female colleague was travelling with them. Many women in Amy's shoes, especially if it were someone junior in the team, would be uncomfortable having that conversation, grin and bear. Some women may put up with it, because they 'share a good relationship' with the team and would be scared to make their male colleagues unhappy or appear uncool by complaining.

Alisha's situation was risky because it involved a third party at the client site, who was also a female minor. Should the parents have taken exception to the fact of two strangers hitchhiking in the car, and asking personal questions, the matter could have snowballed into a major crisis for the organization. Imagine the headline, 'Employees of XYZ Organization force a teenager to give lift, ask uncomfortable personal questions. Parents file complaint'. Employees are often not aware of the fact that gamut of sexual harassment extends not just to employees but a broad set of stakeholders such as clients, vendors, visitors, etc. Andy clearly demonstrates a clear lack of discretion and judgement, which could lead to future issues, even if this particular incident per se was not harassment. The bigger problem was that the incident was reported but ignored, keeping alive the possibility of future issues. Ideally, this should have been reason enough for HR to conduct a short awareness session on potentially problematic scenarios that feet-on-street staff encounter—and what to be careful about.

In the case of Anne, there was no reason for Anthony to ask her for a hug. This is a typical scenario when a behaviour can be passed off as 'harmless' but upon looking closely it will be found to be an act of indiscretion. Both Anthony and Anne were Indians. Hence, they didn't belong to a culture where hugging is the usual way of greeting, especially between genders. Some people do hug each other, but that depends on the nature of personal rapport the individuals share. Anthony and Anne had a good rapport, but that did not extend to a physical hug. Anthony was out of line in asking for it. Most importantly, Anne was uncomfortable. It is difficult to ascertain Anthony's intention, and that is immaterial. He demonstrated lack of a nuanced understanding of boundaries. Hug is a high-physical-contact greeting, and in workplaces, across genders, can easily mean unwanted touching in many cultures.

Often organizations limit themselves to minimum-required-by-law investigation under POSH and overlook numerous such scenarios that are too small to be raised yet are daily irritants. This is where we hear stories about the creepy manager who insists on hugging everyone, until one fine day, five female employees make a joint complaint and a major issue erupts. Unless a formal grievance is lodged, organizations may turn a blind eye to such matters even when incidents are known. This leaves female employees no option but to resort to avoid-the-manager strategies, instead of focusing on work (if they are unwilling to go through the process of raising 'sexual harassment complaint'). Sometimes, all that is required is an informal conversation to make someone aware of a potentially problematic behaviour. In fact, managers could be equipped to have these conversations, as HR talk can be seen as intimidating. In this scenario, the manager's manager could make them aware of the behaviour and advise course correction. Harassment is a continuum. Seemingly small but daily acts of offense distract employee attention that should otherwise be focused on achieving business outcomes. Therefore, broadening the definition harassment to include a range of situations of varying degrees, and deploying strategies to deal with them, must be a business priority.

Mindset of No

I had a good friend at work, with whom I shared a great rapport. Once, he cracked a joke with a slight sexual overtone involving me, in front of another common friend. I believe it was one of those moments when you utter a pun spontaneously, without giving it much thought. Since we were good friends, I was okay to overlook it this one time. However, the problem I had was that this joke was said about me, in my presence, to a third common friend. I could overlook even that, but I didn't want a repeat of this in future. Hence, I decided to mention it to my friend and ask him to be more cautious in the future. In my mind, it was meant to be a normal 30-second conversation. But I was mistaken. My friend was offended. He ranted for 10 minutes after that. He never once said, 'I am sorry, I didn't realize it offended you, won't happen again.' That's all I needed. I felt worried and anxious that I had 'ruined our friendship'. I asked him later if I indeed had damaged our rapport by objecting to his joke. He said, 'A little; earlier we were 100 per cent friends, now we are 95 per cent friends.'

In the discussion of sexual harassment, 'consent' is most talked about. However, equally important is the discussion on 'mindset of no'. 'Consent' is checking if the woman is okay with a certain act. 'Mindset of no' is observing, acknowledging and respecting her position when she is not comfortable. Presence or absence of consent is a key deciding factor of whether something is considered sexual harassment or not. Determining consent is a critical part of the grievance 'redressal' process. On the other hand, establishing the 'mindset of no' is key to 'prevention' of sexual harassment in organizations. Another fundamental difference between 'consent' and 'mindset of no' is that 'consent' is studied only from the perspective of the woman. However, 'mindset of no' needs to be looked at from the lens of:

1. The person saying no
2. The person being told no
3. Others

Saying and accepting no, in general, is a difficult thing to do for human beings. The level of discomfort varies across cultures. Cultures akin to low-context communication, that is, saying things as they are, may be open to communicating a *no*, directly. However, cultures akin to high-context communication, that is, saying things loaded with context subject to interpretation, may find it more challenging to communicate and accept no. 'Saving face' is important to many cultures, which may add to the discomfort of saying no. For example, one of the common 'saving face' examples in an Indian context is saying, 'I will try my best to come,' in response to an invitation you are not in a position to accept. In such cultures, people may feel even more inhibited to express discomfort with a behaviour, for the fear of making offender lose face, in private or, worse, public. Another factor that makes saying no challenging is when the organizational or institutional cultural identity is cult-like. Anyone calling out a problematic behaviour which is accepted as a group norm is seen as a traitor, to be ostracized and ganged-up against, causing many to bottle up or vent on social media later. This cult-like culture can be observed in colleges and even businesses. We discussed this aspect of organizational culture in the chapter 'Dissent and Diversity'.

In the context of sexual harassment, *no* refers to communicating behaviours one is not okay with and would like the other person to course-correct. It's important to observe that, given the unique nature of sexual harassment, which involves a lot of shame and embarrassment, communicating no is a universal challenge that women face in every culture. #MeToo, which rocked the Western world, demonstrated that even globally successful women found it difficult to share their angst for decades. One can only imagine the challenge of women in low-power positions in communicating *no*, that too proactively. She would be told, 'come on don't make an issue out of it' or pay a price for raising the issue, through work-related bullying, if the offender is a senior in the organization. Regional and specific workplace culture can serve to compound the universal discomfort women experience in saying *no*.

The attitude towards communication of *no* is important to understand and deal with in workplaces, particularly in the prevention of sexual harassment. This must be addressed, as we mentioned earlier, from the following perspectives.

The Person Saying No

One of my seniors in an organization, in a leadership role, told me that her male peers use cuss words while talking, which is something she is not comfortable with. However, she has to grin and bear, else she won't be accepted as 'one of them'. This is a widely documented reason for women to put up with and even adopt behaviours they may inherently be uncomfortable with. When women in even leadership roles succumb to the pressure, they may be less empathetic towards women in lower ranks facing the same situation. This creates roadblocks in women leaders being able to play a constructive role in combatting sexual harassment in workplaces. We will talk about this in greater detail later in the book. In my case described at the beginning of this section, I was dealing with a colleague who was also a good friend. I myself experienced apprehensions of 'ruining my friendship' and was duly punished for communicating boundaries with '5 per cent ' deducted from my friendship. There are many reasons why women don't say no:

a. Act is offensive but too small to be called 'sexual harassment' (This goes back to our earlier point of not having more words to describe the continuum of offensive behaviours. In my case above, I wouldn't call the stand-alone joke as sexual harassment. However, it was a problematic behaviour. If repeated as a pattern, it would qualify as sexual harassment at a later point in time. This is why small acts should not be wished away, but they often are.)
b. Fear of embarrassing the person (the one who made them feel uncomfortable)
c. Fear of being shamed (i.e., 'don't be so sensitive', 'grow up', etc.)
d. Hurting the relationship (mentor, senior, manager, colleague)
e. Fear of being seen as a person who is a 'troublemaker'

One of the *most critical, and equally neglected* area of prevention of sexual harassment is helping women find the courage to tell their colleagues, mentors and managers that they do not like it when someone stands too close, or cracks the 'non-vegetarian' jokes, or touches them while talking, or comments on their 'slim figure', or uses profane language in general. For women on the growth path, the fear of being seen as a 'troublemaker' is particularly high and not unfounded. It is not unusual to hear hush-hush conversations on, 'it was her' (i.e., the one who raised an objection). Unfortunately, HR is also party to such informal exchange of feedback during key organizational promotions. One of the key things in creating a mindset of no is to aggressively manage the perception around saying no and have a clear commitment to women not being penalized at work for communicating boundaries.

I was chatting with a leader about the need to do organization-wide, dialogue-based, mixed-gender sessions including the executive team. He said, 'Let's not open the Pandora's box.' The truth is, many business leaders may pay lip service to prevention of sexual harassment and have their marketing teams put up emphatic 'safe workplace' corporate messages. However, their own convictions are akin to the 'Pandora's box' sentiment. Hence, they concede with doing the minimum required 'trainings' to be legally compliant, while being careful to not have any more dialogue that may lead to increase in number of complaints. This only creates a ticking time bomb, waiting to explode as #MeToo. Creating a safe environment for women to express their discomfort, without being penalized or ostracized, serves to proactively tackle sexual harassment—and not create additional trouble for the organizations, as many leaders falsely fear.

The Person Being Told No

There is an often-used dialogue in Bollywood movies, '*Ladki ke naa mein bhi haan hoti hai*', meaning when a girl says *no*, it includes a *yes*. The line is cliched yet significant in understanding a deep-rooted mindset towards the seriousness accorded to an expression of no, by women. In the chapter 'Equal not Same', we discussed about women being traditionally expected to be coy. Therefore, a *no* need not be taken seriously at once, unless it is emphasized upon or said repeatedly. We hear lot of accounts by men, when they admit to not recognizing a no. Let's refer back to the instance shared at the beginning of the chapter, when male managers in the session felt 50–90 per cent of sexual harassment cases result out of 'misunderstanding', whereas female managers felt all of it was deliberate. This gap is worth researching. A plausible reason could be the inability or unwillingness to read the signs of no.

I was travelling for some workshops and was put up at the guest residence of the client. Meals were served in a central cafeteria. Another team was also staying at the guest house and came to the same cafeteria. One of the evenings, a man from that team tried to strike a conversation with me. I wasn't interested and gave polite monosyllable responses and moved on. The following morning, I was early to breakfast and was the only person in the cafeteria. Two more people came in shortly, one of whom was the same person from last evening. He greeted me, I nodded and moved away. I prefer eating in silence before a workshop and chose an obscure table hidden behind a pillar to have my breakfast in peace. After five minutes, I find the man take a seat at that very table, on a chair right next to mine, out of the 40-odd tables and 200-odd chairs that were vacant at that time. I had no option but to be rude and walk away to another table.

This incident is not an example of harassment. But it's an example of how routinely we fail to recognize and acknowledge a *no*. I had given enough non-verbal signs that I wasn't interested in a conversation across both meetings. Yet, the person was persistent. Sometimes *no* is expressed verbally.

Often, it is expressed non-verbally. When you are standing too close to a woman, she will look uncomfortable, try to pull some objects in between (a purse, a chair) or cross her arms. When someone replies in monosyllables and makes little eye-contact, it shows they aren't as interested in that conversation you are trying to strike. Ideally, this is not rocket science. These are universal cues that human mind is wired to understand. However, non-verbal can be easily ignored or tagged as confusing, lacking the concreteness of spoken and written word. Even when *no* is said verbally, if the tone is friendly and said with a smile, it ends up not being taken seriously. Unless one says it rudely, people refuse to get the point. One of the areas of awareness that is necessary but, again, ignored is about various ways a no is communicated and the need to take cognizance of them. All expressions of *no* are to be respected as a *no*. During my workshops, I hear objections to this mindfulness with the argument, 'how can we communicate freely with each other if we have to think so much?' The answer to this is fairly straightforward, especially when the question comes from managers and leaders. Having the ability to observe and empathize with another person's reaction is a key soft skill required in all interpersonal communication. Many business scenarios such as sales, negotiation and customer conversations require these skills. Anyone who finds observing signs of discomfort in a woman tedious, may even lack overall people skills required for key business roles.

Apart from being able to recognize a *no*, another aspect is being graceful to *accept* a *no*. In my own case, my friend took offense to my expression of *no*, instead of understanding my point and sentiments. Often, response to a *no* is defiance. A rewiring is required to understand that an expression of *no* is an opportunity for dialogue and should not be taken as an insult. We need to transition our responses from:

- 'You are making an issue out of a small thing,'
  to 'Sorry, I did not realize my action offended you, I will be careful in future.'

- 'You are so sensitive,'
  to 'Sorry, I should have been more sensitive to it.'

- 'Grow up, are you a child?'
  to 'Sorry, I should not have behaved that way; I will do better next time.'

The Others

Of all things we fail to address in building the mindset of no, foremost among them is the role of 'others'. Others are colleagues, friends, managers, employees—that is, the third party witnessing an incident. All of us have played that role in the past:

- Sometimes, we witness a wrong behaviour and turn a blind eye to it (*'Why should I get into it, the offender is my friend'*).

- We discourage the expression of *no* by joining the shaming (*'Chill, don't take it so seriously'*).

- Knowingly or unknowingly, we partake in the act of harassment (*Indulge in gossip mongering about the 'character' of a female colleague*).

'Others' may directly witness an event unfolding or have second-hand information (for example, you hear the account of what happened at the office party last night from a colleague who attended it). 'Others' have the inclination to form their opinions about a scenario based on their biases towards the parties involved. In all the high-profile #MeToo cases, people have openly taken sides and handed out character certificates to both parties, whether good or bad, such as:

- 'I never had this experience while interacting with this person, the accusation must be wrong.'
- 'I have heard not-so-good-things about this person, the accusation must be right.'
- 'She has a B-grade career, so she must be doing it for career gain or publicity.'
- 'She has made such allegations in the past. Why does it only happen to her all the time?'

One can see the folly of such assumptions and character certificates which are based on partial knowledge of facts and our personal biases towards the parties involved. The only right things to do, as 'the others', in case of a sexual harassment are:

a. If you are witnessing it, intervene to stop it, and enable the expression of *no*.
b. If you get to hear of it, don't take sides, and let the process do the fact-finding.

Those incharge of prevention of sexual harassment need to create enough awareness of everyone's role as 'others' in creating a culture where saying no is easier. Not participating in gossip mongering, not shaming a person calling out a behaviour, objecting to anything inappropriate 'others' witness (even if done by a friend) are all important parts of building a mindset of *no*. Those driving prevention of sexual harassment cannot afford to not leverage the power of 'others'.

Overall, some of key ways to build the *mindset of no* in an organization, across the three roles of (a) person saying *no* (b) person hearing *no* and (c) the others are:

1. Role modelling mindset of *no,* at the leadership level
2. Building awareness of various ways, a *no* is expressed, verbally or non-verbally
3. Building awareness of our role as *the others* in any scenario
4. Capturing and sharing organizational anecdotes on expression and respectful acceptance of *no,* and how that improves rapport between colleagues, instead of damaging it

---

I was meeting friends after a long time at a restaurant. Some of us were seated on sofas around a table. A friend (male) sat next to me. I moved slightly away. He immediately sensed it and said, 'Sorry I think you are uncomfortable.' I clarified to him that I moved away to give him more space to sit comfortably, and not because I was uncomfortable with him sitting next to me.

This did not happen within a workplace, but is a great example of a communication of *no.* My friend was sensitive to non-verbal cues, and I in turn could clarify. The communication just lasted 15 seconds. When the culture and mindset is that of respect and understanding, communication of *no* (saying or listening) is uneventful. It can be as effortless as saying, 'pass me the salt'. Far from making opposite genders uncomfortable with each other, it improves inter-gender communication and makes for stronger relationships at workplaces.

Redressal Is Not Equal to Prevention

A low *number of complaints* is often taken as the pseudo-indicator of an organization's success in preventing sexual harassment. Given how under-reported sexual harassment is, it will be fair to call *number of complaints* what it is: a *metric of denial*. Since redressal of sexual harassment directly falls under the purview of law, organizations take a regimented approach to its communication. Ironically, while all organizations call their efforts as Prevention of Sexual Harassment, their interventions are, in effect, focused only on the *redressal* process. *Prevention* is largely ignored.

Both prevention and redressal are prerequisites for attaining the goal of a safe work environment. However, both need (a) separate attention and (b) different approaches. An accessible, credible and efficient redressal process acts as a deterrent to sexual harassment. Focus on redressal is necessary (and also mandated by law) but not sufficient by itself. At this time, organizations are a long way from even being able to establish and communicate a process that is respected by all employees. While businesses pull up their socks on that front, the whole different dimension of prevention needs to be worked upon. Abuse and subsequent shaming for calling out abuse has been normalized for long. To change that law alone will not help unless the mindset is worked upon. The only true metric of the success of prevention of sexual harassment is when organizations have been able to normalize the *mindset of no*. Where if someone says, 'Hey I am not okay with this,' the only response is, '*Sorry, it won't happen again.*' The skill sets required to drive redressal and prevention could be different. Prevention would require high capability to drive difficult conversations and dialogue on ground.

Some of the key differences in approach to redressal and prevention are as follows:

Redressal of Sexual Harassment	Prevention of Sexual Harassment
Overall focus: Driving a credible and effective grievance redressal system as per law	**Overall focus:** Building a culture of safety including, but not limited to sexual harassment
Communication: • **Content:** Legal purview, process, policy • **Style:** Instructional • **Frequency:** Periodic • **Delivery:** In-person, e-learning • **Driven by:** HR/safety team	**Communication:** • **Content:** *Mindset of no*, principles of inter-gender communication, non-verbal communication, attitude towards sexual harassment and safety • **Style:** Dialogue based • **Frequency:** Continuous • **Delivery:** In person, cross-sectional audience across gender and levels • **Driven by:** Business leaders, managers, employee volunteers—facilitated by HR
Interventions: Awareness trainings, campaigns, posters, mailers	**Interventions:** Dialogue-based sessions, round tables, focus groups, experience sharing on positive behaviours, communication of organizational anecdotes, utilizing informal expression mediums such as skits, inviting stories, proactive briefing during office trips, parties, etc.
Measure: 1) Actual handling of grievance: Efficiency, transparency plus discretion, communication 2) Credibility of the process and people driving the process	**Measure:** 1) Employee experience of safety in the organization 2) Employee experience of ease of communicating discomfort to each other, managers, leaders without apprehension

(continued)

(continued)

Redressal of Sexual Harassment	Prevention of Sexual Harassment
3) Level of awareness and access about the grievance redressal mechanism 4) Successful prevention of direct or indirect retaliation to complainant irrespective of the outcome of the complaint	3) Culture of safety is made a shared accountability across all levels of the organizations (could also extend to being included in the balanced scorecard of individuals) 4) Communicating norms of behaviours to customers, vendors, visitors, etc.

Leadership and HR—Do They Lead by Example?

I had joined the HR team recently. We were out for a team dinner. All the HR senior management was a part of it. One of the directors was a part of the POSH investigation committee. Sometime into the dinner, I heard a few of them make jokes about some of the sexual harassment complaints that had been raised. It has since left many questions in my mind about the sanctity of the role and conduct of HR in prevention and redressal of sexual harassment.

HR is tasked with driving the prevention of sexual harassment within organizations. It is absolutely critical that they possess the skill and credibility to do so. It's a fair expectation for HR to be above the board, given the level of information they can access and their role in the process. Yet, HR teams seldom receive the training and mentorship required to handle complex situations. It is assumed that they already know the requisites, because they have an 'HR degree' or 'experience'. However, *doing something* and *doing something well* are two different things. If prevention of sexual harassment is an important goal, the capability and conduct of HR has to be looked into carefully.

Conduct

- Not engaging in gossip mongering
- Not passing on case information to business leaders with whom they share a good rapport
- Not turning a blind eye to harassment they may be aware of, unless explicitly raised
- Not engaging in acts of harassment themselves

Capability

- Ability to probe and collect data
- Ability to document findings and file a robust report
- Ability to have difficult conversations
- Ability to facilitate tricky discussions
- Ability to maintain objectivity without succumbing to one's own biases

In-company sexual harassment investigations are quasi-judicial processes and require specific skills of fact-finding, probing and communicating to stakeholders. If the case has been reported in media, then crisis management capabilities are also necessary during the redressal process. To enable prevention of harassment, skills to facilitate difficult dialogues in one-on-one and one-to-many conversations are critical. These skills cannot be developed by one-odd training but need long-term focus. An indicator of the seriousness of any organization in prevention of sexual harassment is whether they have invested in developing these capabilities in the HR team.

Another practical challenge for HR is their low-power position in the organization relative to business leaders. HR is a support function, and a rather insecure place to be in. HR metrics that can prove its value as a function beyond being the 'caretaker of the organization' deserves a book of its own. The moot point here is, HR is often dependent on the 'good will' of business leaders saying good things about the function. This becomes problematic when a case of harassment involves senior, powerful and high-performing business leaders. This has been observed in cases reported in the media, including Uber's Susan Fowler[2] case and HSBC's Mike Picarella case.[3] Fowler, in her viral tell-all, shared how HR along with senior management had been actively covering up for errant managers, forcing women engineers to change teams or stay on to get poor performance reviews. Mike Picarella's account, reported by Huffington post, in the article 'Inhuman Resources', talks of how HR not only didn't initiate investigation on senior bank executive Eileen for sexual misconduct, but also breached the identity of the complainant who had raised the concerns in confidence. The head of HR was said to have 'close friendship' with the accused. These are not one-off cases but representative of a wider organizational dynamic, where HR is systemically incapacitated to act independently. Further, it also boils down to the individual, as is the case with anything in life. It will take an HR head of exceptional character to stand up to powerful business leaders and call out rampant harassment. In all probability, such an HR head himself or herself will be shown the door under the guise of non-performance or something similar. One of the solutions could be to consider forming a safety team comprising of people with the right skills and mindset, who are further groomed for the role. Additionally,

---

[2] https://www.susanjfowler.com/blog/2017/2/19/reflecting-on-one-very-strange-year-at-uber
[3] https://highline.huffingtonpost.com/articles/en/hsbc-sexual-harassment-hr/

a dotted-line reporting to the board can be considered, just for the purpose of grievance handling when very senior executives are involved. However, none of this will matter unless there is real leadership backing, which brings us to the most critical point on the role of business leadership in prevention of sexual harassment.

When the 2008 downturn hit the economy, it opened the can of worms on business practices in Wall Street. A skeleton that tumbled out of the otherwise haloed closets of top financial institutes were stories about prostitutes and escorts being used for entertainment of clients, high-flying bankers and brokers. Business meetings being held in strip clubs was prevalent even pre-COVID, with corporate cards being used for expenses.[4] The fact that a company (under Amour Inc.) specifically banned strip clubs as a valid expense on a corporate card,[5] indicates prevalence of the practice. The problem isn't limited to financial firms but also extends to other businesses such as law firms[6] and Silicon Valley.[7] These are hallowed industries that millions of young graduates, both men and women, dream of joining. The elephant in the room is the question: What will be the real level of sexual harassment prevention in such organizations where business practices lend themselves to an environment of harassment? Google has been accused of being secretive about sexual harassment complaints against top

---

[4] https://www.bloomberg.com/news/articles/2018-11-15/strip-club-business-meetings-are-alive-and-well-in-age-of-metoo
[5] https://www.bloomberg.com/news/articles/2018-11-05/under-armour-bans-strip-club-expenses-in-metoo-moment-wsj-says
[6] https://www.wsj.com/articles/BL-LB-909
[7] https://www.independent.co.uk/life-style/gadgets-and-tech/news/eric-gilmore-silicon-valley-startup-turvo-strip-club-lawsuit-a9249146.html

executives including Andy Rubin, the brain behind Android.[8] Media reports suggest executives, against whom grievances were raised, were given generous exit deals.

We mentioned earlier about how business leaders like to be hands-off in the sexual harassment arena, viewing it as some Pandora's box. This begs us to ask the fundamental question: Why do you care about prevention of sexual harassment? Do you really care, in the first place, or is it because of a legal mandate? Any leader who speaks on diversity should realize from a practical standpoint, if not a moral one, that a safe workplace is a pre-requisite for diversity to be nurtured. Prevention of sexual harassment is, therefore, key to that strategy. One cannot afford to take the approach of 'do the minimum to tick the boxes'. Leaders need to have greater involvement in the prevention of sexual harassment, if they really believe that women bring value to the table. Without demonstrating resolute commitment to building a harassment-free workplace, any leadership rhetoric on diversity is mere hogwash. In November 2018, 20,000 Google employees marched out of Google offices around the world[9] protesting the company's handling of sexual harassment and demanding for structural changes.[10] One of the tasks of the protesters has been to issue a public report on harassment cases. On paper, Sundar Pichai and leader of people operations at Google have emphatically stated their commitment to fighting sexual harassment, quoting statistics such as 48 people who were fired

---

[8] https://www.nytimes.com/2018/10/25/technology/google-sexual-harassment-andy-rubin.html?auth=login-email&login=email

[9] https://www.nytimes.com/2018/11/01/technology/google-walkout-sexual-harassment.html

[10] https://www.nytimes.com/2018/11/01/technology/google-walkout-sexual-harassment.html

had never received exit packages.[11] However, this is where the commitment of business leadership needs to be scrutinized closely. If lower-rung employees are fired for harassment but powerful senior executives are protected and given handsome pay-offs, it mars everything. This is the same Google where Pichai cancelled a part of his vacation to personally fly in and fire James Damore for a memo. Why should the treatment differ for powerful executives, no matter how smart they are?

A notable case of firing was that of Phaneesh Murthy, who was sued for sexual misconduct and fired from Infosys, nearly two decades ago. Phaneesh Murthy was known to be a brilliant mind and a high performer, having contributed to Infosys' business growth and was supposedly the blue-eyed boy of both Narayana Murthy and Nandan Nilekani. Unless decisive actions are taken against powerful business leaders engaging in sexual harassment, irrespective of their level of brilliance and contribution, all efforts of prevention of sexual harassment will fall short. It's not clear if Phaneesh Murthy was fired because it was thought to be the ethically right thing to do or because it had exposed Infosys to legal risks. Perhaps, this is why large number of tech and other companies in the USA require employees to sign *forced arbitration* where employees cannot sue the company and must agree to an in-company procedure. For everyone criticizing #MeToo movement must know that a lot of genuine stories never come out as a result of these agreements. Google agreed to scraping of its forced arbitration policy for future cases of sexual harassment, following the employee protests.[12] We are unaware of the current status of the

---

[11] https://thewire.in/tech/google-gave-android-creator-andy-rubin-a-90-mn-exit-package-after-sexual-harassment-allegations

[12] https://www.vox.com/technology/2019/2/22/18236172/mandatory-forced-arbitration-google-employees

policy. Laws per se vary across countries. For example, in India, a woman has recourse to civil redressal under the guidelines of the POSH Act as well as redressal under criminal laws.

The moot point here is, we are a long way from any significant improvement in prevention of sexual harassment, unless there is a well-intentioned introspection and change at the business leadership level, beyond managing legal compliance and public perception. Key indicators of real leadership commitment to sexual harassment would include:

1. Ensuring no retaliation to those raising complaints about harassment by senior management or criticizing the policies (In large number of cases, complainants have experienced retaliation and felt compelled to quit. For example, there have been reports on Google's culture of retaliation.[13] Claire Stapleton[14] and Meredith Whittaker were two of the organizers of the Google employee walkout protests. Both have claimed facing retaliation including demotion of roles and creation of hostile environment by manager.)
2. Strict punitive action on senior executives, especially those wielding power, in case of proven sexual harassment complaints against them
3. Executive team being the first to attend sexual harassment training alongside employees
4. Ensuring no discrimination against sexual harassment complainant during hiring or promotion, whether or not the complaint was proven, to remove the taboo around raising grievances

---

[13] https://www.bbc.com/news/technology-48024849
[14] https://www.wired.com/story/google-walkout-organizers-say-theyre-facing-retaliation/

Sexual harassment issue exists only because there is a lack of leadership will. Unless leaders can come clean and stop protecting their kin, employee activism and #MeToo are just the beginning. This is not scepticism but merely the stark truth of 'prevention of sexual harassment', without tokenism. There is no other way of saying this. The buck simply stops, at the top.

#MeToo, a Weapon against Men?

Around the time Susan Fowler shocked the world with the account of abuse and harassment at Uber led by Travis Kalanick, another gut-wrenching account was posted by someone who took the alias of Amy Vertino.[15] As Amy described her, if not systemic, then system-aided, belittling as a woman and human being, including being called a 'whiny bitch' in meetings, to facing sexual overtures, readers of her account could feel something churning at the pit of their stomach.

For anyone who wondered if #MeToo was a tool to get publicity and leverage, last lines of Amy's blog have the answer. She ends with saying, 'Even though I don't work at Uber any longer, the damage that was done to me by Uber's work environment ruined my spirit. It damaged what was most precious to me: dignity and self-respect.' Sexual harassment is so prevalent that almost *every* woman has experienced it at least once in their life—be it that male colleague, who forgot he is only supposed to be looking at your face while talking to you; or that one who stands just a little too close to you every time, despite you being visibly uncomfortable; or that one who cracks a lewd joke with you as the subject and quickly says,

---

[15] https://medium.com/@amyvertino/my-name-is-not-amy-i-am-an-uber-survivor-c6d6541e632f

'Hope you don't mind; btw I respect women a lot.' Jacinda Ardern, in an interview,[16] was responding to a question on whether she personally had experienced sexual harassment. She said, 'Show me a woman it hasn't happened to.'

I don't need a Harvard study to tell you that a woman will *always* notice when your gaze shifted, and she will *never* forget that look on your face. The worst part of sexual harassment, even the mildest incident of it, is that it reduces women to mere objects with just a look, a word, a touch. This is probably why sexual harassment is also a tool to control women in society. We said earlier, not all harassment is sexual harassment. But sexual harassment merits the most urgent, immediate and decisive action because it's the most debilitating and dehumanizing form of all harassment.

Alisha, a high-performing, high-potential employee, was in a brief relationship with her manager, Axel. The manager was bound by organization policy to declare any relationship he had with someone reporting to him. He flouted the policy and kept the relationship a secret. While in the relationship, he wanted to get physical but Alisha didn't. There would be days he would treat her very harshly at work. Later, Axel admitted to Alisha that his behaviour was a result of his frustration. Both felt it was best to end things amicably and move on. Both Axel and Alisha were passionate about their work. Little did Alisha know things would go downhill for her soon.

As Axel started getting more growth in the organization, he panicked about what he had done. Instead of doing the right thing and managing the situation with fairness and dignity, he resorted

---

[16] https://www.youtube.com/watch?v=dQivl4oneOA

to emotional manipulation and using his authority to create what is the very definition of a hostile environment for Alisha. He started insulting her in front of colleagues. He nit-picked her mistakes, criticized her heavily. He kept her out of meetings she should have been part of. He did not keep her posted on matters concerning her areas of work. He would ignore her every now and then, knowing fully well it would impact her. In private, he often took the liberty of raising his voice and talking to her aggressively. While his public insults would be about work, his private insults belittled who she was as a person. He refused to support and coach her for a new role she had taken up. If she hung out with colleagues outside work, he accused her of doing so, because she wanted to talk to others about him (i.e., his constant fear was that she might tell all). He suggested her to move to another team. Alisha had no reason to agree with it, because she really liked her current role and had worked hard at it. She didn't consider it fair for Axel to make such a suggestion for his personal convenience. It wouldn't be in the best interest of the organization either, because Alisha was good at what she did.

On one occasion, Alisha tried leaving the organization, traumatized by the routine insults. Axel convinced her that HR should not see her as unstable and that her resignation should mean something. He set up a meeting with HR, communicating to them that she was unhappy with her growth and had resigned for that reason. Alisha was not privy to the communication made by Axel to HR and learnt about it later. Given she had been a good performer, HR even made a case for her promotion and took it to Axel. He played a masterstroke and told HR that he did not think she was ready for the move. Alisha didn't realize until much later, how she had been methodically manipulated and taken apart, by the very person she continued to, rather foolishly, trust and have feelings for. Axel was already laying landmines in her way, should she ever raise a case of harassment against him. He was an expert in posturing and had carefully worked on constructing a public perception that all was well and if not, then he wasn't the problem. Axel had recommended Alisha for recognition certificates on one odd occasion, while having refused her even a discussion on career planning. He mocked her in person for asking for a career discussion. Axel was carefully destroying all future prospects and hopes of Alisha.

Alisha finally left, as Axel wanted her to. Her performance had dropped as the incident unfolded. She should have grown in the organization by virtue of her work. She wasn't allowed to, simply because her presence was a constant source of discomfort for Axel. She had become inconvenient to his organizational ambitions and was dispensed with.

Answer to the question, 'Is #MeToo a weapon against men?' as sceptics call it, is not easy, simply because the allegation itself is not straightforward. Beneath that accusation lies layers of:

1. Misconceptions
2. Prejudices
3. Lack of understanding of the redressal process
4. Lack of empathy for the human impact of sexual harassment

Therefore, let's go through the entire drill of understanding what happens when sexual harassment takes place and then get to addressing the #MeToo-a-weapon-against-men question.

We could have chosen to share another story—one where Alisha and Alex had not dated each other. But this is how real-life cases are, all unique circumstances, each different from the other, with a heady concoction of emotions and events, one connected to the other. We picked this case because it digs deep into key aspects of nature of sexual harassment, investigation and, most importantly, human impact.

First, let's discuss the nature of harassment. This *is* a clear case of sexual harassment. Bear in mind Alisha and Axel had a brief affair. That was consensual. The fact that Axel, being a manager, failed to disclose the affair, would be considered as a policy violation but not sexual harassment per se. However, two parts of his behaviour were gross acts of sexual harassment. First, when he treated Alisha harshly at work because of frustration of wanting a physical relationship. Second, the entire sequence of activities when he decided to force Alisha out of the organization, after they ended their relationship, because of his fears. Each case of sexual harassment is different. The nature and extent of harassment and punishment is decided after an exhaustive enquiry process by a panel, if the grievance is raised with the organization as a part of civil process. There is also a criminal recourse available in India, which will have a different procedure.

Second, let's discuss the nature of investigation. As readers, at this point in time, we have a *full view* of the case laid out for us. However, if we were witnessing it as a colleague or HR or a work friend of either of the two parties (the others), one would only have a fragmented view of things. Further, people perceive the facts based on their own biases, familiarity and loyalty to either of the two parties. In the case of a manipulative individual, misleading perceptions can be constructed and situations planted to influence opinions. This is what we said earlier about the dangers of doling out judgement and character certificates as a third party, based on very limited view of things. As much as we think we *know* about a case, it's best to remind ourselves that we *don't*. Now, imagine the task set for the investigating panel. All of these events will have to be reconstructed through series of interviews and innumerable questions to multiple parties. Uncovering the truth of each incident will require painstaking effort.

The African movie *Citation*,[17] said to be broadly based on true events around sex-for-marks incidents in Nigerian universities, depicts the challenges of a sexual harassment hearing process. In the movie, a professor starts with subtle sexual advances to an intellectually gifted student. His frustration increases as she resists him. Finally, he attempts to rape her after a house party of students. She escapes the incident only to find that her dissertation paper he had praised highly earlier was now being trashed by him. During the investigation hearing, the professor manipulates the narrative of every incident documented in the complaint, in a way to prove that the student was infatuated with him and had offered sex to him, while *he* was the one who turned it down. It took a lot of grit and determination from the student, with support from a lawyer, to get the right witnesses and turn things around. The professor in the movie was a highly acclaimed and respected scholar. It was to the credit of the panel to not be swayed by reputations and stick to the evidence. The tediousness of an investigation process is often neither understood, nor appreciated at large. Often, there is a perception that as soon as a sexual harassment complaint is filed, the 'man's life is spoilt'. It doesn't work like that. There is a long-drawn tedious process of fact-finding. If a man is punished, then it is based on the findings of investigation and not on a mere complaint. On the other hand, people also accuse panels of taking time to reach a conclusion. A credible investigation process is thorough and seldom easy. Alisha's dossier, had she complained, would have run into hundreds of pages. Her initial complaint itself, documenting months of harassment, would run into several pages.

---

[17] https://www.imdb.com/title/tt11481312/

Third, the human cost of sexual harassment. It took Alisha two years to come out of the trauma. She had nightmares and disrupted sleep for a long time after the incident. She would often break into tears abruptly and found it difficult to focus on any work. Given the nature of the issue, Alisha did not confide in anyone else in the family and, thus, had no emotional support. It's particularly important to understand the nature of emotions she experienced. Her first emotion was pain for having been subjected to the harassment by a person she trusted. She also had an underlying emotion of severe anger for the humiliation she was subjected to. However, she did not allow herself permission to feel the anger, for a long time, because of her earlier relationship with Axel. This added a third emotion of guilt, for feeling anger. Finally, Alisha experienced shame for having allowed such a thing to have happened to her and not called it out. The four emotions of pain, anger, guilt and shame tore her apart. Alisha was not a doormat. She was a bright young girl, full of ambition, confidence and one who could speak her mind. Yet, this happened to her. She did not 'pull a #MeToo'. Nor did she raise a sexual harassment complaint. She lost precious years of her career because of Axel's ambitions, while her own ambitions were sidelined. 'I kept trying to forgive him. I will never let this happen to me again,' Alisha rues.

It's important to understand that the emotional trauma of harassment happens at many levels. It's particularly difficult when the perpetrator of harassment is someone the woman knows, looks up to, respects—a mentor, a colleague, a manager, teacher. Just like in the case of Alisha, women experience a mix of pain, anger, guilt and shame. While pain and anger are understandable emotions, guilt and shame are unexpected but typical. Women tend to blame themselves for a scenario: 'Did I do something to bring it upon myself?' 'Was I too friendly?'

'Could I have done something differently?' It's the self-imposed *lajja* that we discussed in the chapter 'Equal, Not Same'. At a personal level, we feel that Alisha had been naïve and emotionally gullible, in a way that her intelligence did not justify. But her offense was to her own self. She had been unfair to her own career for allowing things to go on for so long. There was nothing for her to blame herself for the debilitating treatment meted out to her. What was *done to her* was wrong. The shame should have belonged to Axel, whose life went on unbridled as he fulfilled his ambitions, at the same time that Alisha's life stopped still. Yet she was the one experiencing both guilt and shame, just like millions of women professionals in a similar situation.

Fourth, about the question people frequently ask about #MeToo: 'Why are women speaking after 10 years or 20 years?' 'Why didn't they speak then?' 'Why didn't they file a complaint earlier?' In fact, often these questions are raised not with a spirit of inquiry seeking to understand but more in the sense of questioning the credibility of the complainant. Many have claimed, rather foolishly, that the scores of women who spoke out during #MeToo (out of millions who didn't) were doing so for publicity or some other gain. It is argued that if a complaint is genuine, it should have been raised earlier. Let's understand why women don't complain or, sometimes, prefer raising it on social media, rather than follow a formal complaint procedure. We have discussed in the section on *mindset of no* the reasons women don't speak up while facing day-to-day harassment. For gross harassment, as in the case of Alisha, additional dynamics come into play. There are four primary reasons.

- To begin with, it's the shame women experience. It seems cognitively illogical as to why the woman going through harassment experiences shame, while the perpetrator doesn't. Think of any other crime on earth—theft, fraud, murder. The victim isn't the one ashamed. This phenomenon is unique to sexual harassment. That's why contrary to what many assume about #MeToo being a threat to men, we have a *very long* way to go, before millions of women can come out of their shame to raise the complaints that they should.

- The next reason is the fear of judgement and ostracism. We discussed this aspect earlier, and the point cannot be emphasized enough. The tendency of 'the others' to take sides and pass judgements based on assumptions is the biggest injustice to facts of a case. Some of the common judgements are:

  - The woman is a 'B grade', 'small time' so-and so
  - The woman is looking for a payout

This kind of rhetoric, by both men and women, makes one wonder if there is a legal perquisite specified in the law for a woman to be A-grade in her profession to raise grievances. Interestingly, when Gwyneth Paltrow, admittedly an 'A-grade' actor, had to speak on Harvey Weinstein, she hesitated to do so publicly at the beginning and sought to find out if many women could speak out together.[18] She was already dealing with a controversy with her fashion brand and did not want to add to the controversy. She feared that her story will be treated as 'trashy tabloid expose'. Even an 'A-grade' career woman could not speak out without apprehensions about her credibility being questioned; one can only imagine the plight of millions of 'B, C...Z grade women', as they are called, by 'the others' (i.e., all of us). This is why women *don't* speak up more

---

[18] https://www.insider.com/gwyneth-paltrow-hesitate-to-accuse-harvey-weinstein-goop-controversy-made-2019-9

often. The point on 'women looking for payout' leads one to wonder if it was indeed such a lucrative payday, how come millions of women, who have experienced sexual harassment in the hands of rich and powerful men, suffer in silence? In professionals like Alisha's case, a typical discrediting happens under the guise of 'she wasn't given the promotion she wanted, so the complaint is retribution.' Axel exploited this typical mindset in creating that perception with HR, before Alisha realized she had been set-up. We must introspect as 'others' when we take this line of thinking, on our assumptions about the capability of women. Are women not capable of getting promoted or earning money on their merit that they must resort to such a painful and arduous path as raising a sexual harassment complaint? Do such allegations make sense? Now, let's say a woman is ambitious. Does presence of ambition in a woman make her less credible? Does it automatically follow that an ambitious woman raises a sexual harassment complaint only because she wants to realize her ambitions? In fact, an ambitious woman might choose to swallow the bitter pill and not raise a complaint. The next point explains why.

- The third reason women don't speak up is that once they make a sexual harassment complaint, that is all they are known by. That is all that 'the others' want to know and talk about them. It becomes the most defining aspect about them—'a victim of sexual harassment' or 'the one that complained'. This also translates to real career challenges for women. The writing on the wall is—no one wants to hire someone who raised a sexual harassment complaint. This is why it takes exceptional courage for women to fight for justice. Our hypothesis is perhaps this is why women who may have nothing more to lose are more likely to speak up, while those who have things to lose in the process stay quiet; that is, women at the very top and bottom of their career may be in a relatively easier position to speak than those in the middle, which is the majority. This goes back to our point on role of leadership in prevention of sexual harassment. Until we reach the day when leaders take a stand that no woman who has raised a sexual harassment complaint will be discriminated against during hiring and promotion, we are light years away from women feeling comfortable to seek justice. This is why women speak only when they are unable to take the trauma any more or have the support of many other women speaking up. This should answer the question of 'why didn't the woman speak earlier', 'why are they speaking now suddenly, all at once?'

- The final reason why women avoid seeking justice is the process of justice itself. Contrary to what many imagine that it is just the matter of raising a complaint, the redressal process is very tedious. The experience of sexual harassment itself drains out energy, hope, self-esteem, focus and time. Seeking justice for it is additionally taxing on all those parameters. Raising complaints, providing evidence, dealing with gossip takes a toll on resources, mind and soul. All of this is without any promise of justice. We go back to the instance we shared at the beginning of this chapter, where the business leader talks about a senior HR person helping a senior leader accused of sexual harassment, avert arrest. These are real cases. If women don't feel confident about the process' credibility, they may be further discouraged from going through the additional pain of the process, that comes with no guarantee of justice. This is why we said earlier, in the section Redressal Is Not Equal to Prevention, that a credible redressal process can act as a deterrent to sexual harassment. Organizations, whether in India or the USA, are far from achieving that level of credible, impartial and fair redressal system. We might hazard a guess that perhaps this is why women resort to a social media #MeToo, instead of filing a formal complaint. Often, we quip, 'If she is serious, why didn't she go to the police?' The question seems to be dismissive of the inhibitions and mental block women may have to visit a police station, which is not exactly like going to a coffee shop. Perhaps, this makes women more comfortable with reporting a #MeToo on social media, from the comfort of their home, where they can put forth their story, in the court of public opinion, hoping for some support. It also provides some protection from powerful individuals influencing the redressal process in their favour. Many women first report an incident on social media, then follow it with a formal complaint, probably to ensure that their case is not sidelined. This should help us overcome the ill-informed perception of 'women do #MeToo for publicity'.

All the above was the long answer to 'Is #MeToo a weapon against men?' The short answer is, #MeToo is not even a tiny tool sufficient to safeguard women, let alone be a weapon against men. It's not that #MeToo is insignificant. It's just that the problem is of a mammoth scale, in comparison. For every woman who has shared a #MeToo experience, there are tens-of-thousands of women who haven't. The number of prosecutions resulting from #MeToo has been low, as it's difficult to establish facts of incidents that happened decades ago. Famous prosecutions like that of Harvey Weinstein and Larry Nassar were enabled by testimonies of multiple victims. For solo complaints, legal battles become an uphill task. #MeToo is still too small an aberration in the pattern. Far from being a weapon, given the scale of changes required, it is a mere twig of hope in the septic sea of widespread sexual harassment.

Role of Women in Prevention of Sexual Harassment

No one took her seriously. She had a big mouth and a loose talker. She indulged in open flirting with men. Being a bubbly girl, in her early 20s and hardworking, people overlooked her chatter as harmless banter. In her farewell thankyou speech, she pointed at all the department heads and joked, 'I have slept with all of them' (it was indeed a joke, to the best of our knowledge). Let's call the girl, Anne.

Now, reverse the gender and turn Anne to Andy. Let's say Andy jokes in this farewell speech, pointing at all female heads of departments, 'I have slept with all of them'. Is it still the same harmless banter, or did something change in the dynamics of the situation? A few year ago, I had written an article on LinkedIn titled[19] 'She Has Good Figure: Why Creating a Safe Workplace Takes More Than Sexual Harassment Policy'. It was about the many too-small-to-report harassment incidents

[19] https://www.linkedin.com/pulse/she-has-good-figure-why-creating-safe-workplace-takes-swati-jena

that sexual harassment policy cannot tackle. This goes back to our argument on *mindset of no* earlier in the chapter. Many readers commented on the post appreciating the perspective. However, few said that it did not talk about 'the other side', perhaps implying the men's side of the story. I have come across such comments on many social posts and heard men mention it in workshops and conversations. They seldom elaborate the questions they think should be explored on 'the other side'. At times, we hear things like, 'But what about men getting harassed?' So, lets discuss a little bit about 'the other side', and put women on the hot seat. The questions we will explore are:

- What is the role of women in prevention of sexual harassment?
- Are there things women do, to hurt the cause of tackling sexual harassment?
- Can women be abusers too?
- What about men getting abused?
- How do we make sense of sexual harassment in light of the above?

One of the solutions often talked about, to counter bro culture and resulting cases of sexual harassment, is to 'induct more women' in the teams and leadership. There are fundamental assumptions we make about women, while proposing that idea:

- Women don't perpetuate, aid or abet sexual harassment, they are fundamentally against it
  (they are sort of nicer people)
- A woman understands another woman's plight better

Let's look closer into both those assumptions.

First, sexual harassment is often equated to an abuse of power. Sexual crimes are often described, unlike other crimes, as crimes to control and subdue. If that be the case, women at this point in history are indeed far less likely to participate in sexual harassment than men, given their low-power status in society. In future, when that power equation shifts, it will be interesting to observe if the 'fairer sex' does better than men, in not letting power corrupt them. This makes for an interesting subject of research for social psychologists. However, can we use the generalized assumption, women-are-less-likely-to-participate-in-sexual-harassment-than-men, to conclude that simply adding more women leaders will help prevent sexual harassment?

In HSBC's Mike Picarella case, we mentioned earlier, the perpetrator of sexual harassment was a senior executive at the bank, a woman. The article gives the context that the executive had to fit into the existing boy's culture and ended up becoming 'one of them'. She would routinely engage in sexual talk and particularly harass a junior in Mike's team, another woman. The junior would be asked to accompany the executive to client meetings and parties and offered as a sexual bait. The executive would further engage in gossip about this at work. This was an alleged case of a woman harassing a woman and a man. We have highlighted the issue of women feeling compelled to fit into the bro culture, earlier in the book. That holds good for sexual harassment as well. At colleges with cultures of severe ragging, female students also participate in ragging junior females, just as harshly or more, in order to fit into the boy's gang. These female students, with that kind of mindset, go on to become successful professionals and be tasked with being guardians of prevention of sexual harassment. In widespread cases of HR towing the line of business leaders in protecting offenders, especially when they are in senior roles, statistically, more HR professionals are women. We have shared anecdotes where female HR directors, who are members of POSH committee indulge in gossip mongering. Their gender does not stop them from being party to subverting the grievance redressal process. Hence, we cannot make the blanket assumption that mere addition of women leaders or professionals will improve the sexual harassment situation. We need the *right kind of women and men* take up leadership positions, who are willing to role model and build the right culture.

Secondly, the assumption, or rather expectation, that a woman will empathize with another woman's plight better need not always be true. A factor we overlook in female-to-female dynamics is 'familiarity breeds contempt'. Women could, at times, be less empathetic to other women as a result of that. We googled 'trolling *by* women on social media'. It's almost as if Google itself was in denial, and all search results were talking about 'trolling *of* women on social media'. It's like we don't even ask that question. Finally, we found someone who seemed to have studied this.[20] UK think tank Demos analysed 10,000 tweets targeted at 6,500 users. It was found that 50 per cent of the trollers were women. The use of 'slut' and 'whore' by women for women was common. It might be naïve to generalize the findings to all of social media, without further studies of larger sample sizes, especially given that it's difficult to verify gender of profiles. However, we can safely conclude that women do participate in actively demeaning other women, whether or not the frequency is at par with male abusers.

There are two implications of this. First, rooting out the problem of sexual harassment will need deep introspection on

---

[20] https://www.cosmopolitan.com/uk/reports/news/a43626/women-half-online-trolls/

the part of women as well, on the role they play as colleagues, leaders, in HR. Second, we cannot afford to blindly trust just about any woman with the responsibility of driving prevention and redressal of sexual harassment without assessing their capability and mindset, in the same way as we should do for men. Third, women will need to take more responsibility in defining and communicating their boundaries at home, in society and workplace. It's not going to be easy, and they will continue to be shamed in the foreseeable future, by men and women. However, if we are serious about creating an environment where we can work, have good conversations and go back home safely, then women will need to bite the bullet and speak up. This also means Anne will need to be counselled on her loose talk and harmless banter at workplace, in the same way as an Andy in her place.

This brings us to the unanswered question, 'What about men getting harassed?' Let us complicate the question, before we answer it. This question is often asked on social media by men, as a counter to #MeToo and women sharing their stories. The tone is typically argumentative, and the question is, in some way, meant to cancel out 'women getting harassed'. The base assumption in the question is that if men are harassing women, then women are harassing men. This question represents the biggest folly in the sexual harassment narrative, that is, looking at it from binary lenses. So, here are more sub-questions:

1. Yes, men face harassment too, but who is harassing men? Women or men themselves?
2. What about women harassing women? Does that happen as well?

The issues of male or LGBT community harassment is under-represented in the narrative. In fact, organizations and those incharge of managing sexual harassment might be ill-equipped to handle such scenarios. Any man getting harassed, by another man or woman, in no way negates any women getting harassed. It's not that we can focus only on one, at the cost of other. Sexual harassment of anyone, irrespective of where they are on the gender continuum, is a matter that needs attention. Recurring questions of 'what about male harassment' only shows we have taken a narrow view of sexual harassment, focusing mostly on men-to-women harassment, ignoring men-to-men, women-to-men and women-to-women harassment. The scale of each type of harassment may vary. But every person deserves protection from harassment, whether or not that occurs frequently. Therefore, just as much we want men to change, we must reflect on the role of women in being party to and preventing sexual harassment. Which brings us to our last point: Sexual harassment was never about women versus men.

#MeToo Isn't 'Battle of the Sexes'

Genuine critics along with those seeking to discredit #MeToo often state examples of how the movement is used to bring powerful men down. Now, let's say that happens in a few cases. Here's what it does or does not mean.

- In principle, every law on this earth has been abused by those who can. If we want to have a real conversation on misuse of sexual harassment laws, we must begin with accepting the universal follies of human nature. We can realistically accept that people may try to exploit the law. So, let's say a politician used a woman to make false sexual harassment complaint to discredit his rival. What does that establish? Does it prove that another woman raising a genuine grievance against a politician is making a false accusation? Or that all complaints must be discredited on the basis of few cases of misuse? Men and women abuse laws all the time. Does it mean there are no genuine grievances and all the laws anywhere in the world should be done away with? No. Therefore the argument of misuse of #MeToo is naïve and misdirected.

- Second, claims of misuse of sexual harassment laws are used to pit women against men. But it doesn't work that way. In the chapter 'Equal, Not Same', we shared the example of a man using the 'woman card'. Much in the same way, fake sexual harassment complaints involve both women and men—whether their husbands, next of kin, business partners or in case of political or business rivalry, the man who commissions the fake complaint. Therefore, it is not one gender versus the other. It is people who misuse the law for personal gain, both men and women, and people who don't—again, both men and women.

#MeToo is a movement for anyone who felt too marginalized, too afraid to speak, irrespective of gender. It's up to us, to make sure that we listen with respect, seek to understand and push for an effective mechanism to deal with grievances swiftly and fairly. Men, whether straight or gay, must also find the courage to come out with their stories. Many industries such as entertainment, media and fashion are known to have rampant harassment of men as much as women.

#MeToo is not about women versus men. It never was. It is about men and women, who perpetuate, aid, abet abuse of power, versus men and women who seek to have a safe workplace both for themselves and others. It is about men and women who shift accountability to others versus men and women who are willing to introspect their role in creating a culture of safety. It is about men and women who mock anyone trying to say, 'I am not okay with this', versus men and women who respect and accept an expression of no. It is about leaders who pay lip service to prevention of sexual harassment versus leaders who are really committed to it.

Safety is a prerequisite for any organization—whether diverse or not. Especially those who declare diversity as their goal must reconsider their entire approach to prevention of sexual harassment before they can even talk about diversity. It starts at the top, it starts with mindset, it starts with willingness to tackle sexual harassment without tokenism.

BIG IDEAS

1. *Harassment is a continuum:* Women experience many too-small-to-complain cases of harassment, which go undetected. Organizations must widen its definition of harassment and build mechanisms to tackle them.

2. *'Mindset of no' is key to prevention:* Determining consent is necessary to the redressal process. However, building a culture where people can freely express what they are not okay with (mindset of no), without being shamed and ostracized, is the key to prevention of sexual harassment.

3. *Prevention needs separate focus than redressal:* Despite using the word 'prevention', most organizations focus on redressal and communication of redressal process, with a view to being legally compliant. Prevention requires a separate set of interventions and different skill set.

4. *Leaders need to be above the board:* Executive team needs to lead by example in role modelling behaviours and show concrete commitment by holding senior business leaders accountable in case of complaints against them and ensure zero retaliation against those who speak up.

5. *HR needs to be equipped and empowered:* HR may be constrained due to organization structure to act against business leaders who hold sway. A dotted-line reporting to the board may be considered for the safety-related accountabilities. Specific skills required for prevention must also be built in the HR team.

6. *'Low number of complaints' is a metric of denial:* Sexual harassment is a grossly under-reported grievance in organizations. Tracking 'number of complaints' as an indicator of safety is misleading. More meaningful metrics must be looked into separately for redressal and prevention.

7. *Induction of more women won't necessarily reduce harassment:* Despite popular assumption, women too might be prone to perpetuating and supporting harassment in positions of power. It's necessary to find the right kind of women and men for leadership roles.

8. *#MeToo is not women versus men:* Reducing #MeToo to a gender war hurts the cause of tackling sexual harassment. There are both men and women who abuse the process for personal gain and men and women who work towards a safe workplace for themselves and others. #MeToo should give voice to anyone who has faced harassment, irrespective of gender.

Bias Is Pervasive

*Our comforting conviction that the world makes
sense rests on a secure foundation, namely, our almost
unlimited ability to ignore our ignorance.*

—Daniel Kahneman, Psychologist, Economist and a
Nobel Prize winner in economics

This is an interesting story that a senior executive at a start-up
that had attained 'unicorn' status recently told us:

I was sitting in a workshop on diversity that was specially
organized for the leadership team by the head of learning and
development, who also informally doubled up as a kind of
chief diversity evangelist. Some of the founders failed to turn
up. Knowing them, it did not mean that they were not open to
diversity. From what I knew of them, it just meant they thought that
you didn't need to attend a workshop to understand the obvious!
For them, being open to diversity was no different from being
ethical and fair! They may, perhaps, have been naïve and had
shut their mind to what they thought were 'new-fangled' ideas. Or
maybe they were simply uncomfortable opening up and debating
a contentious topic in an open workshop in a democratic set-up.

An attitude of 'what I don't know does not matter' reflects eventually as a 'not invented here' syndrome. Such companies are generally scared of hiring smart people because smart people would come in and tell the company what to do. And if by chance they ended up hiring smart people, they would tell them what to do or pay lip service to 'listening' instead of genuinely learning new things from them. This executive further told us, 'This attitude of "what I don't know does not matter" resulted in lost opportunities for our company; and competitors successfully built very valuable businesses in adjacent categories right under our nose.' The inability to recognize that you have some blind spots and acknowledge that others may be seeing what you don't can eventually harm business. Therefore, an ability to harness dissent begins with an open mindset. We have discussed this at length in the chapter 'Dissent and Diversity'.

He continued the story:

The rest of the management team and some of the more senior mid-level managers were present at the workshop. During the course of the discussion, one of the management members, who was perceived as soft-spoken and benign, smugly remarked with a sly smirk that women tend to be more conscious about their appearance and often preen before entering a meeting. It was a Freudian slip, and like all Freudian slips, it was a subconscious thought. There was stunned silence. He didn't even know how to be politically correct! Even if you have worked all along in male-dominated companies, it was difficult to imagine that someone could be so blindsided to believe that the comment would draw enthusiastic approval from the men, and coy smiles from the women, around the table. Seeing how dumbstruck everyone was, he quickly realized what he had said and beat a hasty retreat.

Women jumped at the comment, including the ones who would have deferred to authority under normal circumstances. In the face of hostility towards the comment, including from the male members, he was profusely apologetic and quickly accepted that he was wrong. Obviously, the fear of being seen as regressive was what made him retract, but deep-seated beliefs don't go away like that. They just get concealed and disguised better. One of the women had to actually point out that in reality most women go out of their way to look natural because of such biases their male colleagues carried.

And this was a company where there were explicit policies against discrimination and where many male leaders clearly articulated that they wanted women to advance in their careers, but the flippant comment smacked of a deep-rooted bias in the mind of the individual.

Most outwardly balanced and progressive individuals, and companies, can carry prejudices that are never brought to the fore excepting in situations like these when the guard is down. These companies can otherwise come across as extremely benevolent and fair. But when it comes to evaluation of women leaders, they tend to carry deep-seated biases like the one that surfaced in the workshop, or others such as—they are 'overly aggressive' or 'overly emotional' or 'overly given to tears', which imply a 'not like us' syndrome. They are tolerant, and even supportive, of women as long as the women don't question the patronizing attitude or demonstrate ambition.

The Subliminal Persuasion

I (Hari) grew up in Sunabeda, a small township in the southern part of India's eastern state of Odisha. Nestled in the middle of the Eastern Ghats, with the nearest rail head being more than a hundred kilometres away, the town and the outer reaches were pristine in their natural beauty. Wordsworth's lines 'Let the moon shine on thee in thy solitary walk; and let the misty mountain winds be free to blow against thee' came to life every day of the year. For those not entirely familiar with India's geography, the Eastern Ghats are a discontinuous range of mountains along India's eastern coast. They run from northern Odisha, through the states of Andhra Pradesh and Tamil Nadu in the south, passing some parts of Karnataka as well as Telangana.

My father worked at the Hindustan Aeronautics Limited (HAL) factory at Sunabeda, which during those years manufactured the MiG-21 engines. These engines were moved by road to Nashik, a town in India's western state of Maharashtra, where they were fitted to the airframes in HAL Nashik. MiG-21 aircraft is a single-engine, single-seater, multirole-fighter/ground-attack aircraft of Russian origin and formed the backbone of the Indian Air Force for several decades. During the later years, due to unavailability of quality spare parts, there were a series of accidents and the aircraft attained unparalleled disrepute. HAL was one of India's premier PSUs. India's PSU townships were some of the best places for children to grow up in—company run schools that were highly subsidized, large playgrounds, lazy Sunday mornings, neatly laid-out neighbourhoods, along with a cosmopolitan and liberal culture. One got to celebrate India's incredible diversity and experience the common threads that held the seemingly diverse elements in one single piece. No wonder India has been referred to at different times as a subcontinent and a salad bowl.

I studied in a co-ed school and saw teachers of both genders in equal numbers. Most of the lady teachers were wives of

HAL officers. The HAL hospital had just one lady doctor. She was a graceful and stylish young woman, and we had never seen her husband for a very long time. We had imagined that he would be an equally smart and fashionable young man to be married to someone like her. When we got to see him, we were disappointed. He was inelegant and clumsy. The nursing staff was largely women, mostly from the southern state of Kerala. There were no women in the HAL factory, neither on the shop floor nor in the engineering and design division. The only woman who worked in the factory was a receptionist. She was single, wore makeup and was good-looking. Some neighbours looked at her as if she were a loose woman and some others as if she was an alien from outer space. No woman drove a powered vehicle in town, until an officer from the Indian Air Force was deputed to HAL. His wife would drive a scooter of Italian make (Vespa) and none of us could take our eyes off her when she drove by.

Some of the ideas that unconsciously took shape, and root, in the collective psyche of the children that grew up in the town were: Girls had an equal right to education as the boys, but women should be happy being housewives and supporting their husbands and children (Betty Friedan's *The Feminine Mystique*). It was perfectly normal for them not to be working outside the home. It was alright for women to work as nurses and teachers, and maybe as doctors too, but not as engineers in the factory. The factory and the engineering office were an exclusive male bastion. Women who were single, worked in a male-dominated workplace and wore makeup were loose characters. On the other hand, men were the bread earners. They had the freedom to pursue any career—teaching, medicine, surgery, engineering, operations or anything else one could think of. These were some of the unconscious opinions and viewpoints that children of my generation in the township grew up with.

It is interesting how opinions tend to form at a very early stage in life by what you see around you. Most of these are formed quite unconsciously. It is quite likely that nobody explicitly drills these into your head or even hints at these. They are based on what we see every day. Seeing is believing may sound clichéd, but the wisdom behind a cliché remains elusive until you go through something that suddenly transforms the cliché from the commonplace to the extraordinary.

Unconscious Bias: Boon Turned Bane

Daniel Kahneman's book *Thinking, Fast and Slow* is a real masterpiece. He demonstrates beyond doubt that we are not the epitome of rational thinking we assume ourselves to be. This book is a *must-read* for anyone who wants to understand the tricks the human mind plays on us all the time. Many of these tricks did serve a purpose during the course of evolution, and some still do. But most of them are well past their expiry date, and in today's world, they cause more harm than good.

Unconscious bias based on any factor (gender, race, colour, language, etc.) is a set of unintentional, unconscious and involuntary mental associations based on that factor. These associations stem from traditions, upbringing, values, culture and conditioning. Such unconscious and instantaneous associations come in the way of a more thoughtful assessment of individuals and instead result in decisions based on stereotypes. Organizations need to take steps to counteract these biases. These unconscious biases are as harmful, if not more, as explicit sexism or discrimination. And the reason is simple. You can act on explicit sexism and discrimination because it is easy to spot, whereas, most of us fail to spot unconscious bias, and we are victims and perpetrators at the same time.

As per an International Labour Organization (ILO) research note, there is a strong association between women and adjectives such as 'emotional', 'mild', 'pleasant', 'sensitive', 'warm', 'affectionate' and 'friendly', and between men and adjectives such as 'dominant', 'achievement-oriented', 'ambitious', 'self-confident', 'rational', 'tough' and 'aggressive'. This is an unconscious and automatic association created over decades through a combination of various factors. The strange thing is that this association exists in most parts of the world. If a job description is peppered with words that are associated with men (ambition, dominant, rational, etc.), then men tend to benefit from this unconscious association. Similarly, if there are words associated with women (mild, sensitive, warm), then women tend to benefit from this unconscious association. And job descriptions for most jobs in management are liberally sprinkled with adjectives that are unconsciously associated with men, and from here begins the unconscious bias that men are more suited than women in management roles.

Unconscious bias has deep origins in evolution and, hence, not easy to wish away. The human mind is in constant search for stories. Stories serve a purpose. They make the world look coherent and comprehensible. The brain is extremely proficient at using limited information, and data, to create a coherent story by filling in the missing pieces. The brain of a zebra—or that of a primitive man—can/could almost instantly assemble the image of a lion behind a bush just by observing a few patches of yellow. This gives the zebra a split-second advantage in escaping. But so wonderful and impartial is nature's camouflage (as well as the ability to see through the camouflage) that both the predator and the prey are equally disguised from one another (and equally discoverable by the other). The delicate balance is what aids the survival of both.

The ability to spot patterns quickly with very limited data also helped humans take quick decisions (intuition we called it) in the past and, to an extent, even to this day. But in the world we live in today, the narratives created by these patterns cause more harm than good. The lion, in today's world, has been replaced by characters like the boss, a peer, a competitor, etc. The patterns that the human brain constantly conjures up are more often than not inaccurate and incorrect. Kahneman sums it up beautifully with the quote at the beginning of this chapter: 'Our comforting conviction that the world makes sense rests on a secure foundation, namely, our almost unlimited ability to ignore our ignorance'. Another book that explores this topic beautifully is Dan Ariely's *Predictably Irrational*.

This inexorable quest for a story explains the proliferation of business books that profess to explain in hindsight, for instance, as to why Amazon or Google are such great companies! Theodore Levitt told us in his epochal article—that is part of the mandatory reading list for every student doing a master's in business administration—in the Harvard Business Review titled 'Marketing Myopia', that companies often do not spend enough time understanding what customers really want. He goes on to suggest that if only the buggy whip manufacturers had defined their business as 'transportation', as opposed to defining their business as 'buggy whips', they may have survived. As students, we were all awestruck by the sheer brilliance of this deduction! But we also wondered how they could have survived by merely defining their business as 'transportation'! Could they have survived by morphing into companies that manufactured ignition switches or carburettors for automobiles? But how could companies that understood how to design and manufacture 'buggy whips' begin to ever understand ignition switches! There was nothing common between the two pieces of equipment, excepting a tenuous and fanciful connection in Levitt's mind. The fallacy in Levitt's argument was obvious, but it sounded so elegant and enticing that the casual reader overlooked the absurdity of the conclusion.

Protagonists of diversity have unravelled the perils of unconscious bias and have revealed some of the stories we have told ourselves over the centuries—narratives which are no longer relevant or mostly dysfunctional in the world we live in today. The 'unconscious biases' that most of us carry with us lead us to taking suboptimal, or even totally wrong, decisions. No preparation for diversity can be complete without a mandatory education on unconscious biases that cloud our thinking. Biases that have been reinforced over centuries do not go away overnight just by attending a training session on unconscious biases. This needs continual reinforcement and a deep commitment on the part of leadership to do so.

A popular story on gender bias that is invariably recounted in any discussion on gender bias, in various forms, goes something like this: A father and son get in a car crash and are rushed to the hospital. The father dies. The boy is taken to the operating room and the surgeon says, 'I can't operate on this boy, because he's my son.' Half of those who listen to this story get stumped because they cannot imagine that the surgeon could be a woman and therefore the surgeon is the boy's mother.

Unconscious biases that one experiences at the workplace are culture specific and vary by country and geography. However, the most common ones are around 'not like us', 'age', 'education', 'gender', 'skin colour', 'communication style' and 'culture fit'. We have discussed some of these extensively in other chapters. In the chapter titled 'Does Diversity Really Help Business', we have discussed the bias rooted in the 'not like us' syndrome and 'culture fit' extensively. We have discussed bias centred around 'age' and 'education' in the chapter titled 'Beyond Tolerance'. It takes great effort to get over these biases. It needs a combination of a deep commitment to 'inclusion' and also a willingness to introspect and acknowledge the bias we display unconsciously in our everyday life.

Two groups of tech leaders evaluate identical resumes for the role of 'principal architect'. Half the group is told that the name of the candidate is Nandini and the other half are told the candidate is Nandan. Would you feel surprised that Nandini is perceived as being less competent for the job than Nandan? Many companies have, therefore, resorted to redacting names of candidates and any other data that could trigger unconscious bias from a resume. Hiring managers, who want to beat the system, however, can find ways of figuring out this information. Therefore, this needs to be reinforced with other methods.

Choice of Words: How It Reinforces Bias

Research has shown that a seemingly innocuous statement like 'women are as good as men in leadership roles' could potentially imply that men are normally better than women in leadership roles, and a statement like 'men are as good as women in nursing roles' would imply that women are normally better than men in nursing roles. There is also strong evidence that men tend to associate more with words like 'competitive' 'driven', 'under pressure', 'whatever it takes', 'high performance', 'proven', 'decisive', 'strong', etc., than women would. Why men associate more with these words than women could be for a variety of reasons, but almost all the reasons have to do with conditioning. Therefore, use of these words in job descriptions tends to attract a higher percentage of men than would be the case by use of gender-neutral words and phrases and, in the process, reinforce the social conditioning. It is exactly the opposite with phrases like 'warm', 'friendly', 'supportive', 'committed', 'responsible', and use of these words tends to attract a higher percentage of women. Language that statistically alters the percentage of women and men who apply for a job could be considered gender biased. Just so everyone is clear, many men can be 'warm' and 'supportive' more than doing 'whatever it takes' and yet be attracted to the latter phraseology; and many women could be very comfortable 'under pressure' more than being 'supportive' and yet may have an affinity for the latter terminology. So, comfort or affinity with specific terminology is no indication of actual displayed behaviours.

Language is a reflection of culture and culture in turn shapes language. It is not surprising therefore that companies tend to use words that reflect their culture and, hence, automatically attract people who fit that culture. Some companies may liberally use words like 'hustlers', 'rock stars', 'ninjas', 'kick ass', while some companies may totally avoid these phrases or words. Does a company flaunt its culture of hustle, late nights and after-office-hours bonding? Watch out for these terms very carefully. Culture bias starts unconsciously and well before hiring managers meet candidates; and language, starting from how the job descriptions are written, could convey coded cultural messages.

Textio is a Seattle-based start-up that helps companies write job descriptions that are neutral around gender, race, etc., and, in the process, help attract a larger number of candidates. It's alarming to note that that as per Textio, 100 per cent of the words favoured by Amazon, Google, Microsoft, Netflix and Uber tend to attract male candidates. Textio also found that

Amazon used the word 'wickedly' 33 times more frequently in their job descriptions than the next closest company; similarly, 'maniacal' appeared 11 times more frequently in Amazon job descriptions. According to Textio, 'wickedly' and 'maniacal' statistically result in a higher proportion of applications from men. While framing a question, a hiring manager at Amazon may state to a candidate, 'You would be surrounded by people that are wickedly smart and ....'[1]

A tool like Textio can help create a gender-neutral vocabulary. While this is necessary, it is not sufficient, because the gender-loaded vocabulary reflects deep cultural biases that need to be overcome.

Let's assume Amazon, Google and others have chosen to use a set vocabulary that tends to attract a specific set of individuals. What's wrong with this if that's what they want and that's what they believe is good for them? If they are unconsciously using such vocabulary, then it spells trouble and they need to listen to the experts and be guided by them. However, if they are consciously trying to attract a particular set of individuals, then isn't it their choice? Who is anyone to pass judgement? Is it, or is it not, as simple as this? Our position on this is that in the ultimate analysis, diversity and inclusion is slowly becoming a fundamental value, as fundamental as the national motto of France—'liberty, equality, fraternity'—adopted in different forms by several countries. All dictators in history may have also thought that who is anyone to judge them and their autocratic notions? But the people, and history, did judge them. The writing has been on the wall for a while that the world is growing increasingly intolerant of unfair and

---

[1] https://www.inc.com/betsy-mikel/amazon-is-33x-more-likely-to-use-this-wickedly-bizarre-word-in-their-job-descriptions.html

inequitable practices. Organizations that aren't making the effort to draw the line between necessary business choice and compulsive bias are doing so at their own peril.

It's not just about men and women. Every profession tends to develop their own culture that is communicated through a unique vocabulary, phraseology and set of frameworks and constructs. This tends to keep away those who are not familiar or comfortable with this since the feeling they get is 'I don't think I'd fit in.' The vocabulary and phraseology used by venture capital professionals is different from what is used by, say, marketing professionals in an FMCG company. And the vocabulary of early-stage venture capitalists is different from the late-stage venture capitalists. The problem that this 'insular' vocabulary solves is ease and speed of communication, but it could keep away some of the best minds from the profession by creating psychological entry barriers. A good way to access the best talent is to cut out jargon and have a conversation around the underlying problems, ideas and principles.

Fair and Lovely—Duplicity is Ubiquitous

Sometime in June 2020, Hindustan Unilever Limited (HUL—the Indian arm of Unilever) announced that they had repositioned the 'Fair and Lovely' brand from 'fair' to 'glow'. This was both a practical joke and a hoax! Do the attributes of a product change just because you call it something else! If the product helped induce a pastel shade in dark skin, would it stop doing so just by rebranding it from 'fair' to 'glow'?

After exploiting, and reinforcing, the prejudice against dark skin and a dusky complexion for 45 years, the brand gave in to increasing social pressure. HUL Chairman Sanjiv Mehta claimed that the decision to abandon the moniker of 'fair' had nothing to do with the Black Lives Matter movement in the USA and that the timing was just a coincidence. Who would believe that! They had displayed a cavalier attitude to the same demand made by Indian social activists for long by insisting that they were just offering what consumers wanted! They even had the temerity to create a 'Fair and Lovely foundation' to enhance the self-esteem of women in India! It is surprising how large corporates can get away with such brazen disingenuity. Companies, the world over, were being called out for pretending to support social causes like Black Lives Matter but promoting products that promised light skin. This time, the pressure on them to address this dichotomy was immense. We have reflected on the phenomenon of woke-washing in the chapter 'Discrimination and Diversity'.

We would argue that merely taking off the word 'fair' from the brand was nothing short of deception. And the logic is straightforward: If what HUL claimed for 45 years was true (using the product lightens the skin), then the brand (irrespective of what you name it) would continue to lighten the skin. Therefore, what did HUL achieve by renaming the brand and 'repositioning' the brand promise from 'fairness' to 'glow'? Nothing! The product would continue to lighten the skin of its users, and hence the brand continues to promote fair skin and perpetuate the myth of the superiority of light complexion. However, what is more likely is that the product never really induced a light tone in the first place, and HUL fooled and fleeced a billion people for 45 years. In which case, the product had never delivered on its promise.

Therefore, if HUL admits that the product never induced a light tone in dark skin, then it is damned for lying and cheating users for 45 years. If they say that it did induce a light tone, and they have done nothing to change that, excepting dropping the word 'fair', then too it is damned. Therefore, when the same Sanjiv Mehta announced HUL's goal of getting to achieve full gender parity by 2022, one was left wondering whether there was a dichotomy somewhere. To take a charitable view of both HUL and Sanjiv Mehta, the topic is especially confusing given the inherent contradictions. Should a company cater to consumer needs and not bother to judge whether these needs were a result of certain unconscious and not so desirable beliefs (like, say, the superiority of fair skin)? And even reinforce these beliefs through advertising? Or should a company display activism and engage in socially responsible behaviour? These are difficult dilemmas to deal with. We guess the common problem many of these companies face is wanting to come across as socially conscious and responsible but, at the same time, maximize financial returns to their stakeholders by pandering to consumer needs, irrespective of how 'ethically right' these needs may be!

As our friend, Professor Chandradeep Maitra of IIM Calcutta, wrote in afaqs.com, the fair thing for HUL to do would have been to (a) completely and immediately discontinue the brand, not just rebrand it and remove the word 'fair' from it (while everyone already knows the brand and product, what's it's formulation, what it's meant to do and continue selling and profiting from it), while using another surrogate word like *'glow' or 'radiance'* (and their vernacular equivalents) that everyone would easily understand. It's not just the superficial naming of the brand but the underlying product, formulation and core promise that is at the root of the larger problem, and (b) publicly own up and apologize for creating and selling these brands and variants all these years. In this entire episode, HUL's double standards became visible. It is not just about HUL. Many other companies displayed similar duplicity in terms of their public posture for social causes and the prejudices they created and reinforced through their products.

Logical Fallacies—The Twin of Unconscious Bias

A logical fallacy is defined as an invalid or otherwise faulty reasoning in the construction of an argument. It is quite easy to be taken in by fallacious logic unless you train your mind to sniff it out. Logical fallacies are deployed by people both unconsciously and intentionally in arguments, sometimes innocently and sometimes with mala fide intention. Politicians have used these logical fallacies to attack opponents. For instance, when a rival politician attacks the economic policies of the party in power by saying, 'What would a finance minister who has never had a formal degree understand about economics?' is saying nothing about the economic policy of the government but is an attack on the personality of the finance minister. This logical fallacy is commonly referred to as 'ad hominem'. Of all the logical fallacies, this is possibly the most crass and petty.

Many of these logical fallacies have been generously deployed in arguments 'for' as well as 'against' diversity, and it is important to see through these and avoid being tricked. We will briefly discuss a few.

There was a common belief during the Middle Ages in Europe that lice were good for health because lice were rarely found on sick people. The truth behind this was that lice are sensitive to temperature, and even a slight fever would induce the lice to leave a host. Lice deserted those who became sick. Therefore, the belief that lice were essential for good health was not true! This is an example of the 'false causation' fallacy also referred to as the 'correlation–causation' fallacy. Another often quoted example that points to a false sense of causality is this: Ice cream sales correlate with death due to drowning. This does not indicate any causality obviously. However, the most plausible explanation is that ice cream sales spike in summer and that's the season when people go out in large numbers for swimming; and hence both are outcomes (spike in sales of ice cream and deaths due to drowning) that are closely related (and correlated) to each other because of their independent connection with a common underlying cause or set of causes, with neither 'causing' the other.

Use of the false causation fallacy can impress and persuade folks who don't have a deep grounding in logic or statistics. Over the last decade or so, this has been called out so often that smart speakers and writers, even when they intentionally use this fallacy to imply something, are quick to add that 'correlation does not imply causation', hoping of course that the listener (or reader) is not attentive to the disclaimer in fine print. We have discussed examples of how liberal doses of this fallacy has been used in arguments in favour of diversity and, on some occasions, in arguments against diversity. Consultants like McKinsey and Boston Consulting Group have been at the forefront on this.

Some studies show that companies run by women CEOs deliver lesser shareholder returns than those run by male CEOs, and some studies show that companies with gender diversity in their top management deliver better returns than those without gender diversity. Neither of these correlations indicate causality.

Another logical fallacy is the 'anecdotal evidence fallacy'. A statement like, 'I have heard that women who are nominated to boards to meet diversity standards or requirements are subpar', smacks of this fallacy. We discussed this in the chapter 'Women in Senior Management'.

It is important to spot these fallacies and call them out. Poor arguments using logical fallacies are very common, but if you are cognizant of these, they are reasonably easy to spot; and with awareness, and some mental training, you can avoid being fooled.

In conclusion: Bias is all around us. Bias is prejudice of some form. It could be both conscious and unconscious. Unconscious bias is also referred to as implicit bias. Unconscious biases can remain suppressed and may surface under stress or when teams collaborate on projects with tight timelines and handoffs. Cross-cultural contexts need seamless collaboration between teams, and this scenario is also the perfect condition for nurturing and feeding unconscious bias. Leaders need to, therefore, play an important role in helping people see their own biases and in overcoming them. The topic of implicit bias has been extensively researched and well understood now. Training programs that expose people to their implicit biases are now easily available.

BIG IN THE CHAPTER
IDEAS

1. *Biases about women are deep seated and unconscious:* Unconscious biases are difficult to detect and accept. Companies, otherwise benevolent towards women, may not realize they are being patronizing and unaccepting of women demonstrating traits such as ambition.

2. *Biases take root early in a person's life:* No one explicitly gets instructed on stereotypes and biases. As children, the mind is unconsciously conditioned based on what they see around them.

3. *Biases can be both boon and bane:* Some biases can lead to positive association for certain job roles and be beneficial. On the flip side, the same association can lead to prejudice in selecting candidates who don't fit the gender stereotype.

4. *Unconscious bias can lead to conflicting values and double standards:* Many organizations demonstrate duplicity in behaviours by asserting vocal support to something and acting in direct contradiction to it while conducting business.

5. *Logical fallacies feed into biases:* Common fallacies include confusing correlation of two things as causation and using anecdotes as evidence rather as means to understand something.

Beyond Tolerance

*The only way in which a human being can make some
approach to knowing the whole of a subject is by
hearing what can be said about it by persons of every
variety of opinion, and studying all modes in which it
can be looked at by every character of mind. No wise
man ever acquired his wisdom in any mode but this; nor
is it in the nature of human intellect to become wise in
any other manner.*

—John Stuart Mill

Inclusion in its most pristine form is acceptance of individuals
for who they are. In the early stages of the worldwide push for
diversity and inclusion, the primary focus was on gender, race
and ethnicity. Over a period of time, the theme was extended
to include diversity in age, nationality, political beliefs, sexual
orientation, mother tongue, education, life experiences, etc.
The wider the definition of what you consider important, the
more difficult it is to select or comply. Let's take an example.
When you recruit an enterprise salesperson, what do you look
for? You might look for a strong achievement orientation, an
ability to deal with rejection, see a problem from a customer
point of view and have a consultative approach to selling.
If you stretch the definition of a good salesperson to include

honesty, truthfulness, articulation, collaboration and all the other good human values you could think of, you are in effect making your own life difficult. This is neither necessary nor helpful. Prioritization is important. The lack of prioritization, in this context, would dilute the core requirements of the job just as the lack of prioritization in providing feedback reduces the efficacy of the key messages.

To some extent, this is what has been happening on the D&I discourse.

Let's take how companies view diversity in 'education' when it comes to staffing roles. Most companies specify a particular education requirement (like say a bachelor's in accounting or a bachelor's in engineering) as a prerequisite for a role. Some people have argued that this goes against the grain of diversity since what matters is the ability to do a job well, and that is not necessarily correlated with the type of education a candidate may have had. The truth is that you can always find someone who does not possess these degrees but is fully competent to do the job; but to be able to discover this individual, or a handful of such individuals, you need to cast the net really wide. This would slow down the hiring process. So, organizations have used education as a 'filter'. The trade-off that organizations have consciously made is between speed-to-hire and getting a perfect candidate at the perfect price point. Now, does this go against the grain of diversity? Are candidates at liberty not to disclose their education and yet expect to be considered for the role? We'll come to this in a bit.

Let's first apply the same argument to 'age'. In a start-up where the founders are, say under the age of 25, would it violate the principles of inclusion if they prefer equally young colleagues and do not spread the net wide enough to identify candidates who are 50 years or older? On a similar note, what about a company, where the management team is all over 50 years of age, that does not spread the net wide enough to look for 35-year olds for the role of a CXO? While there are very competent 35-year olds who are fit to be CXOs, and equally competent 50-year olds fit to be CXOs, their acceptance in a company has generally depended on the demographic profile of the leadership team in the company.

It is easy to take a politically correct position and argue that you should always spread the net wide enough, extend your search process and not layout any education or age barriers. Some organizations have taken these politically correct positions and have baked it into their hiring process. However, even these progressive organizations have not applied this process with equal rigor for entry into the sanctum sanctorum of the organization—the executive team. In these organizations, the recruiter redacts the resumes for the details for age, education, gender, etc. (if they happen to be there) before sending them to the hiring manager. Now, many hiring managers in these organizations have figured out ingenious ways to suss out these details and organizations have learned to train a blind eye to this. So, being politically correct just introduces dishonesty in the system. Instead what is needed is an open discussion to arrive at a pragmatic approach.

When does a pragmatic approach to hiring that tacitly or explicitly calls out education and age restrictions metamorphose to 'exclusion' and 'discrimination'? When leaders in a company forget that these restrictions are not cast in stone and merely serve as a guideline to get to a shortlist quickly. When they begin to blindly turn down candidates who fit all the other criteria, that's when the pragmatism has ossified to discrimination. By focusing on the most visible indicators of diversity such as gender, race and ethnicity, are we ignoring the less visible and, perhaps more foundational, elements of diversity? This is a question that we will try and address in the following section.

Is the Focus on the Visible Indicators of Diversity Misplaced?

The most common imagery associated with the idea of diversity and inclusion is a group of smiling men and women with different racial features and skin colour gathered around a table in a conference room giving the appearance of a diverse, collaborative and well-knit team. At one level, this is a powerful image and succinctly conveys what diversity and inclusion are all about; but like any imagery, it is a bit of an oversimplification and conceals the nuances.

For instance, in countries where radically different skin colours, or races, are not common (like in India, Scandinavian Countries or the Middle East), the readers or participants in D&I training programmes may wonder what diversity in their context means. Or even in countries where a range of skin colour is common, the obvious question is, 'Is there more to diversity than skin colour, gender or race?' By focusing on the visual identifiers of diversity, are these images camouflaging the less obvious but more foundational aspects of diversity? This is an important question, and we'll come to that in a bit. But first, some insight into the difference between the two terms—'diversity' and 'inclusion'.

One of the thought leaders on the topic of diversity and inclusion, Andres Tapia, had observed that 'diversity is the mix and Inclusion is making the mix work'. If you have ever spoken to even an amateur in D&I, you would have heard this in one form or another. When faced with the challenge of explaining an idea that is inherently difficult to comprehend, one of the most powerful approaches is to use an analogy from a different context that is more easily comprehensible; and then use that understanding to create clarity around the original idea. Story tellers, marketers and communicators have used this approach for centuries. We will try and do the same.

In March 2019, St Martin's Press published a book authored by Safi Bahcall titled *Loonshots: How to Nurture the Crazy Ideas That Win Wars, Cure Diseases, and Transform Industries.* This is one of those truly defining books that lucidly explains the recipe and chemistry of 'innovation'. Also, it offers parallels one can draw in entirely different contexts. One framework that Bahcall uses in the book to explain the enablers of innovation is helpful in understanding diversity and inclusion. Bahcall says that for organizations to innovate, they need to (a) separate teams that are preparing the organization for the future from teams whose primary focus is running the current business. The nature of their work is different and so is the rhythm and time sensitivity of what they do. Therefore, it is not surprising that these two sets of individuals require different talents, and (b) the quality and intensity of interaction between these two distinct groups needs to be high. The interaction helps develop mutual respect and test new ideas on the ground. And new ideas don't constitute 'innovation' until they are tested and commercialized.

If either of these two conditions is not met, the organization would fail to innovate and would soon become obsolete. If only the first of the two conditions are met, then all great ideas will languish and eventually be buried forever because the group that is responsible for testing these new ideas on the ground is not sufficiently invested in them, and the two teams do not have respect for each other. If only the second condition is met, great ideas are never conceived, and the organization would be lost in noisy incrementalism or caught in a series of 'activity traps'.

The first condition, namely the need for different types of people to perform the two different sets of activities or work, is the equivalent of 'diversity' and the second condition, of creating high quality and mutually respectful interactions and relationships between these two groups, is the equivalent of 'inclusion'. Innovation does not happen without both coming together.

In the context of D&I, diversity without inclusion results in dysfunctional conflict, excessive friction, poor exchange of ideas and bad execution. On the other hand, without inclusion, diversity is worse than homogeneity. Aiming for diversity without creating the groundwork of inclusion is putting the cart before the horse. Bahcall explains that the difference between Steve Jobs in his first stint at Apple before 1985 and in his second stint after 1996 was that he had learned to love both his 'artists' (Jony Ive) and 'soldiers' (Tim Cook) in his second stint. Being the quintessential 'artist' that he was, he had demonstrated utter disdain for the 'soldiers' at Apple in his first stint. He had realized during the intervening years that mutual disrespect and disdain between these two critical parts of the organization was what had proved harmful. We all know that what Apple accomplished during Jobs' second tenure was truly magical. The first stint was dotted with serious incidents of disrespect, conflict and friction which made innovation excruciatingly painful or even impossible.

Right to Equality—A Long and Arduous Journey

Let's come back to the question we raised at the beginning of this chapter: 'Does the excessive focus on the visible identifiers of diversity camouflage the more foundational aspects of diversity?'

Maybe in the world we live in today, it might seem that there are other aspects of diversity that don't get the attention they deserve because of the excessive focus on some of the more visible identifiers of diversity. True, but to be fair, discrimination on the visible identifiers has been rampant until recent times, and therefore, the focus is not entirely misplaced. The world is far from being a fair and equitable place even today. Discrimination on the grounds of gender, race, ethnicity, language, religion, sexual orientation, caste and skin colour has been common and even accepted as fait accompli until recently. While discrimination is banned by law in most civilized parts of the world, society at large is yet to wholeheartedly embrace it in spirit.

It needed concerted effort by heroic and lionhearted leaders to fight these battles. Many of them were ignored, ostracized, physically attacked, mentally tortured and even assassinated. Those born after 1980 were born into a much better world and may not have seen or experienced this first-hand and, hence, might wonder what this fuss is all about. Training on D&I could include a brief history of the long and uphill struggles of different minority groups for equality and fair treatment; and women are not even a minority, but their struggle has been the worst of all and needs to be told separately. Only with an understanding and appreciation of this struggle comes the required empathy and understanding of this emphasis and focus.

Maria Wisława Szymborska was a Polish poet, essayist, translator and recipient of the 1996 Nobel Prize in Literature. Her poem 'Vietnam' powerfully symbolizes the state of women in society. Her only identity was that of a 'childbearing machine'.

'Woman, what's your name?'
'I don't know'

'How old are you? Where are you from?'
'I don't know'

'Why did you dig that burrow?'
'I don't know'

'How long have you been hiding?'
'I don't know'

'Why did you bite my finger?'
'I don't know'

'Don't you know that we won't hurt you?'
'I don't know'

'Whose side are you on?'
'I don't know'

'This is war, you've got to choose'
'I don't know'

'Does your village still exist?'
'I don't know'

'Are those your children?'
'Yes.'

Even in the USA, it was only as late as in 1964 with the passage of the Civil Rights Act 1964 that discrimination based on race, colour, religion, sex or national origin was outlawed. The word 'sex' was not even there in the original version of the Act and was added at the last minute because of intense pressure that the feminist movement, which was then at its peak, had piled on. In fact, even in 1964, the powers given to enforce the provisions of the Civil Rights Act were weak, though these were supplemented during later years. Passage of this Act was not easy, and there was considerable opposition in both the Senate as well as the House of Representatives! As late as in 1994, in the O. J. Simpson (OJ) trial, an open and shut case of double homicide was skilfully sidetracked by the defence into a 'Black celebrity being framed by a racist Los Angeles Police Department' narrative. This trial divided civil society into two—those who believed OJ was innocent and those who believed he was guilty. The fact that the public at large fell for this deceit on the part of the defence so easily and the fact that the majority of the jury believed that OJ was 'not guilty' showed the extent to which society was still polarized, and how easily unscrupulous folks could use it to their advantage and get away with horrific crime.

Most folks would be shocked to hear this, because it goes so much against the common belief about the liberal and progressive nature of civil society in the USA. It would be interesting to note that the USA has lagged behind many countries in the developing world when it came to inclusion, minority rights and treatment of working women. Even to this day, women are not entitled to government mandated paid maternity leave in the USA! There is something called the FMLA (Family and Medical Leave Act, 1993) as per which eligible employees can take up to 12 work weeks of unpaid leave during any 12-month period to take care of a newborn child. In order to be eligible for FMLA leave, an employee must have worked for the employer for at least 12 months, have worked at least 1,250 hours over the past 12 months and work for an employer with at least 50 employees. In contrast, just across the border, Canada has had a liberal policy of providing a year of paid maternity leave. And countries like India have mandated a 26-week paid maternity leave with no constraints. A woman could join a company and proceed on maternity leave the very next day.

The American Dream symbolized equality of opportunity, and that anyone, regardless of the circumstances of birth, could achieve success through risk-taking and perseverance. The USA had attained independence in 1776, and by 1964, the American democracy was nearly 200-years old! The reality was that the great American Dream until recently was exclusively for the privileged!

When India attained independence in 1947, the world had already made progress towards creating a more equal society. A century of colonial rule played a not-so-insignificant role in creating the right legislative framework. The Constitution of India explicitly called out the 'right to equality' as one of the seven fundamental rights that are enforceable under the constitution. However, the reality on the ground, like in most countries that legislated equality, was different and has been changing at an excruciatingly slow pace.

It is interesting to note that where governments had failed, a few private, for-profit companies and businesses showed the way. In India, Tata Steel enacted the eight-hour work day in 1912, the leave with pay policy in 1936, the Workers' Provident Fund Scheme in 1920 and maternity benefit (paid maternity leave) in 1928—all of which were subsequently adopted by the ILO and enacted by law in India! As late as 1960, in the USA, a woman could be legally let go from employment if she became pregnant. The common belief though is that it is the ILO that set standards that the world adopted. Tata Steel has always been a microcosm of a liberal India, and Jamshedpur, the town where the main steel works are located, was built as a secular and harmonious community. The word secular is used to convey an ideology where the state is neutral in matters of religion and is embedded in governance as a structural framework for supporting religious inclusion. Another quote of J. N. Tata speaks volumes of how a visionary leader can show the way:

We do not claim to be more unselfish, more generous or more philanthropic than other people. But we think we started on sound and straightforward business principles, considering the interests of the shareholders our own, and the health and welfare of the employees, the sure foundation of our success.[1]

This single quote is a lifetime of wisdom for any corporate leader!

The plight of women has been particularly appalling and the long road to even basic equality has been arduous. Women's rights movements across the world have made progress, but it is quite a revelation to see how even something as elementary as the right to vote was granted to women decades, or even centuries, after men got that right. A quick summary of how this unfolded in different countries would highlight the extent of the problem and the recency of the changes which, in today's world, most of us take for granted and assume have always existed.

Swiss women won the right to vote in federal elections in 1971! In Australia, non-indigenous women won the right to vote in 1902 and the indigenous Australians didn't get the federal right to vote until 1962. Canada passed a legislation in 1918, expanding suffrage to female citizens but excluding Asian Canadian and aboriginal women, who did not win the right to vote until the 1940s and 1960s, respectively. Women in Greece have had the right to vote since 1952. Japanese women got the right to vote in 1945, thanks in part to Lt Ethel Weed, an American officer who advocated for civil code reform during the American occupation of Japan after the cessation of hostilities in the Asia–Pacific theatre at the end of Second World War. In

---

[1] http://www.tatacentralarchives.com/tata-legacy/recollection.html

France, women became enfranchised through legislation passed in 1944. In the USA, although some states enfranchised women before 1920, the 19th Amendment, which was passed that year, granted all female citizens in the USA the right to vote. From all accounts, in spite of this, it was a well-acknowledged fact that election officials often kept women and people of colour from voting with literacy tests, poll taxes and intimidation. In 1965, the then-President Lyndon B. Johnson signed the Voting Rights Act into law, which made such tactics illegal but did not end them.[2] So, tactics that made it difficult for women and people of colour to vote wasn't even illegal until 1965. Now remember that it takes a long time for a law to percolate down to the ground and get implemented wholeheartedly. You don't have to go much deeper than this to understand how things have been stacked against specific communities, and women in particular, for centuries. Overcoming centuries of bias, discrimination and prejudice on the ground takes far more than mere legislation. The next time one wonders why there is excessive focus on these visible indicators of diversity, it would be helpful to recall the history behind this.

Women at Work

Diversity is multidimensional, but gender is by far the biggest dimension for the simple reason that it is universal, and women are *not* a minority. Therefore, this particular aspect of diversity needs a deeper understanding. Amnesty International, in its charter, has said something that is very interesting and insightful:

When looking at women's rights, it's helpful to have an understanding of feminism. At its core, feminism is the

---

[2] https://www.insider.com/when-women-around-the-world-got-the-right-to-vote-2019-2

belief that women are entitled to political, economic, and social equality. Feminism is committed to ensuring women can fully enjoy their rights on an equal footing with men.[3]

Feminism, for some strange reason, has received some unnecessary flak. Unnecessary because feminism at its core is what Amnesty International has defined it as, namely ensuring women enjoy rights on an equal footing as men. No sane individual could possibly be opposed to it. Therefore, men can, and should, be feminists too! Hence, men who are opposed to feminism can rightfully be seen as being sadistic and women opposed to feminism are probably being masochistic.

Second World War, for the first time, pulled women out of homes on a large scale and thrust them into jobs that were originally exclusive to men. However, after the war came to an end and the men began returning home from the battlefront, this trend lost steam and women were back to being confined at home. Sometime in the early 1960s, when the world was slowly forgetting the war, the feminist movement began gathering momentum and women began organizing themselves and agitating in the USA alongside the Civil Rights Movement by the Blacks. At this point of time, in the USA, a woman was not eligible to hold a credit card unless approved by her husband and could be legally let go of from employment for becoming pregnant.

In 1963, Betty Friedan, a feminist, wrote a book titled *The Feminine Mystique*. The book struck a chord with the women in most of the Western world and went on to inspire change. She coined the term *feminine mystique* to describe the then

---

[3] https://www.amnesty.org/en/what-we-do/discrimination/womens-rights/

widely held belief that women did not need anything other than a happy marriage, passive sexuality, upbringing of children and housework for leading a life of joy and fulfilment. In the social milieu I was a part of in childhood, many of the women in our own lives (mother, aunts and others) explicitly or implicitly endorsed this belief. The extent of brainwashing had reached a level where women themselves advocated this for other women. The reasons for endorsing this belief were many, and one of them was the need to maintain harmony by not upsetting the status quo.

Betty Friedan interviewed hundreds of housewives for her book and discovered that what was perpetuated by the media, and accepted as common wisdom, as the perfect recipe for everlasting happiness and fulfilment, namely an unswerving and unconditional devotion to their husbands and the family, was totally false. Strange, but true, that you needed a rigorous study to conclude the obvious!

She uncovered that unable to attain the feminine mystique, many women spent years with psychologists, who tried to help them adjust to their 'feminine role', or they took to tranquilizers and alcohol to ease their feelings of emptiness. The other notion that has persisted in societies across the globe is that the more educated a woman was, the more unhappy and unfulfilled she was likely to be with her role as a housewife. This was a common theme in the early days of cinema. This observation would be equally true for men too. The more educated a man is, the more frustrated he is likely to be if confined to household chores or other monotonous jobs. Instead of figuring out how society could create fulfilling careers for women, the prescription applied almost universally was to curtail education for women!

It is difficult to believe that Cambridge did not grant degrees to women as late as in 1948. And the only career option for a brilliant English scientist like Cecilia Payne was to become a teacher. Realizing this, she migrated to the USA. She received the first PhD in astronomy from Radcliffe College for her thesis, since even Harvard did not grant doctoral degrees to women. As an interesting sidebar, in her doctoral thesis in 1925, she proposed that the sun was composed largely of hydrogen and helium. Many years later, her 1925 thesis, titled 'Stellar Atmospheres', was famously described by astronomer Otto Struve as 'the most brilliant PhD thesis ever written in astronomy'. However, when Payne's dissertation was reviewed, astronomer Henry Norris Russell, who stood by the theories of American physicist Henry Rowland, dissuaded her from concluding that the composition of the sun was predominantly hydrogen, because it would contradict the current scientific consensus that the elemental composition of the sun and the earth were similar. She was forced to acknowledge that her results were wrong. Russell himself later realized that she was correct when he derived the same results by different means. In 1929, he published his findings in a paper that acknowledged Payne's earlier work and discovery; nevertheless, he is often credited for the conclusions she reached.

Friedan's own solution to the problem was radically different from the prevailing view of the day. She rejected the feminine mystique and suggested that women develop a new 'life plan.' Rather than being treated as a 'career', housework was to be finished as quickly as possible. Friedan further contended that a woman could have a successful career as well as a family. Education, in her estimation, had less to do with reinforcing the feminine mystique than with the outright emancipation of women.

Over a period of time, the feminist movement began getting nuanced. For instance, the early feminist movements were led by White women and a new form of Black feminism emerged, which argued that sexism, class oppression and racism are inextricably bound together, and hence, any attempt by the feminist movement to overlook racial discrimination is bound to fail. The feminist movement began losing steam in 1980 when under Ronald Reagan; there was a push to go back to 'family values' which was a euphemism for confining women in homes. However, at the turn of the millennium, the feminist movement became much more inclusive by highlighting the stories of women's oppression in other parts of the world, especially Asia and Africa. With young women leaders like Yousafzai Malala, a brave young woman from Pakistan, standing up and speaking up, the movement got a lot of teeth. The power of the social media helped women organize, highlight and coordinate their movements globally, creating a huge amplification. However, social media also allowed the opponents of women's equality to hide in anonymity and threaten women with assault and rape and get away. The trolls could unleash their venom without any consequences.

Society has not abandoned the 'feminine mystique' completely. It continues to operate at an unconscious level and, even in this day and age, is the underlying driving force behind some regressive decisions regarding education and marriage.

Role of Literature and Films

I (Hari) recently finished reading two very interesting books. *The Liberation of Sita* by Volga and *The Palace of Illusions* by Chitra Banerjee Divakaruni. Volga is a feminist writer in Telugu and has published more than 50 novels, plays and short-story collections. Chitra Banerjee Divakaruni teaches creative writing at the University of Houston and is an enchanting storyteller who has written several best-selling novels. Volga and Divakaruni are at their sublime best in these two books. These books provide a very powerful insight into possible reasons as to why the world views men and women the way it does. Literature is a powerful medium that can influence people and society and can even change them. Both these authors have taken the epics of the Ramayana and Mahabharata, essentially male-dominated stories, from the perspective of some of the female characters in these stories and provided a fresh set of perspectives that are as daring as they are fascinating. Many of us grew up with a certain understanding of the characters of the key male protagonists in these epics. As a child, I recall reading abridged versions of these epics and remember listening to the various subplots in great detail. But what remains etched in my memory is that these epics were the stories of brave men, their conflicts, their struggles, their values and their wars. Women were just appendages with nothing more than ornamental value and a source of conflict between the male protagonists. In contrast, in Volga's *Liberation of Sita*, it is Sita who embarks on a journey of self-realization after she is abandoned in the jungle, when she was in the family way, by *purushottam* Rama. On this arduous journey, she ends up meeting some of the women characters in the epic like Surpanakha, Ahalya, Renuka and Urmila, who have broken free from their husbands, sons and their notions on chastity, beauty and desire. In the process, she finds unexpected resolution.

After reading these two versions by Volga and Divakaruni, most readers are forced to review their long held opinions about their heroes. I couldn't help wondering whether women have always read these epics differently from the men. Did they understand and interpret the characters of Sita and Draupadi (the central female characters in these epics) differently from the way men did? Did they deify the male heroes in these epics and have the same unconditional reverence for them as their male counterparts? I can't help but feel the answer to the first question is a 'yes' and to the second is a resounding 'no'.

In 1949, *The Second Sex*, a ground breaking book by Simone De Beauvoir, was published in Paris, and it became an instant success selling over 22,000 copies in the very first week of its release. The book brought her a lot of international acclaim. Women across the world resonated with her thoughts. The book also earned her disrepute and abuse. Never before had the case for female liberty been made so forcefully, boldly, unabashedly and successfully. Never before had anyone explored this topic so diligently, exhaustively and painstakingly. In her book, she brings out the forces from history, biology, anthropology, politics and philosophy that had come together to create this condition for women. The book is about the 'feminine condition', a condition she had been contemplating for a long time and become acutely aware of, namely, the all-pervasive domination of man over woman. The story of women's struggle for equality, not just economic but also psychological and social, has been very different from the struggles of say the Blacks, the Dalits, the workers, the Jews or, for that matter, any other group. Unlike these groups, women are not a minority. Their lives are so intertwined with the lives of those who have denied them the rights that even understanding that they are oppressed takes a while. The complexity of the situation can be understood from the fact that many women have themselves not been great supporters of the feminist movement because they believed that if women took up the jobs of men, their husbands could be unemployed! We started the book with Virginia Woolf's quote: 'The history of men's opposition to women's emancipation is more interesting perhaps than the story of that emancipation itself.' To this, we'd like to add that women's opposition to women's emancipation is, perhaps, even more interesting and insightful and illustrates the complexity of the issue and the extent of challenges that anyone who has championed equality for women has had to overcome.

De Beauvoir writes (paraphrased a bit to make it succinct for this context),

> *Her whole education system conspires to bar her from the paths of revolt and adventure; all of society, including her parents, lie to her about the value of love and devotion … and that is the worst of crimes committed against her; throughout her life she is corrupted by the temptation that giving up her freedom in exchange for a stable family life of love and devotion is meant to be her vocation.*

Fighting for their rights for women was literally about living with the enemy and still fighting a battle. Black women have had no choice but to be part of the Black man's struggle against the White, the Dalit women had no choice but to be part of the struggle of the Dalit men against the upper castes. Yet, there were woes that both these groups of women had in common that needed them to come together and fight. And many of these woes were shared by the women folks from the oppressor groups whom these minority groups were fighting against! By being dismembered and scattered as part of different male groups, they truly lacked the means to organize themselves into one group to fight for their common rights. The reality has been that women's agitations have mostly been symbolic and they have won what men have been willing to concede to them. We will briefly touch upon the feminist movement later in the chapter. Understanding of 'diversity and inclusion' without a knowledge of the history of some of these movements will always be shallow and incomplete.

In 1977, *Bhumika*, a Hindi film directed by one of India's finest film-makers, Shyam Benegal, was released. The film was based on the autobiography of one of India's most sought after and bohemian actresses of her time—Hansa Wadkar. The book *Sangtye Aika* (in Marathi) was published in 1970. It instantly won universal acclaim and became a bestseller. The film went on to garner awards for best actress (Smita Patil), best screenplay and best film. The film shows the female protagonist bound in a patriarchal society, exploited by family, husband, her director and other characters in her life. The theme was bold and explored uncharted territory. In India, parallel cinema directors brought social issues to the forefront, and actresses like Smita Patil and Shabana Azmi portrayed roles that would begin to change the way society—even the women in society—perceived women. In their films, these actresses played characters who were independent, fearless and represented an intelligent femininity that stood out in stark contrast to the contemporary cinema of the times which was male dominated, where women were nothing more than objects or appendages.

Inspiring feminist writing bloomed in several languages. Men contributed to it as well, and over time, many male celebrities across the world went on to advocate feminism. The world has a lot to thank these audacious writers and daring film-makers who raised awareness on a large scale. Awareness is the first step to a resolution.

Religion too is full of male prophets and male gods. This has, at a subliminal level, undoubtedly influenced some of our beliefs about men and women, as well as the way we think and act. Religious texts across the board and the world's most respected philosophers have all played an active part in women's oppression in society. Simone De Beauvoir brings this out with innumerable examples that would shock the sensibilities of anyone in the civilized world.

Changing the way society thinks about social issues and overcoming unconscious biases is a slow process and needs, among many other things, a change in storytelling and a diversity in the storytellers. Organizations may typically focus on the visual identifiers of diversity at beginning of their journey. Companies invariably learn the importance of this kind of diversity reasonably quickly. Also, this kind of diversity is inevitable and almost a given if a company wants to access a wider talent pool or as the nature of the business and its geographical dispersion becomes complex. What may not follow automatically is wholehearted acceptance. And there is a difference. Acceptance merely means that individuals from these diverse backgrounds (skin colour, ethnicity, race, nationality, gender) do get recruited. Wholehearted acceptance means that individuals from these backgrounds can expect to advance in their careers based on merit, contribute meaningfully to decision-making process, etc. Focusing merely on visible indicators of diversity, without focusing on building systems and processes that leverage the diversity, is likely to yield limited results for businesses investing effort in this area. In the chapter 'Rewiring for Diversity', we have outlined the broad stages of diversity implementation.

Should Diversity Follow Inclusion or Vice Versa?

Most advice on this topic seems to endorse the approach that inclusion is more fundamental and needs to precede any agenda on diversity. But there is a small problem with this advice. Our experience in learning and development has led us to the conclusion that people assimilate and internalize a concept or framework well only if there is an opportunity to apply these at work. If they are introduced to concepts for which there is no immediate application, the concepts remain of academic interest or are quickly forgotten. So, a training program on inclusion may not help if there is no opportunity to apply it at work or even appreciate its importance.

Therefore, some element of diversity needs to precede a training initiative on inclusion to make the training meaningful and non-trivial. For instance, a push for inclusion, including a training intervention, may be very helpful right after your company expands into a new geography. Individuals and teams from the two geographies that need to interact on a regular basis will immediately relate to the concept and power of inclusion and the consequences of not paying attention to it. Diversity can then be further stepped up after the groundwork on inclusion is done.

Beyond Tolerance

Becoming tolerant organizations, with commitment to non-discrimination and fairness, implemented through policies, is not the highest goal. It's just the starting point. Businesses could begin with introspecting on fundamental processes, practices and behaviours such as:

- In a company where everyone is soft-spoken and does not express disagreement openly, how does the company treat people who are outspoken and vocal? Does the leadership involve them in decision-making or finds ways to keep them out? Or if the majority are vocal and outspoken, does the leadership treat those who are reticent as individuals without opinions or do they try and encourage them to express their opinions?
- In a company that has just begun hiring leaders laterally, how does it assimilate them, especially if they come from different backgrounds and have not been drinking the company Kool-Aid?

- Is your management council for real or does it exist on paper, with all key decisions being made by a much smaller group of like-minded individuals, especially when it comes to topics where there may be multiplicity of opinions?
- If your company is headquartered in a particular country and the team is distributed across countries in different time zones, do you send leaders from HQ to run operations in other countries or do you hire local leaders? Or even something as trivial as scheduling conference calls—do you schedule calls at a time that is convenient to the folks at HQ or do you inconvenience everyone by turn?
- What mechanisms are in place to ensure that everyone at the table have had the opportunity to share their opinion freely? People stop sharing ideas if undermined or ridiculed. Does the culture explicitly discourage actions that would force good people to start feeling they are not valued and, hence, inducing them to become reticent and indifferent?
- Do leaders spend more time with team members who are in closer physical proximity than with the others?
- Are there subtle political undercurrents that reinforce various forms of the 'not like us' syndrome, that are ignored by the management? And worse still, is management complicit in perpetuating these syndromes either actively or through a studied silence? As Edmund Burke, the Irish statesman and philosopher, had once said, 'The only thing necessary for the triumph of evil is for good men to do nothing.'
- Has the leadership team attended workshops on, say, 'unconscious ias', and have they spent time trying to understand in what ways the 'not like us' syndrome could manifest in their context?

- Irrespective of the nature of the business (tech led, marketing led, R&D led, manufacturing led, etc.), is there a relationship of mutual respect between functions?

At one level, there has been a lot of progress made in the last 50 years towards eliminating inequalities and prejudices, and the world is a much better place today than it used to be. Only those who had reached adulthood half a century ago and belonged to some minority community (or were women) would truly appreciate the extent of change. Change was a result of legislation as well as shift in mindsets, and corporates, too, were quick to mirror some of the positive changes in society. Some companies, especially those with a global presence, began focusing on diversity and inclusion and realized it could become a potent weapon if executed well. However, execution on scale is always a challenge, and D&I initiatives suffered from poor understanding and faulty execution.

The explosion of social media at the turn of this millennium and the ability of social media companies to manipulate human behaviour and spread fake news have polarized the world faster than any of us could have imagined; and it is far easier to create a tipping point in a political movement or build a political career on a divisive platform than an inclusive platform. As per Twitter, on an average, fake posts have a six times larger reach than genuine posts. While one set of prejudices is being erased, new ones are constantly taking shape. It is like taking two steps forward and one step backwards or, who knows, maybe two steps backwards. Therefore, those who understand the acute criticality of diversity and inclusion in the present times and are committed to the cause need to enable fundamental rewiring across systems to make businesses and the world, at large, become truly inclusive, beyond mere tolerance.

BIG IDEAS IN THE CHAPTER

1. *Diversity without inclusion is worse than homogeneity:* Organizations must work on an environment of inclusivity before working on diversity to ensure high-quality interactions, instead of friction.

2. *Critics of feminism fail to appreciate the constraints of 'feminine mystique':* Feminine mystique was a term coined to define what women want in life to be happy—marriage, children, house work and suppressed sexuality. The stereotype still exists, which is why feminism is necessary to break out of it.

3. *Film and literature play an important role in changing stereotypes around women:* Biases are difficult to overcome, and storytelling can play a powerful role in helping society to do so.

4. *Inclusion and diversity need not be worked on sequentially:* Initiating some diversity interventions, alongside work on inclusion, will help employees see the relevance on building inclusive mindset and give them an immediate opportunity to apply the principles.

5. *Harnessing diversity requires organizations to move beyond tolerance:* Many organizations may begin with visible indicators of diversity, which are easier to learn. It's necessary to move beyond mere tolerance towards more fundamental rewiring over a period of time.

Rewiring for Diversity

Human communities depend upon a diversity of talent,
not a singular conception of ability.
And at the heart of the challenge is to reconstitute our
sense of ability and intelligence.

—Sir Ken Robinson

A World Wired against Diversity

The pursuit of diversity is a swim against the tide because our wiring as individuals, organizations and society, at large, is increasingly geared towards what we may call *non-diversity*. Google Ngram shows trends of words searched online. 'Diversity' has shown steady rise in the last two decades. Interestingly, identity-based searches such as 'woman of colour' and 'find your tribe' too have shown an unprecedented spike. They have moved from being hardly searched words to highly searched words in the recent past. Words such as 'White', 'Black' and 'Asian' have shown a rise as well.

We quoted Andres Tapia earlier, 'Diversity is a mix, inclusion is making that mix work.' Developing a mindset of inclusion is easier said than done. Globalization and social media would have been expected to help the human race find a shared identity and facilitate inclusion by making us aware of one another's stories and challenges. Unfortunately, it has led to a stronger and narrower boundary of personal identity. The rise of identity politics in the world around White, Black, man, woman, Hindu, Muslim, liberals and conservatives is testimony to this phenomenon. The divide is not just on strong personal identities but also on ideologies. Social media has provided a veil of anonymity for vitriolic exchange of disagreements on all matters, significant or insignificant, with no willingness and patience to listen to each other. We increasingly want to be with 'like-minded' people and stay away from those who don't think or look like us. None of these augur well for diversity and inclusion at a societal level.

Our systems, both schools and businesses, when looked at closely, also reveal a similar wiring against diversity. Late Sir Ken Robinson, in his TED Talks, has shared how the schooling system was created to fulfil needs of industries resulting in a still existing class system of subjects, with sciences on the top, followed by humanities and fine arts right at the bottom. Think of how many 'good students' in the world are expected to pursue science even if they were interested in humanities, simply because 'good students' are supposed to study science. Humanities are for the ones with lesser academic capability. The seemingly new fascination for science, technology, engineering, and mathematics education is nothing new. Science has always ruled the roost, with humanities being the poorer cousin. Fine arts are seen as a hobby and not something that requires any significant level of intelligence. Despite thought leaders such as Daniel Pink pointing out that the future belongs to right-brained thinkers, education is a long way from acknowledging or implementing that. In the context of our discussion on diversity in organizations, the concern for us is that education, by and large, does not recognize diversity in thinking or ability, neither incorporates interdisciplinary learning in a meaningful way. This is pervasive across how students are taught, assessed and generally valued. Malcolm Gladwell has spoken about bias in standardized testing towards certain kind of thinkers.[1] He inquired why we put strict time limits on standardized tests instead of allowing students as much time they need. What is gained from getting students to complete the task faster, instead of focusing on the quality of responses? Gladwell's interaction with test designers did not lead to any concrete explanation on what is achieved by designing tests with a bias towards those who can solve it faster. Gladwell's quip is—students doing well in timed tests need not necessarily be smarter. His observations hold true for a lot of test designs of common entrance exams around the world, which focus on scoring the most in lesser time. Anyone who has attended coaching classes to crack engineering or MBA exams would know how candidates are taught several techniques to maximize correct responses and avoid negative marking. If students are just smart enough to solve a given number of questions correctly—and more importantly, avoid the ones they are likely to get wrong, one can fare well in such exams. This approach can very easily throw false negatives for students who have the intelligence to solve deeper problems. These are just some examples of how the core teaching and learning process across K–12 and higher education does not support diversity in thinking and calls for some deep introspection.

Now, let's look at how workplaces are wired vis-à-vis diversity. Let's take the example of job descriptions. It will not be wrong to describe most job descriptions (JDs) as documents

---

[1] https://www.youtube.com/watch?v=SKlcEZzbZic

which got created 100 years ago, mostly inspired by someone else's document (i.e., 'benchmarked'), seldom updated or reflecting the reality of a job. The job specification, that is, qualifications, skills of the candidate are often so specific that unless candidates have the exact experience in that very job, they will not make the cut. In fact, we suspect that one of the reasons organization faces a dearth of candidates is severely narrow and impractical job specification. All of these aspects of the JD point at a few behaviours that are roadblocks to implementation of diversity in organizations.

- Jobs are not seen as dynamic and evolving with the business environment.
- Candidates are being considered from a stereotypical lens.

Take, for example, how marketing has evolved over years. Even a decade ago, marketing used to be this function responsible for running cool campaigns. If you have been friends with any senior marketing professional on Facebook, you would often find them posting pictures with celebrities that the company has signed for endorsement. In contrast, sales function has been the one to generate revenue and, as a natural outcome of it, a powerful department within organizations. Finding concrete metrics to measure the revenue impact of marketing has not been straightforward. A campaign can be successful but not necessarily lead to commensurate revenue generation. A third player has become prominent in the recent past, that is, the product function. A shift to productization and focus on 'design a product that is its own advertisement' are all significant inflections in the changing equation between product, sales and marketing. Increasingly, companies, especially tech companies, no longer work with the rationale of 'create a product' and then sell hard using a sales team that can 'sell ice cream to eskimos'. Today, companies have realized that the starting point needs to be asking, 'Does the eskimo want an ice cream at all?' As a result of this, both sales and marketing have had to rethink their approach. Further, social media and digitization have significantly changed how products are branded and sold. Rise of content and product marketing is testimony to the changing role of marketing within organizations. I was moderating a panel on the 'Role of AI in Content Marketing' at a product conference. Panellists were heads of marketing and experts in the area. One of the questions I posed to the panellists was whether marketing, in the digital marketing era, can still get away with being a cost function, with budgets to spend on campaigns but never directly responsible for revenue. There was a unanimous view that marketing is increasingly being held accountable for hard business outcomes. The new term 'growth marketing' is a reflection of that shift. However, while organizations have been quick to adopt the lingo, their marketing JD still retains its antique charm.

Someone on my LinkedIn contacts posted something which was funny and sad, at the same time, and reflective of what we are discussing here. He was commenting on a job post that asked for '10 years of Python experience' for some junior-level coding role. He was amused at the recruiter's expectation of finding many eligible candidates for that kind of experience. There were many comments on the post, about how the recruiter must have replaced some other coding language with 'Python' in an old JD and posted it. Several marketing JDs give a similar impression. One finds the words 'growth marketing', 'content marketing', 'digital marketing' sprinkled here and there, but job specifications are from the earlier JD version of 'MBA in marketing' ... '10 odd years of experience', etc. There's a whole new generation of digital marketers who have emerged not from B-schools but 'learning on the street'. These are products of the gig economy who have slogged it out without organizational support. However, such profiles, the ones who really have the new-age skills, can never compete with alums of, say, MICA (a premier institute in India, in demand especially for marketing, media and advertisement roles) or any other premier institute, who are limited by the experience their organizations offer them. Even at the same experience level, with real skills, the 'outsiders' will never make the cut for these marketing roles. Even if they do, they will never be paid as much. Ironically, many of these 'growth hackers' are hired either directly as vendors or through agencies who in turn act as vendors to organizations. The question here is simply this: Does it not make sense to build a marketing team with a variety of profiles, that is, a mix of those with formal degrees who have worked within organizations and those who have picked up the skills in the open market? In fact, when it comes to new skills emerging in all areas of business, one is likely to find them in the free market much more than within organizations. Then why do we have a constricted view of jobs and who can perform them well, given how quickly jobs are changing?

Another case in point is the bias against hiring entrepreneurs. Let's say one needs to hire a procurement director, with about 15 years of experience. One candidate meets the exact requirement, that is, 15 years of organizational experience in procurement. The other candidate has 10 years of procurement experience and 5 years of experience in trying to set up a supply-chain business which gets some traction but ultimately does not scale. In the current scheme of things, the latter will not make the shortlist in all likelihood. Five years of entrepreneurship will be taken as a break or deviation from the exact requirement. But wouldn't such a person be a value-add in the team? What if all departments were to have 15–20 per cent of their teams as people who have certain years of core functional experience but rest of the years with diverse experiences in entrepreneurship or other functional roles or even something as having opened an NGO, worked on books. Why are these seen as a 'break in continuity' instead of 'experiences on a different continuum'? Here, we are looking at diversity from the perspective of roles and competencies, more than demographics of the candidate. The reason we consider JDs to be a good indicator of an organization's wiring is because this angle of diversity has nothing to do with forced morality or legality of anti-discrimination, equal opportunity employer laws. Even for an organization that does not believe in all of that—this approach to diversity is for business' sake.

Diversity as a Shared Accountability: Role of K–12 and Higher Education

Much of D&I's success depends on one of the toughest things to change about human beings, that is, mindset. Yet, it's surprising that there is not even the slightest impetus on diversity and inclusion during phases of human life where mindsets are still shaping up, that is, stage of education. Let us put a cautionary note here right away. We aren't in the least talking about 'diversity and inclusion' being taught as a subject in schools and colleges. Creating a subject and conducting exams builds knowledge. Here, we are talking about building the mindset. It is the same mistake schools make in teaching 'values'. Just as we can't inculcate values through books and exams, we cannot build an inclusive attitude with an academic approach. Building a mindset of diversity and inclusion at schools and colleges requires the same level of rewiring as organizations. Let's take the instance of how students are grouped together. Schools have a system of multiple sections in every grade. In many

Indian schools, children are divided across these sections as per academic achievement. For example, Grade IV-A might have all the top students, while IV-C may have struggling learners. The stated logic for such demarcation is that children can be taught as per the needs of their respective levels. Let's map this scenario to organizations or the real world, for that matter. Is it that all top performers work in one team and medium and low performers work in their own separate teams? In real life, you can end up with anyone. Also, is it that one student who is good in one thing is necessarily good in everything? A 'good student' by definition is someone who scores well in core subjects. But does it mean they are the best thinkers? Or are they as good at theatre and fine arts? There are two problems here. First, the definition of 'good student' itself is skewed. It's based on a very narrow set of metrics. This fallacy continues in the hiring process, where employees are shortlisted based on college pedigree, marks, etc. Second, especially in context of building the mindset of inclusion, this kind of 'student-class system' leads to specific issues.

- Students grow up as adults who believe the best way to work is to team up with similar people. So-called smart ones want to team up with those similar to them. So-called average ones stick to their kinds and want to remain in their comfort zones. (This inculcates a non-inclusive mindset very early on in a person's life, which is very difficult to change just through workshops.)
- Students are unable to expand their thinking by working with peers who might be good at different things (not working in varied-capability groups early on in life deprives youngsters from experiencing first-hand the benefits of diversity and inclusion and learning skills to find common ground and leverage complementary strengths).

The behaviours continue in higher education as well. Back in my MBA days, I remember feeling fascinated at how a class of 60 could form project groups almost within seconds of the professor asking students to do so. It's like group contracts would be signed through some eye-contact code language. Mostly students, when given a choice, preferred working with those they were friends with. All the biases we have discussed in this book can be seen among youngsters, right from 'not like us', regionalism, racism to gender stereotyping. These biases continue into the managerial, administrative and leadership roles and impact how organizations hire, appraise, reward, frame policies and processes. Consider the following scenario:

- What if we could work on these unconscious biases and hardwired thinking before all of these stakeholders enter the workforce?
- What if a significant part of education is redesigned to build mindset, rather than cramming knowledge?
- What if more time and thought is given to making each student work with every other student during the year and consciously reflect on it (instead of creating an academic class system and non-diverse mindset)?
- What if we could get students to reflect, at the beginning and end of each activity, on questions such as:

  o Why did you choose, or not choose, to work with certain peers? What assumptions did you make about that person? On what basis did you make those assumptions? How does your expectation *versus* real experience of working with the person compare (pre- and post- project)? What did you learn?
  o What if you end up being in the same team as the person you want to avoid? How will you feel? How will that feeling and your assumptions about

the person impact your behaviour? What can you do to make things work?

o   What assumptions do others make about you? How do you know? How do you feel about it?

Needless to say, these discussions will need to be handled with finesse and by creating a psychologically safe environment. We are not getting into modalities here. But imagine what kind of students will emerge from an education system where they have constantly reflected on their behaviours and assumptions about people, as a core part of their learning process. Imagine the commitment of such students to create such safe environments in workplaces where differences can be resolved and leveraged, with respect. So far, we have simply assumed education's role to be limited to contributing scholarly research (which most often only scholars can access), or teaching courses on 'diversity for business leaders'. Educational institutes simply cannot take the easy route of being the preacher, instead of practising diversity. Educational system is far better positioned than organizations to build mindsets, because they operate in the formative years of a person's life. If the 15–20-odd years we spend in schools and colleges are not utilized in building the right mindset—and, on the contrary, actually spent perpetuating a siloed thinking and working—then expecting organizations to fix the problem is simply setting them up for failure. Admittedly, education has been slow to change. Therefore, we need to take a practical view of how we can involve them in the larger diversity agenda. There could three possible ways.

1. Governments could consider incorporating mindset building in education policies. Further, educational leaders and teachers across K–12 and higher education could be equipped to build the mindset of diversity and

inclusion through behaviours, without turning it into yet another subject with exams and grades.

2. Organizations, as recruiters in the placement process, could urge educational institutes for such mindset to be built in students. Businesses could also lend expertise to colleges in facilitating workshops and sharing actual organizational scenarios.

3. Thought leaders could drive conversation at an ecosystem level among key stakeholders to create awareness about the role of education.

Finally, educational institutes are workplaces too. Just as we expect businesses to create a diverse environment for their employees, educational institutions also need to step up to that goal. Else, it will be difficult for teachers and staff to create a mindset of diversity for learners, if they have not experienced it themselves. As we see it, if educational institutions can be both enabled and compelled to build their teaching and learning process in way that incorporates diversity and inclusion, it will serve the dual role of grooming *sharper minds* and *better mindsets*.

Invest before Harvest

One of the misconceptions propagated, either explicitly or by implication, in pro-diversity literature is that the benefits of diversity are realized immediately. Earlier in the book, we have discussed extensively how studies on diversity seem to directly attribute better financial results to a diverse leadership team, without clearly establishing a causal relationship between the two. The unconscious expectation is, therefore: *Hire a diverse leadership team and see profits soar*. We can all agree that diversity, if implemented thoughtfully, will eventually lead to tangible benefits. However, our point here is that those benefits are unlikely to be seen in the short term. The underlying reason is that any good implementation of diversity (without tokenism) will need multiple exercises of mindset change; defining goals; involvement of all stakeholders; actual implementation; evaluation and course correction. One of the necessary aspects of a long-term implementation of diversity and inclusion is defining the right metrics.

As of now, organizations mostly use measures such as demographic ratios of manpower (e.g., gender ratio). However, on their own, these metrics don't tell the complete story. For example, an organization with healthy gender ratio may still be employing more women in stereotypical roles such as HR, marketing, corporate social responsibility, etc. Another organization with a predominantly masculine culture may hire women leaders but could often end up hiring women who demonstrate the same masculine style and therefore fit in. Alternatively, they hire women leaders with diverse styles, but the process and culture of the organization sidelines such leaders as outliers. Gender ratio does not reveal the actual truth about diversity and inclusion in these scenarios. In the earlier chapters, we have reflected on whether we must focus on the visible indicators of diversity as race, gender, etc. Our conclusion is that, for some time, the focus on those areas are necessary. Therefore, metrics to measure those areas will also be necessary. Our point here is to say that we need a wider set of metrics, in addition to those that measure these visible indicators of diversity. Also, different metrics would be required for different stages of diversity implementation, which can be broadly defined at the organization and ecosystem as follows.

- **Nascent:** This is essentially stage zero, when there may or may not be widespread understanding of diversity. Even when there is some awareness of it, a *shared*

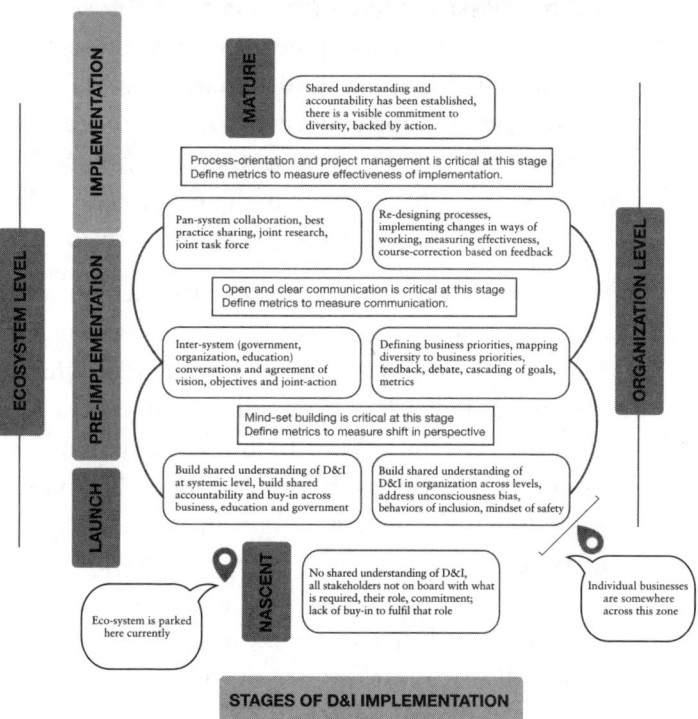

Stages of D&I Implementation in Organizations and Overall Ecosystem

IMPLEMENTATION

MATURE

Shared understanding and accountability has been established, there is a visible commitment to diversity, backed by action.

Process-orientation and project management is critical at this stage Define metrics to measure effectiveness of implementation.

Pan-system collaboration, best practice sharing, joint research, joint task force

Re-designing processes, implementing changes in ways of working, measuring effectiveness, course-correction based on feedback

Open and clear communication is critical at this stage Define metrics to measure communication.

ECOSYSTEM LEVEL

PRE-IMPLEMENTATION

Inter-system (government, organization, education) conversations and agreement of vision, objectives and joint-action

Defining business priorities, mapping diversity to business priorities, feedback, debate, cascading of goals, metrics

ORGANIZATION LEVEL

Mind-set building is critical at this stage Define metrics to measure shift in perspective

LAUNCH

Build shared understanding of D&I at systemic level, build shared accountability and buy-in across business, education and government

Build shared understanding of D&I in organization across levels, address unconsciousness bias, behaviors of inclusion, mindset of safety

NASCENT

No shared understanding of D&I, all stakeholders not on board with what is required, their role, commitment; lack of buy-in to fulfil that role

Individual businesses are somewhere across this zone

Eco-system is parked here currently

STAGES OF D&I IMPLEMENTATION

understanding is missing. Stakeholders lack clarity on what it means to implement diversity and if they have a role to play. At the ecosystem level, let us consider key stakeholders to be the government, businesses and the education system. We have discussed earlier, how the education system is completely missing from the conversation on diversity. Government's role and outlook seems to be limited to laws across employment, anti-discrimination, protection of minority groups and sexual harassment prevention. But is there a shared understanding of diversity among all three stakeholders? Is there dialogue on what other kinds of legislations will help diversity across education and business? Is there investment from government in building the diversity mindset in government funded educational institutes and places of work? Is there discussion on opportunities of collaboration and best-practice sharing among the stakeholders? These questions clearly reveal that the ecosystem at large is in a nascent stage of diversity implementation.

When we look into businesses specifically, a similar set of questions apply. Do all leaders, managers and employees have a shared understanding of what diversity entails (e.g., does a section of employees perceive diversity as 'something to do with women-related initiatives')? Is diversity seen as a shared responsibility in the organization (e.g., do business leaders and managers see it as something only 'HR does')? Have key mindsets and unconscious biases across organizations been addressed? These questions lead us to realize that nearly all organizations are in the nascent stage. This is where some of the 'top XYZ diverse organizations' lists become misleading and set the wrong benchmark. Organizations doing better on visible metrics of diversity may not necessarily have organization-wide understanding of diversity or worked on unconscious bias or ensured that diversity is taken as a shared responsibility. This is not to take away from initiatives implemented by these organizations. We need to start somewhere, and the early movers definitely create momentum for others. There's no harm in appreciating such organizations, as long as we don't lose sight of facts, in favour of rhetoric. Many of such top XYZ organizations might still be in the nascent stage. However, having made progress in some quarters, they are much better equipped to progress to the next stages, as compared to their peers.

- **Launch, pre-implementation and implementation:** The stages of implementation in sequence are *launch, pre-implementation* and *implementation*. The *launch* stage is all about building mindsets about diversity, addressing unconscious bias, defining accountability, nature of role each one can play and level of commitment required, among other things. This is the stage when the groundwork is done to prepare the organization and create clarity around what diversity means, given the context of the business. At an ecosystem level, it means dialogue between key stakeholders from all systems that results in an identification of common ground, shared goals and opportunities to collaborate. *Pre-implementation* goes into more specifics of deciding concrete goals, plans, measures and communication to all stakeholders. Just as the previous *launch* phase is about dialogues, *pre-implementation* is about open communication—which includes debate, feedback and critique. *Implementation* stage involves making actual changes in ways of working, processes and policies. This stage could be spread across different phases. Here, the effectiveness of implementation is most important and must be constantly evaluated.

While the stages are sequential, there might be overlaps among them or multiple cycles might be required. As we pointed out in the chapter 'Beyond Tolerance', mindset building can be more effective when overlapped with diversity initiatives for employees to see immediate relevance in building the right mindset. Also, we can expect diversity implementation to follow the same challenges as any change management programme.

For example, not all leaders, managers and employees may change their mindset or be committed to diversity immediately. Early adopters and influencers within the organization will need to be identified. After the implementation picks up momentum, the cycle is repeated to involve a larger set of employees. A word of caution is to avoid approaching it hierarchically, as is often the inclination. Influencers, early adopters and laggards can be found across all levels of the organization. Finding the right cross section is important for every phase of diversity implementation.

At the ecosystem level, key influencers and thought leaders will need to take the lead across sub-systems to drive the conversation. Early adopters and sponsors will need to be identified to help get traction. The progress of implementation at the ecosystem level will be marked by being able to set joint goals, opportunities to collaborate, best-practice sharing, etc. Research could be an important area of collaboration at the ecosystem level. We have spoken about the limited reliability of diversity-related studies, whether it is industry reports or research on gender behaviours. A lot of what passes off as research are merely surveys, with no established construct validity (i.e., do the questions actually measure what they are meant to?). Also, each survey or study explores a different set of questions, even though they appear to be on the same subject. This renders the studies incomparable. Finally, we also established that implementation of diversity within organizations and mindset building across 15–20 years of education will be a long-term effort. Hence, good quality longitudinal studies will be required to understand the benefits and challenges of diversity implementation over a period of time. Jointly funded research collaboration at the ecosystem level can be beneficial to all stakeholders.

- **Maturity:** *This* is the end station of implementation. At this stage, diversity is deeply embedded in the way of working, processes and decision-making. A shared understanding has been established and everyone understands and buys-in to their role in building diversity and inclusion. Perhaps, organizations who make it to this phase could be crowned as 'role models in diversity'.

One of the factors that can hurt the implementation of diversity and inclusion is leadership change. A PricewaterhouseCoopers 2018 CEO's success study, on public companies, placed the median CEO tenure at five years.[2] If diversity is seen as a serious goal, core to the business strategy, then the board, incoming and outgoing CEOs would need to ensure continuity in the implementation. Diversity is the 'in-thing' in organizations these days. That amount of limelight can also be diversity's bane. If leaders become more interested in who gets credit for diversity, rather than doing what is right for the organization, long-term implementation can get hampered, especially when there is a CEO transition. Breaks in implementation also adversely impact the conviction and commitment of employees towards the overall goal.

Is Diversity Daunting?
(P.S: The Ark Was Not Built in a Day)

As the discussion on diversity broadens beyond the known bounds of improving demographic ratios, the goal may appear a little daunting. Which is why, one last perception around

---

[2] https://www.pwc.com/gx/en/news-room/press-releases/2019/ceo-turnover-record-high.html#:~:text=The%20study%2C%20which%20analyzed%20CEO,over%20the%20time%20period%20analyzed

diversity must be addressed. Diversity is often correlated with chaos and, sometimes, even used interchangeably with the latter. In our minds, we see the relationship as: greater the diversity, more the chaos. That perception might not be completely untrue. After all, with greater diversity comes divergent points of views, different approaches and disagreements. Put together, it gives a feeling of chaos, making diversity appear daunting. However, there is another way to define the relationship between diversity and chaos.

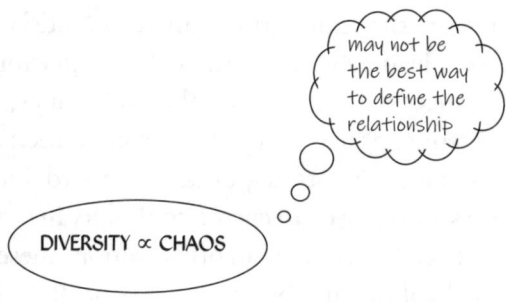

Biomimicry is the approach of learning models of nature to solve human problems. Perhaps, we could rely on the same approach and seek to understand the rules of creation around diversity in nature. Needlessly to say, there is a 'daunting' level of diversity in the universe. Yet, there seems to be order in the cosmic chaos. Endless planetary bodies float in space, move around the sun—and for most parts, they don't collide. Nearly 70 per cent of the world is water, but most of the times it stays in its place. Mountains don't fall off randomly. Every creature lives in harmony with the other, bound by some invisible set of rules. This leads us to a third element in the equation between diversity and chaos. That element is what we will call, 'principles of engagement'. In our context, they are the shared goals, values and cultural norms that act as the inviable glue keeping diversity together in a coherent whole. The common ground allows dissent to be constructive and helps organizations make diversity work *for* them and not *against* them. The interaction between 'levels of diversity' and 'principles of engagement' decides how well diversity can be managed and leveraged. Broadly, organizations could fall into the following zones:

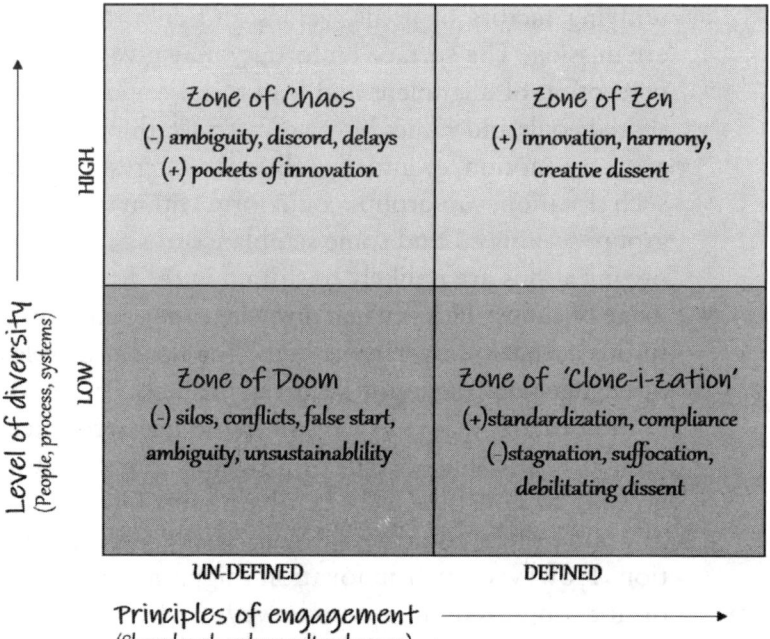

- **Zone of Zen:** This is the zone where nature operates. There is high diversity and well-defined principles of engagement. Organizations that manage to reach this stage (this corresponds to the 'mature' stage in D&I implementation we discussed earlier) can leverage their diversity for innovation, problem-solving and dissent in a way that enables the organization.
- **Zone of clone-i-zation:** This is where organizations choose to be low on diversity and high on defining

principles of engagement. In situations which require uniformity, standardization and compliance, this approach could work. However, since this is a continuum, if diversity is completely stifled and principles become prescriptive, it may lead to employees feeling suffocated and experience repressed dissent.

- **Zone of doom:** This is when diversity is low, and unifying factors of goals, values and cultural norms are missing. The surface uniformity may give the false perception of alignment and lead to false starts. Since shared goals and values have not been set, things which are set in motion, eventually fall apart. Interestingly, in such situation, sub-groups could form within the larger group, seeking to find some semblance of sanity. Such organizations are unlikely to sustain in the long term.
- **Zone of chaos:** This is when diversity can get daunting. In this scenario, diversity is high, but clear principles of engagement have not been established. This leads to discord and delays as a result of too many conflicts and corresponding dearth of processes and common ground to constructively resolve them. Given high diversity, there could be random pockets of innovation. However, such innovation might go unnoticed or not supported in a systemic way.

Therefore, diversity can be chaotic—but only when enough focus is not given on establishing the unifying factors of shared goals, values and cultural norms. When the latter is worked upon, along with building diversity in people, processes and systems, it *can* lead to that proverbial pot of gold at the end of the rainbow that diversity enthusiasts often speak about.

Finally, having said so much about diversity and inclusion all through this book, we want to end with stating the obvious:

diversity is hard work. Perhaps, that is the reason why there is so much tokenism around it. So, let's go back and ask ourselves, why do we bother about diversity? The one common argument in favour of diversity is that diversity helps an organization survive turbulent times. Jim Collins said in his book *Built to Last*, '...it is better to understand who you are than where you are going—for where you are going will almost certainly change.' Diversity is about who we are. Therefore, the only way diversity will work is when it becomes the very way we work, think and take decisions. That kind of diversity cannot be built overnight. It for sure cannot be built easily. Diversity is for *all* organizations, whether a start-up or public company; that is, for *all* businesses that are *being built to stay in the game*. Different businesses can have different starting points, they may take their own path and their own time. But one thing is clear; diversity requires a long-term mindset. Genesis 7 of the Bible says[3]:

In the six hundredth year of Noah's life, on the seventeenth day of the second month—on that day all the springs of the great deep burst forth, and the floodgates of the heavens were opened.... Every living thing on the face of the earth was wiped out; men and animals and the creatures that move along the ground and the birds of the air were wiped from the earth.... Only Noah was left, and those with him in the ark. The waters flooded the earth for a hundred and fifty days.

---

[3] http://web.mit.edu/jywang/www/cef/Bible/NIV/NIV_Bible/GEN+7. html#:~:text=Genesis%207%201&text=And%20Noah%20did%20 all%20that,floodwaters%20came%20on%20the%20earth.&text=And% 20Noah%20and%20his%20sons,the%20waters%20of%20the%20 flood.&text=male%20and%20female%2C%20came%20to,as%20God%20 had%20commanded%20Noah

It is said Noah was around the age of 600 when the great deluge hit the earth. His ark ensured the continuity of human and other species. Did Noah build it overnight, given that he literally had the hand of God on him? Noah received the message around the age of 500, and it took him more than a century to build the ark that survived a turbulence which wiped out everything on earth. It doesn't matter if you read or believe in the Bible or don't. Noah and his ark are an apt metaphor for today's times. Whether it was the 2008 downturn or the COVID virus in 2019—each time it's a new threat; each time it takes us by surprise. Even when there are warning signs, we ignore them. Each time we don't know how long it will last. Building diversity beyond tokenism is a bit like building that ark. It is meant to help organizations sail when all others may drown. Therefore, it has to be built with care, built with time and *while* there is still time to do it. Perhaps COVID could have a silver lining for businesses. Given that all rules of business are being reset, it could just be the right time to layout the blueprint of diversity in the new normal.

Samwise Gamgee says, in *The Lord of the Rings*, in his Hobbit English:

It's the job that never started, as takes longest to finish.

Given how far behind we are, it's about time we get started.

BIG IN THE CHAPTER
IDEAS

1. *World is wired against diversity:* Personal identities based on gender, race, colour, etc., are becoming stronger than shared identity, around the world. This trend is not conducive to the overall cause of diversity.

2. *Education is better positioned than organizations to build mindsets:* It is easier for education to build inclusive mindsets in formative years of a human being, than it is for organizations to break hardwired biases at later stages. Diversity needs to be a shared accountability between education and organizations.

3. *JDs are a good indicator of organization's wiring towards diversity:* Organizations that are unable to redefine jobs differently, given the changes in market, cannot hire diversely merely by adopting diversity-friendly policies.

4. *Ecosystem is at a nascent stage:* There is no shared understanding of diversity or common goals among government, education and organizations. Dialogues need to be initiated among stakeholders at the ecosystem level.

5. *Diversity is a long-term goal, implemented across stages:* A good implementation of diversity may take few years and is spread across multiple stages. Different metrics are important at different stages of implementation.

6. *Jointly funded research collaborations will help all stakeholders:* There is a gap in high-quality, reliable research in the area of diversity. Given the long-term nature of implementation in organizations and mindset building in educational institutes, longitudinal studies will be helpful for stakeholders. Collaboration and joint funding between government, educational institutes and organizations can be considered.

Swati Jena is one of those people who leave you with, 'Aha, I never looked at it that way'. Her uncanny perception and ability to pay deep attention to things help her see often-missed dots and connect them in unlikely ways.

Swati is an expert generalist with 17 years of work spanning across 10+ industries and domains such as learning and development, education, talent management, consulting, product management and entrepreneurship. From going to petrol depots for manpower planning to visiting Rashtrapati Bhavan for arrangements to invite the president of India, Swati's diverse life experiences have shaped her multi-disciplinary outlook. She is the quintessential 'all-rounder', a trait that carried well into her MBA education at XLRI, Jamshedpur.

Swati began publishing her ideas on LinkedIn, on a variety of topics including diversity, which led to her being named as one of, 'LinkedIn Top Voices' of India in 2017. Swati believes that asking the right question comes before the quest for answers. This love for questions was at the core of her TEDx talk 'Life is Like a Google Screen'. Swati's first book, *The Entrepreneur's Soulbook—Is It Your Cup of Tea?'*, is again about questions that aspiring entrepreneurs should ask themselves before starting their journey. The book reached Amazon number 1 bestseller rank through word of mouth. Swati currently runs her venture WriteFor, a one-stop-shop learning hub for domain-specific writing.

T. N. Hari wears different hats—author, angel investor, advisor to VCs and CHRO Bigbasket, among others.

He spent the first 14 years at Tata Steel. Of this, the first 11 years were spent in engineering on the shop floor. The next three years were in HR helping restructure the company to cope with post-liberalization challenges.

The next 18-odd years were with a string (five of them) of high-growth start-ups. The first four saw successful exits (Daksh was acquired by IBM, Virtusa went public on NASDAQ, Amba Research was acquired by Moody's and TaxiForSure was acquired by Ola). In each of these start-ups, Hari has been a part of the management team and played a key role in shaping their growth and exit.

In the last five years, Hari has been an advisor and sounding board to numerous young entrepreneurs and start-ups. He is a mentor at accelerators like Techstars, Silicon Road and India Accelerator. He is an advisor to Arkam Ventures (an early-stage VC fund) and Fundamentum Partnership (a growth-stage VC fund).

He is a prolific author and has authored six books so far.

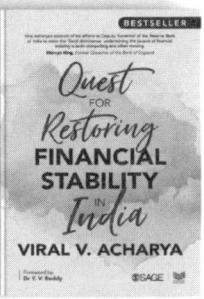